The Face of the Foe

Pitfalls and Perspectives of Military Intelligence

Revised Edition

Kjeld Hald Galster

Legacy Books Press

Published by Legacy Books Press
RPO Princess, Box 21031
445 Princess Street
Kingston, Ontario, K7L 5P5
Canada

www.legacybookspress.com

This edition first published in 2015 by Legacy Books Press
1

Library and Archives Canada Cataloguing in Publication

Galster, Kjeld Hald, 1952-, author
        The face of the foe : pitfalls and perspectives of military
intelligence / Kjeld Hald Galster. -- Revised edition.

Includes bibliographical references and index.
Issued in print and electronic formats.
ISBN 978-1-927537-13-8 (pbk.).--ISBN 978-1-927537-14-5 (kindle)

        1. Military intelligence. I. Title.

UB250.G34 2015   355.3'432   C2014-907232-5
                                                           C2014-907233-3

Printed and bound in the United States of America and Great Britain.

This book is typeset in a Times New Roman 11-point font.

This book does not work for the NSA, will not spy on you in any capacity, and needs a clear line of sight to your computer keyboard.

Table of Contents

List of Illustrations

Acknowledgments

PUBLICATION OF THE revised edition of this work was made possible by the kind and persevering encouragement by Legacy Books Press and its director, Robert Marks to whom this author wishes to express his sincere gratitude.

This author owes much of his insight into military intelligence to long-lasting collaboration with the Royal Military College of Canada, the Danish Royal Defence College and the University of Copenhagen as well as to work with the United Nations and the Organisation for Security and Co-operation in Europe for which sincere thanks is due.

Preface to the 2nd Edition

SINCE IN 2010 this book was first published, the world has seen testimony to considerable developments in scope and practice in the field of military intelligence. Two events have attracted primary attention viz. the American success in locating and assassinating the terrorist leader Osama bin Laden in Abbottabad, Pakistan, and the revelation by Glen Greenwald and Edward Snowden of the worldwide tapping of electronic communications by the American National Security Agency. Though events like these do not in and by themselves change much as far as the historic and theoretical foundations of the spy's trade are concerned, they tell volumes of modern military powers' will and ability to pry into everyone's private life as well as public affairs – the tapping of the German Chancellor Angela Merkel's mobile phone is a revealing example – whether this be done for purely defensive reasons or with underlying malevolent intentions.

Moreover, an update is due not least because of the First Edition's optimistic comments on the strengthening of the European Union's political and military potentials as a consequence of the adoption of the Lisbon Treaty. The much cracked-up new presidency and the introduction of a High Representative for Foreign Affairs turned out to change much less than expected.

For these reasons it appears both appropriate and timely to attempt an update and an expansion of what was written five years ago.

Preface to the 1st Edition

DOES THE ENEMY look cruel? Do we believe him to be omnipotent, possessing unlimited resources and determination to hurt? This book endeavours to describe and analyse the outcome of a complex process that happens every time human beings try to appreciate their enemies. This procedure runs mostly involuntarily as a fusion of facts with intangible matter. While facts originate with basic knowledge and conscious endeavours to acquire precise information, i.e. intelligence, ethereal elements invade the human brain from many quarters and in many forms such as emotions, subconscious material, official rhetoric, religious beliefs, hatred, etc. Although not being historical in its entirety and being eclectic in its point of departure, the work is intended as a probe into the field of military history. Sallies have been made into other scholarly fields – as for instance psychology and sociology – whose distinctive features the author has endeavoured to respect.

For the purpose of supporting the argumentation, historical examples have been employed throughout this book. The guiding principle has been coherence rather than chronology, and the reader should not be unduly surprised to find examples from, for example, First World War and the 2003 war in Iraq in close connection followed by a third one originating for instance in the Boer War. Moreover, impressions from a not so distant past, stored in the memory of the author, have been pieced together to make illustrative examples in order to ease the reader's comprehension.

As far as intelligence is concerned, the terminology used by British intelligence historian Michael Herman has been adopted. Some readers, and probably in particular those of the martial profession, will find that the use of certain terms like "information" and "intelligence" may differ slightly from the traditional military usage. In military parlance raw data is information, and intelligence materialises from processing and interpretation following collection of this data. Conversely, outside the military services all data collected throughout the process are designated as intelligence.

Introduction

"On s'engage, et alors on voit."[1]
– Napoléon

EVERYTHING IS ASTONISHINGLY beautiful – trees, mountains, vineyards, the tobacco fields and the rivulets trickling down from the hills towards the Black Sea. Local tradition has it that it was here that God found the perfect spot for His Eden. The sun is sinking slowly into the calm waters of the sea, and the shadows of the eucalyptus trees are growing longer by the minute. An intense craving for food and cool drinks becomes acutely manifest. Since the early hours of the day, I have meandered through the dusty terrain along rivers, on hillsides, through ravines and back to the sea where I stay in a dilapidated high rise – once an extravagantly luxurious hotel belonging to the armed forces of the deceased Soviet Union. Luxury has now vanished along with the expectations of affluence and equality in the Communist paradise – the power supply is unstable and shuts down our computers at irregular intervals; clean, cold water is rarely available, hot water not at all. The local telephone service is defunct, and our satellite communication is dependent on a small, asthmatic generator, which will supply us with power only as long as there is fuel. When this link to western civilisation breaks down too, we must drive to one of the neighbouring villages, where a telephone switchboard

---

[1] "We engage in battle, and we shall see."

of pre-First World War vintage may, on a lucky day, facilitate connection with Moscow, whence further linkage may be obtained – if the switchboard operator is not too busy.

In September 1993, the Abkhazian autumn is indeed ravishing. However, apart from Nature nothing seems particularly impressive. As we turn into the compound of our so-called hotel, passing the Russian guards lounging lazily on the lawn in their not-too-clean uniforms, we turn left at a monstrosity of a Lenin mosaic set with red, brown, and blue stones and adorned with golden tinsel. The glittering sea reflects the last rays of the setting sun, the wind whispers in the palm leaves, and our jeep, which was white in the morning but now closer to khaki, looks like a commercial recommending the local and disquietingly muddy wine which is delivered weekly in 25 litre plastic containers.

We leave the vehicle to the mechanic and mount the stairs to the bar. Sitting down under the torn portrait of Stalin, we set our eyes on the cool drinks so sincerely craved for. Masha, our multi-national and multi-lingual secretary, pours herself yet another glass of the muddy liquid. She has been seconded by the UN office for Christmas cards, where, apparently, her assistance was no longer indispensable. All of a sudden, a sharp whistling sound penetrates the quiet afternoon. Fractions of a second later a deafening crash resounds. A mortar bomb impacts on the terrace, the windows are shattered, and with a speed which belies her almost 60 years of age Masha, uncharacteristically of her habits, abandons her drink and seeks refuge under a table. Carl Eugen Strålenhielm, a phlegmatic Swedish don, puts his glass down and notices that the ongoing peace talks, which we have travelled thus far to help promoting, have apparently come to a temporary standstill, and intense shooting in the street seems to corroborate his accurate observation. However, though the Grim Reaper seems to be at large in the streets below our shattered windows he shows no immediate inclination of entering our premises.

This is the eruption of violence I have anticipated since I came. The air is thick with "Grad" rockets whistling past our building. Grad is the Russian word for hail showers and also the name of the ammunition of the BM-21 rocket launchers, which are the modern "Stalin Organs," or Katyushas. From the surrounding heights grenades and bombs from mortars, rocket launchers, and all kinds of home made means of delivery pour down on Sukhumi, the "Abkhazian capital." All of a sudden, Colonel Josif Nikolayevich Knaskaftaradze crashes in.

He is an ethnic Georgian and the quite possibly corrupt commandant of the place, mostly exquisitely dressed in tailor-made uniform with gold embroidered epaulets, adornments which are indeed extraordinary with an officer of a rank as modest as colonel. His face is unusually pale and his black moustaches quiver under his voluminous nose as he demands immediate UN protection from the demonic hordes of Abkhaz warriors, and he seems to have very good reason to expect the worst. Others flood the nearby Russian air base to try to get on board one of the ageing Mi-8 helicopters, which fly in and out of Sukhumi on a daily basis, creaking and groaning under the airmen's total disregard of the limits to their lift capabilities.

Colonel Knaskaftaradze

It is September 1993, and the Abkhaz break-away province's self styled government has rallied all men capable of soldierly action for a counterattack. On 13 August the year before, Tengiz Kitovani, born 1938, the Minister for Defence of the former Soviet Republic of Grusia – or Republic of Georgia as its citizens now call it – had made up his surprisingly autonomous mind and invaded Abkhazia. Used to being an Autonomous Socialist Soviet Republic, an ASSR, leading forces in that province had so far tended to believe that, after the fall of the Soviet Union, they might enjoy extensive self-governance running their 'country' from their own capital, Sukhumi, and they had rejected the notion of being remotely controlled from Tbilisi by the Georgian President Eduard Amvrosiyevitch Shevardnadze.

Born in 1928, during the years 1985 to 90 Shevardnadze had been the last foreign secretary of the Soviet Union and his name was then linked with that of Mikhail Gorbachev and the concept of perestroika, as well as with the eventual demise of the USSR. Since then he has been the leader of Georgia, a position which he manages to keep until 2003. As strong central governance is what most leading politicians seem to prefer neither he nor anybody else in Tbilisi support the Abkhaz autonomy. Since leaving the union with Russia, Georgia has endeavoured to leave her past behind. The Russian language has been replaced by Georgian, the Orthodox Church of Georgia – whose confession is different from that of the Russian Orthodox Church – has been reinvigorated, and the schools have changed their curricula. The only thing which seems to be unaltered is the strong belief in the merit of violence as the prime means for solving conflicts. Thus, in 1993 Kitovani tries to accomplish a quick fix to the Abkhaz threat to Georgian territorial integrity. Through a rather smooth military invasion he takes the Abkhaz leadership by surprise and forces their limited militia north to Gudauta and the mountainous area around the town of Gagra. This is a part of the country which is lush and richly covered by tobacco fields and vineyards. Moreover, it borders with the Russian Federation, whose sympathy with Georgia is less than limited. Thus the Abkhazians may look this way for compassion and a certain amount of practical and material support. In the spa town of Sochi just north of the border there is an international airport and a medium size harbour. In Abkhazia, close to Gudauta where the Abkhaz leadership establishes its temporary headquarters, there is an undamaged former Soviet air base still operated by the Russians. From this facility daily flights in and out of Sochi maintain the supply of arms, ammunition, and food to the breakaway republic, and this traffic the Georgians have not got the means to interrupt. The quantities of these sinews-of-war that are coming out of this base nobody knows, but it is obviously a great deal as it allows the Abkhaz militia to strike back, while Russian and Georgian diplomats are still engaged in negotiations on a peaceful settlement.

That day in September 1993 the Georgians in Abkhazia realise that they are in for bloody retaliatory action. They have challenged the apocalyptic beast, which has now risen ready to strike. The Georgians' ceaseless and thorough casting of the Abkhaz population in the rôle as hostility personified with all kinds of horrific qualities now allow their bad conscience as well as their fantasy to play freely. They are aware of the atrocities committed by their own forces and – for that very reason – expect the coming battle to be merciless.

The Abkhaz militia counts merely a few thousand armed men, but they are actively supported by Cossacks, who hope to revive their century-old way of living, and a battalion of Chechen volunteers whose aim is setting up a Caucasian confederation. Moreover, the Russian Federation delivers weapons, ammunition, and certain services. The control of the embryo republic is managed by a group of politicians – the Gudauta Gang as the Georgians call them – under the leadership of Vladimir Ardzindba with local police chiefs, mayors, and military commanders as the subordinate decision-makers. The democratic legitimacy of this polity, however, is not obvious.

Listening to conversations in bars and cafés and talking with those I meet, I get the clear impression that with the image of The Gudauta Gang in their minds' eyes the Georgians produce the portrait of their foe as a fat-headed, black bearded, dark, ominous and self-asserting creature, a figure which fits equally well with the characteristics of Colonel Knaskaftaradze who is an ethnic Georgian and indeed no Abkhazian. They envision a brutal and rude personality, who will rob, rape, and kill as he moves along. Thus, they start portraying the opponent as Devil incarnate.

Ragtag local warriors clad in Soviet uniforms

What they do not realise is that in most respects their adversary is not too different from themselves. Apart from ample admixtures of civilian articles of clothing, the Abkhazian warriors wear the same old-fashioned

Soviet uniforms as the Georgians; but in Georgian eyes the assailants' ragtag appearance metaphorically transform into the 'number of the beast'. "Let him that hath understanding count the number of the beast: for it is the number of a man; and his number is Six hundred threescores and six."[2]

Although in 1993 the Abkhazians constitute a minority of merely 18% of the population in their own province the Georgians fear the worst. The women and children say little, but at the coffee house tables all over Sukhumi the men, who always seem to have plenty of time for chatting, are fiery in their condemnation of the opponent, as they imagine all sorts of horrors to happen within the next few days. They are facing a deluge of long-bearded barbarians, secretly armed by the Russians, and inflamed by equal amounts of vodka and thirst for revenge.

I was no party to the conflict, merely a more or less casual traveller – present on behalf of the United Nations – who had hoped to be able to contribute to a peaceful settlement of the conflict, which, it was said, was petering out. The UN had gathered the parties together in the village of Adler near the Sochi airport to attempt to facilitate a reconciliation. In my capacity as a representative of the institutionalised conscience of the global community, I wandered about in this oriental cauldron a stranger from a world which few of those involved in the conflict had ever seen, let alone understood. Since I was a spectator without even the slightest share in the quarrel I had excellent opportunity to watch and listen. And what I saw and heard made a profound impression on me. Not only because a formerly well organised and comparatively affluent society, albeit not a free one, had perished by throwing itself into infernal chaos and abject poverty, but just as much because I realised the mental metamorphosis happening ubiquitously across the small community.

People who had lived in peaceful and decent cohabitation, although not necessarily as friends, were now brutalised, and they adjusted to the new reality by casting their neighbours in the rôle of the foe. They did so by conveying rumours, demonising, and labelling negatively groups of citizens, whom the changed circumstances had established as enemies of their own faction. A large portion of this vilification comprised characteristics like hue, hair colour, beard etc., which may or may not have been based on reality, but were certainly common to and used by both parties against the other.

As the war progressed and the Abkhaz forces advanced south, the Georgian leadership, and notably Shevardnadze himself, found it advisable

---

[2] Revelation: 13.18

to leave Sukhumi with the utmost alacrity. Every day shooting and the impact of artillery shells were heard and felt in the streets, and frequently I had to step across a dead body when leaving the compound to make my way into to downtown Sukhumi. The local painter, Vladimir Sergeevich Bernadin, knew the affliction of war as he had started his career as a military artist in the trenches of Stalingrad in 1942.

Bernadin's studio

Now, as his studio had got a direct hit by a stray mortar bomb, he was sitting in the forest painting with little shelter from rain, low temperature, and the forces of autumnal gales.

By the end of October Sukhumi was on Abkhaz hands. Now, the enemy images were turned around to describe the Georgians, but they were nonetheless very much the same as before. Of course, the various ethnic groups in Abkhazia were not exactly identical, but most of the basic traits and characteristics were the same. During the Soviet era it had been generally accepted that society was multi-ethnic, but all of a sudden it turned important to be able to prove one's ethnic, linguistic and cultural affiliation with Abkhazia. Any indication showing association with the enemy – the Georgians – had to be avoided. I saw many a sad example of this self-inflicted them-and-us division during that autumn in Abkhazia. It was a well established Soviet practice that a person's ethnicity was printed in his or her official documents of identity, and exactly now some kind of kinship was less appreciated than other. Thus a young mother burned her four year-old daughter's birth certificate to avoid trouble, because not only was she not Abkhaz – she was Russian – but even worse, her ex-husband was Georgian.

While the outer characteristics were much more alike than those engaged in the conflict chose to acknowledge at the time, there were other distinguishing features which were less easily hidden. One of these was the family name. Georgian names tend to end on -svili, -adze or –idze, but such names are unknown amongst born Abkhazians. Another aspect was the traditional Georgian Orthodox confession amongst the Georgians, which was not shared by the Abkhazians who – some locals claimed – were Muslims. However, this subtle distinction of spiritual affiliation makes little sense, since after 70 years of Communist atheist influence religion hardly plays any rôle. Therefore, the enmity I saw was an emotion invented for the occasion, and all available prejudices, rumours and assumptions mixed with random scraps of factual knowledge were employed to serve that purpose. Those cast as enemies might have had distinguishing names and other individual characteristics, but for the impartial outsider all looked very much alike.

Experiences like the ones described above are disheartening and thought provoking in their irrationality, but they are not unique, and they are definitely of no recent origin. They are inherently linked with one of mankind's oldest and most demanding challenges: waging war.

Being among the key emotional tools employed by a bellicose society to characterise aim and objectives of aggression, the prompting of enmity is part and parcel of the logic of armed conflict. The aim in war must be one which is comprehensible to all and sundry, it must have the quality of uniting the people behind the leadership, and it must appear as if lying in the realm of *realpolitik*. The underlying objectives must be such that they may be either conquered or destroyed in order to fulfil the war aim.

However, the object of enmity – the foe himself and the objectives in the war – cannot be defined by abstract or emotional reasons alone. The fighting man and woman must have concrete knowledge about the opponent in order to be capable of fighting effectively, and without well defined objectives she or he will act as if fencing with a blindfold covering the eyes, because the basis for decision-making is missing. Thus you will need to create an image of the face of the foe – the opponent you are actually about to combat – and it will have to show every detail you can possibly detect: how he is, where he is, and what his intentions are. Not until this has been done diligently and accurately, can you tailor your strategy, equip your forces adequately for the task at hand, and plan your operational and tactical moves with any likeliness of success. Victory with minimum losses in the shortest possible time depends on this image, which must be created timely and accurately. If we can make sure that the face of the foe will always be like that, war will be short, sharp and decisive. But can we?

To engage in battle and then see what happens may well be acclaimed as the epitome of military self-confidence. Napoléon Bonaparte may have found such display of panache conducive to the reputation he wanted to cultivate, but in reality he was quite diligent as far as intelligence matters were concerned. He did in fact conduct meticulous preparatory intelligence groundwork prior to all his battles and – as do most responsible war leaders – he made sure that, intellectually, he would always be ahead of the opponent. Though the Napoleonic *bon mot* expresses boldness, which was certainly one of the general's and the emperor's key characteristics, this was actually not the way he went about waging war. Napoleon knew the face of his foe. He was amongst the first of the Modern Era's great captains – as was, by the way, his opponent Arthur Wellesley, the Duke of Wellington – to systematise collection of useful and accurate intelligence on the opponent. As early as possible before battle he established intelligence estimates indicating where the enemy had his weak points, where he was ill-prepared, how his logistics worked, and what he was up to. Thus, Napoléon mostly knew enough of the opposing forces' dispositions and opportunities to allow him to make an educated guess on most of the rest. Based on such foreknowledge he was able to deploy his troops adequately, economise his forces and surprise the opponent at the crucial point in time. Therefore we may assume that "engage in battle and see what happens" was probably meant to impress rather than to describe the Emperor's actual intelligence methodology. Napoleon was not the one to await the whim of the enemy; he spent a lot of effort in being in advance of hostile action, preparing comprehensive images of the situation on hand, thus striving to achieve – to use a modern expression – battle-field awareness as complete as possible. Thus he facilitated planning and execution of operations and provided a sound basis for his subordinate commanders to act on.

The Prussian war theoretician Carl von Clausewitz had his baptism of fire in 1793 when, as a young officer cadet, he took part in the fight against the French revolutionary troops.[3] Later, in the years 1805-15, he fought – first with Prussian units, then on a Russian staff, and eventually with the Prussian colours again – against the imperial French armies and their allies. Thus he gained the experience and the knowledge that enabled him to develop his unique theories on the nature of war. These theories he condensed into the draft for his magnum opus Vom Kriege (On War), which was published posthumously in 1831 by his widow Marie von Clausewitz, née *Gräfin* (Countess) Brühl. Through his practical experiences and his study of military combat during the Napoleonic Wars, Clausewitz came to the conclusion that war is a phenomenon that is too complicated, unpredictable and changeable to allow timely creation of enemy images worth using as bases for the planning and execution of combat. Thus, to "engage in battle and then see what happens" might just as well be a Clausewitzian motto. He was convinced that what mattered in battle was the ability and educated intuition of the commander, "the military genius," and indeed this person's whole comprehension of the forces which are at large in martial activity.

The tools for decision-making have grown considerably since Napoleonic times, and there may be reasons to assume that the technological progress, which now allows us to know of events almost simultaneously with their occurrence, has largely overturned the dictum ascribed to the Emperor. Today, the speed and precision of collection, processing, and dissemination of information and intelligence on the opponent allow the decision-maker to see first, then decide, and eventually engage – precisely and at the right moment. Or rather, this is what is supposed to happen.

As we shall explore in chapters I, VI and VII, modern society at war takes for granted that the foe – once identified – can be discovered, registered, and targeted on the basis of "real time" images and electronic data.[4] The adversary then can be dealt with adequately, timely and accurately. However, this is a view that might be over-simplistic, and the war in Iraq in 2003 indicated that difficulties in knowing one's enemy remain; and combating the Taliban in Afghanistan merely compound this realisation. Indeed, is it possible to understand fully the capabilities and likely behaviour of an adversary? Is the intelligence upon which we base

---

[3] Carl Philip Gottlieb von Clausewitz (1780-1831), Prussian general and war theorist. Author of *Vom Kriege (On War)*.

[4] Such as aerial reconnaissance photos, satellite images, infrared line scan, video, etc.

our understanding as accurate and near to real-time as is needed for casting the foundations of an operation? The American researcher Martin C. Libicki seems to believe so suggesting that, at least in some cases, data may be available and sufficiently accurate to allow engagement without any human interference. This, he claims, might be brought about by transmitting automatically processed information directly from the intelligence collection and processing means to a weapons system. Libicki uses the term "intelligence based warfare" or "IBW," which:

> occurs when intelligence is fed directly into operations (notably targeting and battle damage assessment), rather than used as an input for overall command and control...IBW results directly in the application of steel to target... IBW portends a shift in what intelligence is useful for.[5]

Thus intelligence based warfare seems to be equivalent with the US colloquial term of "sensor-to-shooter."

However, it remains to be seen whether operations that are more complex than a mere artillery barrage can be conducted safely under the similar assumption of the operator – the machine – being in possession of all necessary knowledge and fully updated. Moreover, it is hard to believe than any future high-tech system will be capable of calculating irrational behaviour and unexpected occurrences that invariably materialise whenever human beings are engaged.

This book's point of departure is the hypothesis that "the face of the foe," the image of the enemy, materialises out of pertinent contributions that are being provided consciously by man as well as by machine, but that the depiction is augmented not only by mechanical and electronic input, but equally as much subconsciously by a diverse array of factors influencing individuals that are more or less irrelevant to combat. However, though it has been suggested that the notion of "military intelligence" is an oxymoron: this book will demonstrate that this is not so.

Societies at war rely on perceptions and preconceptions of their enemies when planning their national strategies and their military campaigns. It is often assumed that enemy images are shaped solely by the use of intelligence based on assessments of the tangible aspects of an adversary's war potential. However, as close to perfect as one's intelligence may get,

---

[5] Martin C. Libicki, "What is Information Warfare?" in Thierry Gongora and Harald von Riekhoff, eds., *Toward a Revolution in Military Affairs? Defense and Security at the Dawn of the Twenty-First Century (Westport: Greenwood Press, 2000), p. 41.*

assessments will remain an analytical product of human brains.[6] It is, therefore, reality observed through the lenses of the providers' cultural bias and preconceived ideas concerning the opponent. Information may be collected and processed on such elements as the strength of an adversary's economy, technological acumen, gross national product, defence spending, war fighting doctrines and even the degree of public support for the regime. Nevertheless, alongside these relatively concrete indices of national power are less palpable ones such as psychological and sociological factors, the intentions and war aims of the adversaries, their cultural and religious outlook and a whole host of assumptions that often have little evidence to support them.

An agreed image of the enemy must be arrived at to facilitate rallying the warring or bellicose society in support of its leadership's endeavours and as a point of departure for planning. Bearing on this, American psychologist Robert W. Rieber has claimed that enmification is an essential psychological component behind the mentality to wage war, and that armed conflict is inconceivable without a clearly defined image of the enemy.[7] However, a clear picture is not necessarily a true one.

For the purpose of this book, the metaphor *the face of the foe* is intended to include, not only the looks of the physical enemy, but all information on a hostile or potentially hostile entity as well as the

---

[6] While this book is not about the rôle of misperception in shaping decision-makers, it is recommended to consult the following works on this subject. The groundbreaking work on this subject is Robert Jervis, *Perception and Misperception in International Politics* (Princeton University Press, 1976). On the influence of Jervis' work, see Jack Snyder, "Robert Jervis: Illuminating the Dilemmas of International Politics," (http://www.apsanet.org/PS/sept00/snyder.cfm). The book is also consistent with works on information processing and surprise, notably that of Ephraim Kam and Richard Betts (Richard K. Betts, "Analysis, War, and Decision: Why Intelligence Failures Are Inevitable," *World Politics* 31, 2 (October 1978), 61–89; Michael I. Handel, "Intelligence and the Problem of Strategic Surprise," *Journal of Strategic Studies* 7, 3 (September 1984), 229–81; and Handel, "Technological Surprise in War," *Intelligence and National Security* 2, 1 (January 1987), 1–53. For historical case studies of surprise, see John Gooch and Amos Perlmutter, eds. *Military Deception and Strategic Surprise* (London: Frank Cass, 1982); Abraham Ben-Zvi, "Between Warning and Response: The Case of the Yom Kippur War," *International Journal of Intelligence and Counterintelligence* 4, 2 (Summer 1990), 227–42; D.C. Watt, "An Intelligence Surprise: The Failure of the Foreign Office to Anticipate the Nazi-Soviet Pact," *Intelligence and National Security* 4, 3 (July 1989), 512–34; and James Wirtz, *The Tet Offensive: Intelligence Failure in War* (Ithaca: Cornell University Press, 1991)).

[7] Robert W. Rieber, ed., *The Psychology of War and Peace: The Image of the Enemy* (New York and London: Plenum Press, 1991) p. 4.

environment and milieu in which the armed clash materialises with a view to painting a coherent picture. However, it also comprises the influence on enemy perception of less obvious building blocks. These are provided by the layers of cultural, educational, social and metaphysical baggage present in the human brain. One might suggest that the face of the foe is the synthesis created by the fusion of a thesis, comprising the wish for clarity, and its antithesis, being an intentionally or accidentally opaque picture.

The aim of agreeing on an enemy image is to focus everyone's attention on what the state leadership and the military high command might find conducive to fulfilling the war aims. This will include enmification and similar initiatives aiming at rallying the citizens to the colours of their homeland, but at the levels below the top-brass, i.e. that of war-fighting, the need is merely for a depiction which is precise and timely in order to make the outcome of engagements more predictable and to reduce friction. And here, there is no room for enmification, dehumanisation or vilification. Propaganda, prejudice and superstition have no place in this context. Here, it is important to understand that the accuracy of one's insight into enemy matters or, the extent of misperception of them, may vary with the post a person occupies within the decision-making hierarchy and may be dependent on the particular mental make-up of individuals. Nevertheless, this book will argue that the process of enmification influences decision-makers from top to bottom, although it does so with varying degrees of significance in each individual's overall thought processes. In other words, enmification may not be equally strong amongst all decision-makers or individuals; and its impact, of course, varies with the levels at which decisions are taken and carried out. Persons with incisive and comprehensive knowledge of decision parameters and a high level of awareness of the enemy situation, notably central decision-makers and key intelligence people, may be influenced to a lesser extent than is the common fighting man or woman who has only got the official news to rely upon and no independent source of information. Thus, while enmification may be pervasive within a group or a nation, it may be less central to thinking about the opponent for some individuals than for others.

Amongst the factors contributing to friction in war uncertainty has played, and will always play, a key rôle. To alleviate this, knowledge of the enemy's designs, whereabouts and likely behaviour are required. Some American thinkers argue that, within a concept of network-centric operations, information moves towards being a hundred percent relevant, a hundred percent accurate and a hundred percent timely, thus providing decision-makers with information superiority and decreasing ambiguity.[8] They do not, however, guarantee absolute certainty; they merely mention a trend which points in that direction.

Although the means of collection and processing of information become increasingly sophisticated, the uncertainty caused by the observer's historical, psychological and social background go on forming the mental backdrop to analysis and utilisation. Consequently, uncertainty will never be totally overcome. Therefore, and regardless of the degree of information superiority over an enemy, one cannot eliminate the need to rely partially on assumptions. Some of these may, in the event, be proven right while others may turn out to be erroneous. As a result, surprise and uncertainty will remain critical factors influencing the outcome of armed conflict.

The rationale for creating a specific and coherent picture of the opponent is mostly twofold: to provide a persuasive casus belli, and to tailor adequate responses to the actions and intentions of the foe. While the former provides popular support for the bellicose enterprise, the latter is the basis for military planning. However, any enemy image is created under the influence of the general historical, psychological and cultural dispositions of warring societies and their civilian and military leaderships. These sentiments seem to build up over decades and change but slowly. Thus, after the German Bruderkrieg (Brothers' War) in 1866 the reconciliation of Austria with Prussia-Germany probably took right up to the eve of the First World War.[9] Likewise, the Franco-British animosity, engendered during the Napoleonic Wars, perhaps took even longer to dissipate – possibly from The Congress of Vienna in 1815 to well into the First World War. However, before making a priori assumptions due caution must be exercised. There are, indeed, examples of former foes becoming friends or vice versa in a relatively short time span, and Germany and Italy after First World War or France and Germany after the Second may serve as examples. We may see demonstrations of this in the shifting alliances of the eighteenth century great power wars as well as in the "diplomatic

---

[8] Arthur K. Cebrowski and John J. Gartska, "Network-Centric Warfare: Its Origin and Future" in *U.S. Naval Institute Proceedings,* articles 1998. Cebrowski is a retired vice-admiral of the US Navy and as per 2003 director of the Office of Transformation. Gartska is scientific advisor on the US Joint Staff.

[9] Some may claim that this happened earlier, as the heir apparent, after Crown Prince Rudolf's death in Mayerling in January 1889, Archduke Franz Ferdinand was a keen believer in co-operation with Germany. However, most Austrians including the Emperor Franz Joseph were not reconciled with their northern neighbour until the eve of the First World War.

revolution" that realigned the major European powers in the late nineteenth and early twentieth centuries.

Since the emergence of organised states, enmification has been a means of winning support for armed action and glossing over domestic political weaknesses. Thus for instance, it is commonly assumed that Germany's unification under Prussian leadership was brought about by the Prussian Ministerpräsident (Prime Minister), Count, later Prince, Otto von Bismarck who, following the Blut und Eisen (blood and iron) concept, boosted anti-French feelings amongst the German principalities as a lever for the pan-Germanic conciliation. This process happened at a time of internal, Prussian, political turbulence and strong criticism of the Chancellor's despotic behaviour, but it won him great acclaim and forgiveness for his suppression of the trade unions as well as the social democrat parliamentary opposition.

Historically, societies have created images of their enemies by gathering information on, particularising and re-casting perceived competitors or threats in order to make these appear menacing. Polities and their fighting forces have relied upon, and still require, well-defined notions of the adversary to support war aims, just as much as they need the best knowledge possible of enemy capabilities, designs and whereabouts to reduce uncertainty. This, it may be claimed, leads to a concept linking two diverging tracks. However, these tracks are nonetheless mutually supportive and inseparable. While one is intentionally blurred and biased by emotions and unspoken assumptions, which are needed to bolster the civilian penchant for war; the other, which is incisive and concrete, is meant to provide a precision instrument in the political war leader's and the military commanders' hands. As far as the latter is concerned, it would be but natural to expect the so-called Revolution in Military Affairs to inspire enhanced confidence in the perfection and infallibility of the intelligence gathering, fusing and processing technologies and practices.[10] However, it

---

[10] The term "Revolution in Military Affairs (RMA)" covers the rapid development since the early 1980s of military technology and in particular of military utilisation of information technology. "The term Revolution in Military Affairs (RMA) originates with Marshal Nikolay Ogarkov, a veteran of First World War and, from 1977 to 1984, chief of the Soviet General Staff. Ogarkov argued that emerging technologies would allow NATO to stop a Soviet invasion of Western Europe without having to resort to nuclear weapons. In particular, Orgarkov believed that long-range missiles guided by observation satellites — what he called "a reconnaissance-strike complex" — would deny to the Soviet Army the ability to move freely their mechanised forces that were not yet in contact with NATO ground forces." The concept has been further developed, particularly in the USA. Ogarkov anticipated the further developments of information technology and satellites and the

is not likely that technological means alone will solve the uncertainty dilemma as long as they cannot look into the minds of enemy decision-makers. Moreover, it seems justified to assume that the political motives and general public attitudes, which permeate the whole warring society, cannot be discounted in any quarters, political or military.

While being in British prisoner-of-war custody, Third Reich General Hasso von Manteuffel made that point to the British author Sir Basil Henry Liddell Hart, lamenting the negative influence on operations of Nazi ideology and propaganda. His case was relevant only to his native Germany, but it may be doubted that any wartime political leader will accept that his or her military staff works on a basis of a stringent professional approach totally divorced from the public's conception of the enemy and the political and ideological creed of the country.[11]

Societies at war rely on perceptions and preconceptions of their enemies. In many ways, the perceptions are shaped by the use of intelligence assessing the tangible aspects of an adversary's society. But less palpable indices of national power appear alongside the concrete ones. These may be found amongst psychological, religious, historical, and societal factors, the intentions of one's adversaries, their cultural and spiritual outlook, and a whole host of assumptions that often have little basis in material evidence.

This work deals with the tangible as well as the intangible factors and their interaction in the process of assessing an adversary. Moreover, the book endeavours to answer the questions: To what extent should we expect the enemy image to be clear, accurate, and real time; and how much of uncertainty and inaccuracy will remain?

We shall delve into the matter through a seven-step approach. First we take an overview of historical aspects of the creation of the enemy portrait. Then, we shall look at a number of agencies which are active in the clandestine world. Since the influence of intangible factors seems to be omnipresent we will look at mental, emotional, societal, cultural and religious phenomena, which unavoidably distort the image of the foe in our minds. Taking a glance at psychological factors we then proceed to

---

utilisation of space for intelligence purposes and, thus, suggested a revolutionary improvement of intelligence in the wake or as part of RMA. From http://mca.marines.org/Gazette/2002/02Gudmundsson.html accessed on 1 April 2003.

[11] The Third Reich General Hasso von Manteuffel in his conversations with Sir Basil Henry Liddell Hart. B. H. Liddell Hart, The German Generals Talk (New York: Perennial, 2002), pp 294 ff.

propaganda issues, which are integral parts of any war. Hence, we shall be ready to acquaint ourselves with the methodology and the practical use of intelligence to draw reliable, accurate, and timely delivered enemy pictures, we shall forecast some future developments and, finally, we shall try to extract some conclusion and attempt to cast a glimpse into the foreseeable future.

This book will argue that the face of the foe will always be a multi-faceted one constantly including a human element, and that, consequently, uncertainty will remain a basic condition in war. The technological achievements of modern society will add greatly to the understanding of one's enemy, but hidden assumptions and deep-rooted attitudes will undermine the trend towards certainty. A picture of an adversary will continue to be a mixture of perception and preconception, a synthesis illustrating the enemy image as one built on clearly defined net assessments and intelligence as well as intangible sentiments and prejudices. The instrument that penetrates the minds of enemy leaders is not yet available and it is difficult to believe that such a device will ever see the light of day. In the interpretation of intelligence bias, tradition, ignorance and emotion continue to play significant rôles. Therefore, the image of an enemy is rarely an absolutely true depiction. It ought to be a naturalistic one like a painting by Thomas Gainsborough or John Constable showing everything in great detail, but for many reasons it often looks rather like an expressionistic canvas by Marc Chagal or, may be, like something in between.[12]

---

[12] Thomas Gainsborough (1727-88), John Constable (1776-1837) and Marc Chagal (1887-1985).

Chapter I: Intelligence Then and Now

> "Assess the enemy and determine victory."[1]

Assess the Enemy

PRECIES AND TIMELY enemy images depend on realistic assessment. The way this is brought about today rests on centuries of practice and contemplation, and to provide ourselves with an impression of this development we will start by looking into the evolution of organisation, objectives, and methods. In other words, who has been engaged in this business over the years, what have they sought to discover, and how have they achieved their results?

Without enmity there would be no war. But war is and has always been a basic fact and a frequent occurrence of temporal life. Therefore, it is hardly surprising that in the history of human conflict the image of the adversary has always taken up a central position in the minds of political and military leaders. Since times immemorial, in order to fathom the character, the strength and the intentions of a real or potential adversary, human societies have devised methodologies for collecting and analysing information thus producing necessary intelligence.

The basic elements of the intelligence methodology are of ancient

---

[1] Sun Tzu, *The Art of War: the Denma*, p. 193

origin. Hence many of the methods used by bygone generations for gathering intelligence remain instrumental in developing means, procedures and theories for creating comprehensive images of the threats at hand. In modern military parlance we speak of intelligence as including adversary situational awareness, or red SA; environmental vision, or brown SA; and awareness of various neutral elements, or green SA. In plain English, this means that our enemy portrait should include not only the physical foe but all other features influencing our action such as, for instance, weather and ground. An historical overview may help us realise the centrality of factors like uncertainty, which is ubiquitously present in war, the friction caused for instance by unforeseen events and developments, and the volatility of the situation in combat.

Ancient China

Chinese lore has it that uncertainty generates doubts that are harmful to a war-leader's decision-making. Thus the basic assumption of ancient Chinese wisdom is that you should not engage in war unless you are absolutely certain of winning. Therefore you must make an effort to get knowledge of all factors relevant to a possible conflict before even thinking of deploying your forces – "assess the enemy and determine victory." Through achieving foreknowledge uncertainty might be alleviated and decisions may be taken on a sound and relevant basis. One might ask, then, which factors or concerns such foreknowledge should address. Historically, in the intelligence field Chinese theory has focused on rulers and powerful officials, economic factors and military plans, capabilities, dispositions and movements; factors that remain relevant today.

The sinologist Ralph D. Sawyer has described a Chinese methodology that seems to have worked along lines not far from those governing our present day's military intelligence doctrine:

- We must establish the enemy's as well as our own position, and we must lay down the intelligence requirements of the ruler.
- We should hire and dispatch agencies or agents such as spies, travellers, merchants, defectors and others who can do the collection of information on the ground relevant to our war plans.
- We must collect the data needed and analyse them to determine probable intentions, develop a net assessment and plan possible reactions.
- The decision-maker may utilise the intelligence, thus gained, to solve the conflict, preferably through acumen and diplomatic means and, if that turn

out abortive, mobilise and decide on strategy and tactics.[2]

Although this sequence resembles what today's military officers would call the intelligence cycle – direction, collection, processing and dissemination – the production of the enemy portrait was less formalised then than it has now become. Slow communications hampered the utilisation of intelligence in ancient China, and for more than a millennium this changed very little. As late as the 18th century, transmission of intelligence was still cumbersome, and it was not until well beyond the end of the Napoleonic Wars that telegraph, steam ships and railways alleviated this situation. In the "Spring and Autumn" era, ca. 720 – 404 B.C., Chinese communication was based on foot messengers, as horses were generally not ridden at the time.[3]

Amongst the important sources of information were defectors from the military and the nobility of foreign countries, migrants, diplomats, merchants and the relatively limited number of ordinary travellers.[4]

Today it is a widely publicised fact that, during the Cold War, the KGB *residenturas* were integral parts of Soviet embassies in the western world. It should come as no surprise, therefore, that Chinese diplomats engaged in information gathering and similar clandestine activities. In ancient China diplomatic espionage happened routinely. An early example presents itself in 661 B.C. That year, the state Ch'I wished to expand its territory and, with a view to possible conquest, she wanted to evaluate the situation in the potential enemy country Lu. In Lu the situation was unstable following the recent assassination of its ruler. Thus, a diplomat was dispatched to ferret out the situation in the country, and upon his return he was able to inform his political masters that, under the current circumstances, it would not be possible to topple the Lu government. His reasons for giving this advice were that the potential opponent was capable of defending his territory, and he observed properly the "code of conduct" for decent inter- and intra-state behaviour. Thus, neither would it be possible to turn Lu's own citizens against her ruler, nor did it appear feasible to assemble an alliance from amongst her neighbours. Therefore, the diplomat-spy recommended that

---

[2] Ralph D. Sawyer, *The Tao of Spycraft* (Canada: Harper Collins, 1998), pp. 4 and 302. Sawyer is referring to writings by Wang Chen, a border commander and writer of the T'ang Dynasty (AD 618-907).

[3] Until about 500 B.C. Sawyer, *The Tao of Spycraft*, p. 29.

[4] Ibid., p. 30.

Ch'i should defer military action until such a time when Lu's political leadership might fall apart due to internal disagreement, or if political turbulence would occur when the present ruler died.[5]

The ancient Chinese states did not have elaborate bureaucracies dedicated to intelligence. However, one post in the Chou dynasty's (1045-221 B.C.) governments, the Hsing-jen, did fill the rôle which, nowadays, is played by the intelligence and security services.[6] This official was no humble civil servant. In all the countries, which had adopted the Chou administrative system, the incumbent of that post would rank immediately below the prime minister. His official duties would encompass protocol, foreign affairs, secretary of state and diplomatic courier activities, which must have placed him in a choice position for gathering information. Concurrently, the Hsing-jens were the first covert agents of the ancient Chinese states and their first official intelligence directors.[7]

Moreover, the Chinese developed other spy functions and offices.[8] Thus the *Mu* [shepherd] was to become the officer responsible for intelligence gathering in steppe and regions liable to pay tribute, and a wide variety of similar functions materialised over the years. Military intelligence in ancient China was consistently and consciously carried out with the specific aim of assuring foreknowledge of potential enemies, which would alleviate the rulers' and their army commanders' uncertainty. Though not entirely identical with those employed today, in many respects the intelligence terminology and procedures were close to those of the early 21st century.[9]

As we have already seen, diplomats were useful but they were not the only sources of information. Immigrants and defectors abounded, who sought refuge from oppressive rulers or superiors, who had disgruntled or dishonoured them, hoping to exploit a foreign power's need of information to exact vengeance or perhaps even to annihilate their native communities.

---

[5] Ibid. p. 37.

[6] Hsing = to travel, jen = man.

[7] Sawyer, *The Tao of Spycraft*, pp. 41-43.

[8] Ibid. pp. 47-48.

[9] Ibid., p. 49. In the abundant material of examples: Wu Ch'I makes a 'probing reconnaissance raid' against Cheng in the spring of 630 B.C., a terminology not too different from today's.

This phenomenon seems to have survived comfortably since it was precisely such displeased officers who defected from either side of the east-west divide during the Cold War, and who were instrumental in the efforts of dismantling the risk of nuclear Armageddon. Over the centuries, such individuals have provided pools of ready advisers, and their inside knowledge has been keenly exploited. In ancient China they were regarded as reasonably reliable sources of detailed information on powerful individuals, current policies, likely "fifth column" supporters, troop strengths, military training and discipline, types of weapons and logistical preparedness.[10] During the Spring and Autumn, and also Warring States (403-221 B.C.), periods political defectors and even defeated generals were frequently placed in central positions in their new host countries – some even in active command of its troops.[11]

However, broad observation of the potential threats was not the only measures constituting ancient Chinese intelligence procedures. It appears that, from the period of the Warring States onwards, great emphasis was placed on analysing enemy capabilities and intentions with a view to determining the possibilities of victory before even contemplating war. When this was done, a Chinese ruler would employ his army first by confusing the adversary effectively through clever deception and, subsequently, by debilitating his defences by brutal force.[12] Though largely focused upon human intelligence, the ancient Chinese also attempted to capture enemy communications, interpret battlefield signals and fathom early warning systems.

Sun Tzu, writing in the fifth century B.C., gave much of his attention to the impact on military activity of various characteristic terrain features like water obstacles, defiles, routes of advance etc. He advised military commanders to deploy reconnaissance patrols as far ahead as possible to prevent the main body of the army from becoming entangled in skirmishes, and to find areas that might be expected to hamper manœuvre, hence to be avoided by his own troops. Under the right circumstances these areas could also be utilised as killing zones, where large enemy formations might be bottled up and annihilated.[13] Sun Tzu did not wait until the outbreak of war

---

[10] Ibid., pp. 50-51.

[11] Ibid., pp. 51 ff.

[12] Ibid., p. 87.

[13] Ibid., p 86.

before appraising his foe, and he preferred to construct the enemy image on the basis of appraisals of five factors: moral influence, weather, terrain, command and doctrine.[14] While weather, terrain, command and doctrine will sound familiar to the ears of any keen student of the conduct of war, the "moral influence" may require a somewhat closer examination. Sun Tzu did not explicitly explain this notion, but from his writings it appears implicitly that "morale," which has nothing to do with morality, does indeed affect the overall societal attitude towards the war effort as well as the individual soldier's fighting potential and perseverance. He gives an example:

> During the early morning spirits are keen, during the day they flag, and in the evening thoughts turn towards home. And therefore those skilled in war avoid the enemy when his spirit is keen and attack him when he is sluggish and his soldiers homesick. This is control of the moral factor.[15]

Although military technology, organisation and doctrine have changed dramatically since then, the influence of these factors remains even today. All five factors will have to be taken into account and must be appraised. Based on such an assessment – which in today's military parlance might be called an "intelligence estimate" – the decision-maker defines the courses open to him and picks his choices. Today, just as at the time of Sun Tzu, "an enlightened sovereign and an able general act [on the basis of such an appraisal] and so are victorious over others and achieve merit superior to the multitude's."[16]

To many a modern reader Sun Tze's philosophy may seem dated and mysterious, but there are indeed links to modern theory of war which deserves to be rediscovered. Sun Tzu based much of his thinking upon two notions central to Chinese lore, *shih* and *tao*.[17] The former constitutes the

---

[14] Griffith, Samuel B. *Sun Tzu: The Art of War*. London: Oxford University Press, 1971, p. 63. [The 'Denma' Sun Tzu uses a slightly different terminology (Tao, heaven, earth, the general, and method)].

[15] Ibid., p. 108

[16] Sun Tzu, *The Denma*, p. 59.

[17] Ibid. pp. 70-76 and Griffith, Sun Tzu, p. 63. Denma explains *Shih* as the changing and temporary circumstances of any given state of affairs, the power inherent in a situation, whereas Griffith describes it as 'matters, factors, or affairs'. Also, the Denma translation sees *tao* as the way factors interact; Griffith translates the notion 'moral influence, the way or the

circumstances of a given situation; the latter is the way factors interact in the event. He suggested that even the fullest knowledge of the enemy's proceedings will be worthless if the commander receiving it does not understand when and how *shih* serves his purpose. He advised his reader that a picture of the enemy consists of more than insight into his organisation and weaponry: the potentialities of the situation in its entirety must be taken into account.[18] It follows logically that the information and the advantages tied to a certain occasion should not be expected to bring victory at an earlier or at a later stage. Intelligence must be exploited when the time is ripe – when *shih* is right. In this context, Sun Tzu and the nineteenth century Prussian war theorist Carl von Clausewitz spoke "the same language." Thus it appears logical to claim that Sun Tzu's concept of shih has a certain affinity to the Clausewitzian notion of the *Kulminationspunkt* (turning or culminating point) recognised through the captain's intuition or *coup d'œil*. To both authors, military success was likely only if action was taken at the right time, and if the commander was in possession of insight sufficient to allow him to exercise his coup d'œil, his informed intuition, to determine this moment correctly. This *shih-Kulminationspunkt-coup d'œil* nexus appears to have been central in Sun Tzu's as well as in Clausewitz's writings. What made a lucky captain was primarily his ability to estimate the time when the force ratio would be optimal.[19] In essence, while attacking one must envisage the culminating point, because after this moment the enemy's strength will swell and his vulnerability decrease, and at the same time one's own forces become operationally over-stretched. The ability mentally to grasp when this moment of opportunity had arrived, this *shih*, is the epitome of the commander's *coup d'œil*. It seems reasonable to assume that this will remain so.

Sun Tzu's underlying message was that war is a measure serving the sovereign's interests, i.e. the state's political purposes, which will normally be aggrandizement or enrichment rather than sheer destruction of livestock and property. Therefore he promoted economy of force advising belligerents to conquer as much as possible intact and with a minimum of effort. By implication, this suggests that the enemy image should include

---

right way'.

[18] Sun Tzu, *The Denma*, p. 133. Griffith, Sun Tzu, p. 70 interprets this in a slightly less general manner.

[19] Sun Tzu, *The Denma*, p. 146.

everything necessary for achieving the war aim with no unnecessary destruction and in a cost-effective manner. To limit the damage to otherwise useful installations and to economise one's own efforts, instead of assailing an enemy's strongest fortifications one should find out where weaknesses exist – or in Sun Tzu's own words, "advance so that one cannot be resisted, charge against the empty."[20]

This ancient recommendation appears to have found a true supporter in the twentieth century British war theorist Sir Basil Henry Liddell Hart, who argues – along the same lines – for a strategy of indirect approach following the avenue "of least expectation." To facilitate a strike against the "empty," one must maintain active contact, probe and provoke reactions disclosing enemy dispositions, resources and positions – or in other words, create a realistic enemy image.

Employing present day military phraseology, one may suggest that Sun Tzu treated intelligence as a force multiplier in power politics as well as in warfare, emphasising the necessity of meticulous preparations in that field even before the outbreak of war. His appreciation of the necessity for intelligence estimates still appears to be relevant. This need is equivalent to what Michael Handel and others call "the commander's priority intelligence requirements," and it forms the basis for that leader's planning process with a view to meeting the challenges of foe and battle-space.[21]

Furthermore, Sun Tzu insists that, as a commander, you must "know thine enemy and know yourself; in a hundred battles you will never be in peril."[22] Thus he informs his audience that knowledge of one's own forces is no less important than intelligence concerning the enemy – an increasingly complicated undertaking given the present day's sophistication of military hardware and organisation. For very good reasons, this dual need seems to have become one of the guiding principles in the concept of "network centric warfare" elaborated by advocates within the United States' Department of Defence.[23] That incisive knowledge of one's own

---

[20] Ibid., p. 160.

[21] Michael I. Handel, *Masters of War: Classic Strategic Thought*, 3rd revised and expanded edition (London: Frank Cass Publishers, 2001), p. 231.

[22] Griffith, *Sun Tzu*, p. 84.

[23] David. S. Alberts, John J. Gartska and Frederick P. Stein, *Network Centric Warfare: Developing and Leveraging Information Superiority 2nd Edition* (CCRP publications Series, 2000), passim.

organisation is hard to achieve seems amply demonstrated by the American military authorities' initial ignorance of the behaviour of individual soldiers and NCOs in the Abu Ghraib prison in Iraq in 2003-4.

Renaissance Europe

While in ancient Chinese writings, ever since the earliest accounts of armed struggle, tales abound on how conflict has normally been preceded by systematic information gathering to ensure the best possible foreknowledge of the enemy's disposition and possible courses of action, in Medieval Europe little evidence of such activity exists. About AD 430 Vegetius, or Publius Flavius Vegetius Renatus, publishes his *Epitoma rei militaris* (*An Epitome of Military Matters*) in which he touches briefly on Roman intelligence. However, apart from this opus the process of creating adequate images of the enemy does not seem to materialise in written accounts until the Renaissance.

In *The Discourses*, the Florentine Renaissance writer Nicolo Machiavelli deals with the necessity of and the methods for providing credible intelligence about the foe. He stresses the advantages of having a foothold – in the form of sympathisers, citizens disgruntled by their masters' behaviour, or simply a "fifth column" – in countries where armed struggle might occur. In that context, he mentions that the ancient Romans cultivated extensive contacts with minorities within, what they saw as, potentially hostile societies. This practice provided them with insight into the enemy's camp – its gossip, its organisation, its procedures – and with the opportunity to assess the adversary's possible courses of action. Machiavelli gives us some examples that this was indeed the way the Romans succeeded in many actions:

> Thus we see that with the help of the Capuans they got into Samnium, of the Camertini into Tuscany, of the Mamertini into Sicily, of the Saguntines into Spain, of Masinissa into Africa, of the Aetolians into Greece, of Eumenes and other princes into Asia, of the Massilians and Aedui into Gaul. Hence they never lacked supporters to facilitate their enterprises...[24]

Warmly recommending this subtle kind of subversive activity, Machiavelli suggests that, in the case that a competitor-state is divided internally,

---

[24] Nicolo Machiavelli, *The Discourses* (London, UK: Penguin Group, 1998), pp. 273-74.

support be given to the weaker of the parties, thus facilitating their mutual attrition.[25]

Moreover, in *The Art of War,* where he pondered over battlefield tactics, Machiavelli addresses the practical aspects of the creation of enemy images. Among other things, he points to the value of using light cavalry in a reconnaissance rôle. However, his enemy image – like that of Sun Tzu before and of many a war theorist since – does not only comprise the hostile armed forces and the human brains of their commanders, but also the terrain and the whole battle conditions micro-cosmos. In other words, he encourages military commanders to create comprehensive pictures of the whole panoply of adversity that might be encountered, or the friction in war, as Clausewitz called it. The aim is not merely to ascertain a basis for military planning but also to provide force protection because, "...the Roman generals usually sent some cavalry ahead to reconnoitre the country and scour the roads...where you hourly expect to be attacked you will be obliged for greater security..."[26] He recommends the use of advance parties of pioneers to clear the route of the marching columns and the dispatch of troops of light cavalry still farther ahead to cover the pioneers and reconnoitre the lay of the ground. This measure aims at strengthening force protection since to "avoid being drawn into an ambuscade by the enemy you must be very cautious." The commander "should be particularly circumspect if it [the terrain] abounds with woods and mountains because those are the fittest places for ambushes."[27] Moreover, Machiavelli points out which features of the environment are the most likely to harbour enemy ambush parties thus needing the most diligent vigilance: defiles, vegetations, possible traps, bait left in conspicuous places, and units fleeing for no particular reason. All this, he claims, contributes to providing indications of the foe's designs and of imminent enemy action.[28]

As foreknowledge of the adversary is so immensely important, Machiavelli, like Sun Tzu, reminds his audience of the equally pressing need of knowing one's own forces, which, even today, frequently turns out

---

[25] Ibid., p. 360.

[26] Machiavelli, *The Art of War* (Cambridge, MA: Da Capo Press, 1965), pp. 130-31

[27] Ibid., pp. 142-43.

[28] Ibid., pp. 142-43.

to be a task that is not too easily solved.[29] He draws attention to the war-leader's need for multi-faceted images of the enemy based on multiple, verifiable sources. He observes that the collecting agents must be vetted and their information carefully evaluated to obtain a reliable picture of the threat at hand:

For this purpose, it is necessary to procure by various means several persons who are from different parts and who are well acquainted with those places. He should question them closely and compare their accounts, so that he may be able to form a true judgement of them.[30]

Machiavelli finished *The Prince* sometime around 1500 A.D., when the Middle Ages were quietly transmuting into the Early Modern Era, the Renaissance was at its peak, and the Italian city-states' mercenary armies of the condottieri were entering into their twilight period. Machiavelli saw the looming change in political as well as military matters, and he cautions his reader that neither loyalty nor zeal of one's own troops should be taken for granted.[31]

As mentioned above, and with yet another reference to ancient Rome, Machiavelli suggests that the prince, or ruler, should procure foreknowledge about polities, which he might consider as potentially hostile, by establishing cells or even colonies of sympathisers within these targeted societies. In *Discourses* he lavishes praise upon the ancient Romans and their intelligence practices thus adding historical credence to his insistence on creating enemy images by observation at the closest possible quarter. The informants, fifth column, or sympathisers might even, so he suggested, form the avant-garde for the war's opening skirmishes, should armed conflict materialise.[32] This piece of advice seems to have made sense to leaders like Francesco Franco and Winston Churchill, applying it in Spain during the Civil War of the mid-1930s and on mainland Europe during the Second World War respectively. However sensible this recommendation to support the weaker of two or more parties being active

---

[29] Nicolo Machiavelli, *The Prince*. (London: Penguin Books, 1999), pp. 22-23.

[30] Machiavelli, *The Art of War*, pp. 144-45.

[31] *Condottieri*, literally meaning "conductors," were chiefs and owners of private mercenary troops, which they placed at the disposal of rulers willing to pay, and for as long as they paid what the condottieri found commensurate with the risks involved they served their employer faithfully.

[32] Machiavelli, *Discourses*, pp. 273-74: cf. note 29.

in one's sphere of interest seems, it requires meticulous intelligence collection. And having been collected, this information must be assessed properly to determine to whom, when, how, and how much should be given.[33] This may be taken as a premonition of British balancing manœuvres on the continent of Europe at a much later stage. The numerous examples which exist of successful British support more or less overtly given to partners overseas include The War of Spanish Succession (1701-14), The Seven Years War (1756-63), and the 1st, 2nd, 3rd, and 5th coalitions against Napoléon (1792-1809), when Britain successfully endeavoured to prevent the emergence of a European super power.

The Modern Era

Although intelligence had long been recognised as an important prerequisite for waging war effectively, it was not until the end of the 17th century that dedicated bureaucracies saw the light of day.

In 1792, the French revolutionary regime realised that Austria and Prussia were preparing for war against France. Therefore, on 20 April, they declared war on the German powers in the hope that launching a pre-emptive attack might yield the advantages attached to strategic surprise. The Austrian and Prussian armies moved slowly forward, not expecting too much opposition from an army which was believed to be fraught with organisational chaos in the wake of revolution and the flight of most of the trained officers of the *Ancien Régime*. The Austro-German intelligence and security efforts, therefore, were lax. They should have moved more quickly forward, because as they approached Verdun, the French Revolutionay Army was already in well-prepared positions at Valmy, a state of affairs that a more diligent intelligence work woud hve made evident. Thirty years later, Johann Wolfgang von Goethe, who on the 20th September 1792 – as a secretary of state to Duke Karl August of Weimar – had been present on the Valmy battlefield, described the turmoil in his book *Campagne in Frankreich 1792*. The Germans, who had been sorely remiss as to intelligence activities, did not know where the enemy was, where to direct their offensive efforts, how to arrange their logistics or how to maintain their fighting power. The French military doctrine, the size of the French army and its battlefield tactics: everything was new to the Germans as they had not bothered to keep tabs on the development and deployment of the

---

[33] Machiavelli, *Discourses*, p. 360.

French troops. Although the French army was neither well-trained nor adequately rehearsed, its commanders grasped the advantages of surprise and a favourable force ratio *vis-à-vis* the disorganised German troops. This experience led Goethe to the statement that *"von hier und heute geht eine neue Epoche der Weltgeschichte aus, und ihr könnt sagen ihr seid dabei gewesen* [from here and from today a new era of world history begins, and you can claim that you were present]."[34] Warfare would never be the same, and shortly afterwards Napoléon Bonaparte entered the stage and created a system out of chaos.

Thus as a general, Bonaparte seems to have been the first great captain to develop the trade of intelligence to become a centralised and efficiently run business. He realised the immense importance of getting, more quickly than the opponent, relevant information about the battle conditions so as to be able to act swiftly and exploit the advantage of surprise. For this reason, not only did he organise his strategic, operational and counter-intelligence gathering in effective departmentalised bureaucracies referring to him personally, but he also added new dimensions to the creation of the enemy image. Thus he institutionalised basic intelligence, such as enemy order of battle and doctrine, and open source intelligence derived from newspapers, encyclopaedia and topographical descriptions.[35]

His primary sources of information were the numerous informants he employed and remunerated lavishly, but whose services he guarded carefully from the prying eyes of the opponent as well as from the political leadership in Paris. As early as during the campaign in Northern Italy, 1796-97, he extorted from the vanquished societies large contributions that were kept secret as well. This allowed him to keep and pay a considerable number of informers from whom intelligence trickled into his headquarters on all sorts of matters concerning actual and potential opposition in the field abroad as well as in France.

Moreover, as a general, as *le Premier Consul*, (First Consul), and later as *Empereur* (Emperor), he carried with him during his campaigns volumes of reference works on targeted societies and landscapes. He augmented this information with other overt, i.e. openly available or non-secret, information provided by books and newspapers supplemented by the findings of French diplomats, agents and other individuals spying more or

---

[34] Rüdiger Safranski, Goethe: *Kunstwerk des Lebens* [*Life as a Work of Art*], (Cologne: Carl Hanser Verlag, 2013), pp 372-3.

[35] Douglas Porch, *The French Secret Services* (New York: Farrar, Straus and Giroux, 1995), pp. 7-15.

less candidly against the opponent at hand.

Considering the character of the post-revolutionary French society's conflicts of interests, domestically as well as externally, it is hardly surprising that the counter-intelligence effort was as important as was intelligence *per se*. Dealing with conspiring political factions and individuals competing for power and influence, information superiority or dominance was an indispensable instrument in the hands of the supreme leader. Thus to make quite sure that he was not becoming a tool in the hands of powerful individuals, such as a head of a security service, Napoleon maintained at least two competing secret police agencies. As to the primary, or at least the best known, of these heads of security, no single person played a more central rôle than did Joseph Fouché, later to be created *duc d'Otrante*. With a brief interruption from 1802-4, he occupied the post of Minister of Police from 1799 through 1810. He was an efficient and modern organiser of police business – he developed an extensive network of informants, kept tabs on all persons of any importance, and introduced the *Bulletin de Police* (counter-intelligence report), which was delivered to the First Consul or Emperor on a daily basis. Thanks to his informants, lots of foreign intelligence networks were uncovered and many spies was caught. Moreover, Fouché established the institution of commissaires spéciaux (special commissars) who kept an eye on people coming into France from abroad, especially entering through the Channel ports from Britain. All in all, his methods were so effective that they were willingly imitated by institutions like the Okhrana, the Gestapo, the Stasi, and the KGB. As to the other security service, and as mentioned above, Napoléon saw the inherent risks of having a counter-intelligence organisation as efficient as that of Josph Fouché. Thus, a parallel secret police was set up under the direction of General Michel Duroc, who, through his own informers' network, ascertained that no conspiracies might develop undetected.

The *Cabinet Noir* (the black office) was a legacy from Louis XIV. It was tasked with intercepting, opening, and reading letters to and from foreign ruling families, diplomats and other influential people to glean possible strategic intentions. Napoléon left this business to le commissaire général des Postes (the director general of the postal service), Antoine la Valette, who kept him well informed by tasking the avant-garde of the army with impounding mail as they went, opening it and analysing its content.

Apart from secret intelligence, one particularly important element of the image of the enemy was topography. As Emperor, Napoleon had inherited extensive collections of maps from the Bureau topographique du Directoire (the Directorate's topographical service), amongst which were the works of Cassini and Ferraris as well as collections from Turin and Amsterdam. That, however, was not enough for the large scale European campaigns on which he was soon to embark. Therefore, French cartographers were hard at work providing maps and charts, while additional and extensive purchases were made abroad. Since no aeroplanes or satellites were available at the time, map surveys were time consuming and purchases were an expedient remedy.

However, the military intelligence organisations as well as the homeland security services were by no means the only methods making Napoleon master of events. Officers of his intelligence and security services as well as his diplomats and other emissaries in foreign countries carefully studied every change in society, rhetoric, economy, etc. Thus it came as no surprise when the war was resumed by Britain in spite of the Peace Agreement of Amiens of 1802. In March 1805, the Emperor had been informed that in London everyone talked about war, that Parliament had voted large sums for the Army,that new levies were raised, and that on the south coast of England about forty men-of-war were taking on board huge quantities of weapons. Similarly, the Austrian offensive on 19 September 1805 did not materialise as a bolt from the blue. As early as 25 June, the daily Bulletin de Police had informed Napoléon that on the stock exchange of Amsterdam there had been a considerable boom in gold. This had come about because Britain had started subsidising European partners, which, according to the informant on the ground, always happened when military action was imminent.

Elaborate intelligence gathering activities preceded the battle of Ulm. When the Austrians crossed the River Inn on 19 September, all pertinent measures had been taken, campaign plans had been made, reconnaissance had be carried out, orders had been issued to subordinate formations; and in mid-October the Grande Armée was on the Danube. In the intervening time, hectic intelligence gathering and analysis had taken place. While Napoleon's spy, Karl Schulmeister, bribed himself into a post on the staff of General Karl Mack, the Austrian Army's commander-in-chief; on 25 August Joachim Murat, General Officer Commanding the Cavalry Corps, was ordered to go under the pseudonym of Colonel Beaumont to Mainz, Frankfurt and Würzburg where he would ferret out the enemy's troop movements near the cities of Ulm, Ingolstadt, Ratisbon and Bamberg.[36] He

---

[36] Karl Schulmeister was a shopkeeper of Strasbourg ran a lucrative smuggling business along the Rhine on the side, spoke German as well as French, and provided high-level contacts as, in the case of "Ulm," to the staff of the Austrian Commander-in-Chief Karl Mack. Ibid. pp. 14-15.

would overtly investigate the countryside of Bavaria, while other, more anonymous, collaborators reconnoitred the bridges and roads in and around the anticipated or possible places of battle asking questions about garrisons and troop deployments. Similarly, Général Bertrand was tasked with approaching the Elector of Bavaria to make him reconnoitre the Ulm area and join the Emperor of the French at Strasbourg on 11 September 1805. Acquiring open source intelligence and drawing simultaneously on all available basic information, Napoléon was able to position his forces immediately upon arrival at the scene of battle and, in the end, he managed to win the battle of Ulm more or less entirely through manœuvre without a shot being fired.

The only field in which the French seemed to be somewhat remiss was cryptography. This caused some embarrassing surprises, but by and large Napoleonic intelligence excelled. These conditions were exactly the same that made up the practical background for the theoretical ponderings of Clausewitz as well as those of Jomini. However, while Jomini realised the immense value of effective information gathering and exploitation, Clausewitz ended up with dismissing battlefield intelligence as being largely futile.

Although Clausewitz's theories constitute an impressive overall explanation of war as a phenomenon, as far as personal experiences are concerned he seems to be mired in the intricacies of war fighting at the tactical level only. This may be one explanation for his disbelief in the usefulness of intelligence at the level he most incisively tackled in *On War*. The means of communication at the time of Clausewitz, Jomini and Napoléon made intelligence less practical at the operational or tactical levels than it was at the grand strategic plane, where time mattered less.[37] Clausewitz lamented that "many intelligence reports in war are contradictory, even more are false, and most are uncertain." Thus, he preferred the commander's *coup d'œil*, or educated intuition, to any meticulous effort to finding out what the enemy intended.[38] On the other hand, like Napoléon and Jomini, Clausewitz acknowledged that, at the strategic level, intelligence was the basis for effective war plans and operations.[39] However, although he did not leave any explicit and useful

---

[37] Handel, *Masters of War*, pp. 216 and 228.

[38] Carl von Clausewitz, *On War* (Princeton: Princeton University Press, 1976), pp. 117-18.

[39] Clausewitz, *On War*, p. 117, quoted in Handel, *Masters of War*, p.228.

ideas to posterity as to how, practically, to make up the enemy portrait, a theoretical contribution can, as demonstrated below, be inferred from his more general contemplation on the qualities of the military commander.

To get an impression of how, seen from the Clausewitzian viewpoint, the adversary might look and what his intentions are, one will have to invert the opening remarks of On War. "To impose our will on the enemy is the object. To secure the object we must render the enemy powerless."[40] In other words, the enemy is an entity which is aiming at rendering ourselves powerless in order to impose his will upon us. He will behave in a way aimed at matching his efforts to the opponent's – our own potential or expected power of resistance – up to a certain point, which is determined by our will to fight. This, in turn, will depend on the motives animating our willingness to suffer. However, each opposing side has motives, and up to a point, it will offer the other one resistance. Thus, it may be assumed that the enemy is a creature, which tries to gauge our resolve and our motives for and means of resisting its war aims. Doing so, this foe will adjust his energy and resources to be minimal, though adequate. Since this train of thought is applicable to either side of an armed struggle, it appears, implicitly, that neither belligerent is an abstract or static entity. The war on terror provides lots of illustrative examples. While Middle East air-liner hijacks, Italian Brigate Rosse and German Rote Arme Fraktion once were terrorism personified, the face of this kind of foe has changed over the years now showing the bearded countenance of Osama bin Laden in a prominent position. None of these manifestations is an abstract phenomenon; they are animate and intent on bringing their will to bear upon their opponents. Moreover, Clausewitz reminds us that war is a matter of reciprocity, as both parties will do their utmost to fathom their enemy's intentions and react adequately to each of the opponent's actions to achieve optimal results. This reciprocity Clausewitz explains by stating that "War is not an exercise of the will directed at inanimate matter, as is the case with the mechanical arts, or at matter which is animate but passive and yielding, as is the case with the human mind and emotions in the fine arts. In war, the will is directed at an animate object that reacts."[41]

Alas, creating the true picture of the opponent is not as easily done as merely portraying the enemy commander or the hostile country. The

---

[40] Clausewitz, *On War*, p. 75.

[41] Quoted in Alan Beyerchen, "Clausewitz, Nonlinearity and the Unpredictability of War," *International Security*, 17:3 (Winter, 1992), pp. 59-90.

process comprises every aspect of hostile action, which might be brought to bear, including political, military, moral and other characteristics, as well as non-combat related circumstances such as weather, terrain, public opinion, and the internal cohesion of the war faring society. However, it also takes into account that not all resources can be brought to bear at any given moment. Thus, an image will resemble a patchwork quilt sewn together by utilising all the material currently available, the fighting forces proper, the country, with its physical features and population, as well as its allies.[42]

Although there is no indication of any close familiarity with Sun Tzu on the part of Clausewitz, the Chinese notion of *shih* fits very neatly into his reservations that not all existing means can be employed simultaneously; armed forces might, but such components as fortresses, population, and natural defence lines cannot be moved around to suit a commander's whim. Their utilisation depends on, among other things, season, precipitation, supplies, and mood and health of the citizens. It may be appropriate to remind ourselves that, although in 1941-42 the German *Wehrmacht* was technologically, logistically, and doctrinally superior to Stalin' mass armies, they did not conquer because numbers, weather, and the Russian topography were hostile elements, which Hitler's generals had not bothered sufficiently to take into account.

As intimated above, the situation which the commander does not create alone has a power of its own – its *shih*. Clausewitz concluded that an enemy, situation or circumstance whose nature one wants to understand does not necessarily and at any given time comprise the entire potential of a hostile society. Politically influential factions of the enemy public may sway decision-making away from going to extremes to ascertain the war aims.[43] The goals spurring the citizen's will to fight may not warrant total commitment of the society's resources as the evaluation of the danger at hand, the potential risks and simple prudence might dictate caution. Likewise, chance and flux of public sentiments might produce or cancel opportunities. However, the extent to which the enemy might approach the ultimate effort depends on the motives and the tensions prior to outbreak of hostilities, and the Italian reluctance at the initial phases of First World War may serve as an example. While during the 'Phoney War' of 1939-40 Italy was undecided and many Italians preferred to mind their own

---

[42] Clausewitz, *On War*, pp. 75 ff.

[43] Ibid., p. 79.

business, the impressive successes of the German onslaught on France in May and June 1940 persuaded Rome to side with their Axis ally, Germany. However, whether for lack of enthusiasm, difficult ground or simple, military incompetence this enterprise was not particularly successful. The shih was not right

The motives and the tensions prior to outbreak of hostilities take us back to the political nature of war, which is a central theme with Clausewitz. Politically inspired emotions, for example the need for *Lebensraum* and natural resources, national paranoia and ethnic prejudices combine to form a psychological basis for the enmity that boosts the warrior spirit. In the second book of *On War*, Clausewitz specifically mentions, "all military action is intertwined with psychological forces and effects."[44] As we shall come back to in a later chapter, these and similar considerations do indeed appear to contribute to fuelling the public's martial fervour. Prior to and during armed aggression, political leaders deliberately propagate the centrality of emotional and psychological sides of enmity and their influence on the fierceness, cruelty and willingness to suffer for the attainment of the politically determined war aims.

In the 19th century, Clausewitz saw hostility between states as a wartime equivalent of hatred amongst individuals.[45] This was no less true in the twentieth. The hatred of the authorities or of each other nurtured by citizens or groups has frequently been turned successfully into hostility against external enemies. The Argentine attack on the Falkland Islands in 1982 provides us with a fitting illustration.[46] In his book entitled *War is a Force That Gives Us Meaning*, the American author and war correspondent Chris Hedges tells of his own experiences up to and during the Falklands War and of the reactions to the war amongst his Argentine friends. He notes that a population, who until then had been opposed to the regime, became loyal supporters of the military adventure, not tolerating any further criticism of the ruling military junta:

> The military junta that ruled Argentina, and was responsible for killing 20,000 of its own citizens during the "Dirty War," in 1982 invaded the Falkland Islands, which the Argentines called the Malvinas... The invasion transformed the country. Reality was replaced with a wild and self-serving fiction, a

---

[44] Ibid., p. 136.

[45] Ibid., pp. 137-38.

[46] Ibid., pp. 80-89.

legitimization of the worst prejudices of the masses and paranoia of the outside world... Friends of mine, who a few days earlier had excoriated the dictatorship, now bragged about the prowess of Argentine commanders.[47]

His observation seems to buttress the assumption that war often unites people through shared hatred or hostile feelings towards the adversary, which may or may not be conjured up for the occasion. Political propaganda, censorship and chauvinism promote this purpose strengthening the population's resolve to fight and its will to endure the hardships that war invariably entails.

A comprehensive image of the enemy covers policy, weaponry, logistics, economy and many other elements, but the depiction of the opposing armed forces and, most prominently, their commanders will always be a key component in the overall assessment.

Clausewitz described the military commander as a person possessing certain qualities characterising him as a military genius – though not necessarily a genius in the broader sense of that term. In the enemy commander, therefore, one would expect to find qualities like courage, energy, firmness, staunchness, strength of character, emotional balance and *coup d'œil*.[48] In addition to natural talent, a commander would need a thorough insight in a wide variety of matters pertaining to war. Clausewitz insisted that:

> A commander-in-chief need not be a learned historian nor a pundit, but he must be familiar with the higher affairs of state and its innate policies; he must know current issues, questions under consideration, the leading personalities, and be able to form sound judgements.[49]

By necessity, supreme commanders must understand these diverse factors because it is "in the highest realms of strategy that intellectual complications and extreme diversity of factors occur. At that level there is little or no difference between strategy, policy, and statesmanship."[50] Clausewitz, though, realised that some officers did not qualify for the

---

[47] Chris Hedges, *War is a Force That Gives Us Meaning* (New York: Anchor Books, 2003), pp 43-44.

[48] Clausewitz, *On War*, pp. 100-5.

[49] Ibid., p. 146.

[50] Ibid., p. 178.

designation of military genius because they had simply been unjustly promoted by nepotism, by favouritism or by the lack of opportunity to display their incompetence.[51]

However, a true military genius knows that we need to establish credible, comprehensive and precise pictures of the enemy's features in order to combat him effectively. Thus, the opponent commander will do what he or she possibly can to deceive and mislead us trying to make us believe that he or she is different from his/her true appearance.

For that purpose a wide variety of means may be employed. Just as Machiavelli warned that the enemy might try to deceive us by the use of bait, diversions or stealth, Clausewitz found that a central element in warfare was cunning, though he regarded it as time-consuming and too demanding, because the resources spent in this field would have to be taken from the main efforts. He realised, however, that deception was to be expected and that in this respect we should expect the enemy to be equally as cunning as ourselves.[52]

Finally, Clausewitz discussed the enmity emanating from the belligerents' political aims as manifested in their war plans. Political aims may range from the monstrous all-encompassing designs of Nazi Germany to the modest demands for adjusting borders as it happened between the Russian Federation and Estonia in the late 1990s. War is and will always remain but a "branch of political activity; that is in no sense autonomous."[53] For the sake of that activity, a nation at war will carry on hostilities at a level commensurate with its resources and the opponent's aim and level of resistance. His aim and the level of resistance, at which the foe will abrogate hostilities and give up further resistance, are central elements of the enemy portrait that we need to establish, and it is the task of strategic intelligence to find out about them.

Lieutenant-General Antoine Henri baron de Jomini (1779-1869) was another keen student of the Napoleonic campaigns. He was acutely aware of the necessity as well as the difficulties of creating reliable images of the adversary.[54] For many reasons Jomini's view was different from that of

---

[51] Ibid., p. 111.

[52] Ibid., pp. 202-3.

[53] Ibid., p. 604-5.

[54] Michael Herman, *Intelligence Power in Peace and War* (Cambridge: Cambridge University Press, 1999) p. 16.

Clausewitz. He had served on the staff of one of Napoleons corps d'armée and he had experienced the obvious advantages of combining in one person the powers of head-of-state and those of commander-in-chief. Moreover he had been a keen observer of the Emperor's meticulous efforts in the field of intelligence. Therefore, although he realised the shortcomings of the means of communication of his day, he understood the necessity of incisive intelligence efforts and asked rhetorically, "How can any man say what he should do himself, if he is ignorant of what his adversary is about to do?"[55]

Amongst military commanders today, Jomini is widely regarded as a pseudo-scientist who tried, in vain, to harness positivist thinking for the art of war. However, as far as intelligence is concerned his observations were precise, and he devised four methods of obtaining information on the enemy's operations:

> The first is a well-arranged system of espionage; the second consists in reconnoissances (sic) made by skilful officers and light troops; the third in questioning prisoners of war; the fourth, in forming hypotheses of probabilities... There is also a fifth method, – that of signals. Although this is used rather for indicating the presence of the enemy than for forming conclusions as to his designs, it may be classed with the others.[56]

Although, seen from a modern point of view, the fifth method can hardly be described as intelligence gathering, it makes sense that Jomini mentions it as the value of information heavily depends on its timeliness, i.e. the speed of transmission. Given the means of communication – bugles, drums, and dispatch riders – this was no given thing at the time. And, as we have already seen, precisely the inadequacy of the ways of exchanging messages was the key reason for Clausewitz to dismiss altogether the value of battlefield intelligence.

Apart from one's own intelligence gathering, Jomini acknowledged that some useful information might be collected by freedom fighters sympathetic to one's cause, but he was doubtful as to the value of this source. He found that the presence of and co-operation with partisans on the battlefield was unpredictable, and that "it is almost impossible to

---

[55] Antoine Henri baron de Jomini, *The Art of War* (London: Greenhill Books 1996), p. 268.

[56] Ibid., p. 269 and 272: "the Russian army is better provided than any other for gathering information by the use of roving bodies of Cossacks..."

communicate with them and receive the information they possess."[57]

In *The Art of War*, whose original title is *Précis de l'art de la guerre*, Jomini paints an enemy portrait that depicts the entirety of "the nation to be fought." Thus his 'face of the foe' includes:

> Their military system, their immediate means and their reserves, their financial resources, the attachment they bear to their government or their institutions, the character of their executive, the characters and military abilities of the commanders of their armies, the influence of cabinet councils or councils of war at the capital upon their operations, the system of war in favour with their staff, the established force of the state and its armament, the military geography and statistics of the state that is to be invaded, and, finally, the resources and obstacles of every kind likely to be met...[58]

Jomini's enemy portrayal includes roughly the same elements as does that of his contemporary, Clausewitz. However, one might perceive Jomini's enemy image as being somewhat more complete than that of Clausewitz as he incorporate a specific category, which he calls "military policy" – a discipline distinct from diplomacy, strategy and tactics. In addition, it is noteworthy that in connexion with the military geography Jomini specifically emphasises the need for thorough examination of "permanent decisive points which may be present in the whole extent of the frontier or throughout the extent of the country."[59] It is hard to juxtapose his "permanent decisive points" with any modern military term, but to some extent there is a parallel with the Clausewitzian *Gravitationszentrum* (centre of gravity) as long as this is of a geographical or permanent nature. With reference to Sun Tzu, one may see such points as relevant parts of the *shih* characterising the operational or tactical options, which must be considered by the military leadership for any given military enterprise.

While Clausewitz is adamant that the military measures, which the commander adopts, are always a consequence of political aims and decision-making, Jomini is less convinced. In his opinion, pre-eminence of the political leadership is inappropriate if the political war leader makes his or her decisions in a place that is geographically divorced from the headquarters of the military commander-in-chief. Thus, as a consequence

---

[57] Ibid., p. 270.

[58] Ibid., pp. 38-39.

[59] Ibid., pp. 38-39.

of his disrespect of politicians detached from reality, Jomini sets out yet another specific subcategory, the "political objective point," which is a point that matters to politicians but which is militarily futile.[60] Acquiring most of his military experience under the Napoléonic system, where political and military requirements coincided exactly, as the Emperor embodied the supreme authority in both spheres; Jomini gives some examples from the alliances against France of military disasters caused by politically fixed objective points to be conquered regardless of military prudence. We may illustrate the continued relevance of his observation by one more recent example of political micro-management: the Nazi German campaign in the USSR. In this theatre of war Hitler chose to advance with an unreasonably broad front towards Leningrad, Moscow, and Stalingrad at the same time. While the strategic relevance of the former two was doubtful, the oilfields of the Caucasus mountain range were what mattered. However, Leningrad and Moscow had symbolic value and were – for that reason – politically designated as Nazi German objectives.

Like Clausewitz, Jomini was aware of the importance of psychological factors. "The exited passions of a people are of themselves always a powerful enemy."[61] He paid tribute to the inflammatory talents of Napoléon and Russian General Alexander Suvorov suggesting that "the general should do everything in his power to electrify his own soldiers and to impart to them the same enthusiasm which he endeavours to repress in his adversaries."[62] British Second World War General Bernard L. Montgomery, later Field Marshal the Viscount of Alamein, was well aware that his opponent in the Western Desert in 1942, the German General Erwin Rommel, had perfected that skill, and he went out of his way to wreck Rommel's demigod status with the troops before staging his decisive battles in North Africa. Through meticulous intelligence gathering, Montgomery made sure that no more unpleasant surprises materialised and that the troops regained confidence in themselves through experiencing success.

Although the Prussian 19th century general, Helmuth Graf von Moltke (the elder), was no innovator as far as intelligence was concerned, he was keenly intent on getting his enemy picture right. In his own writings he agreed with many of the ideas put forward by Clausewitz, but he found

---

[60] Ibid., p. 91.

[61] Ibid., p. 41.

[62] Ibid., p. 41. Alexander Vasilyevich Suvorov, 1729-1800.

intelligence both important and practicable.[63] As he wrote his own theories on war in the last quarter of the 19th century, many important changes in European society separated him from the time of Clausewitz. The Industrial Revolution had come to full fruition and – in the meantime – it had provided armies and navies with means of communication, such as railways, steam ships and the telegraph, allowing increasingly effective methods of transmission and mobility. In addition, balloons, which had first been used almost a century earlier, were then put to good use providing military information in the American Civil War (1861-65) as well as during the Siege of Paris towards the end of the Franco-German War of 1870-71.[64] Moltke's appreciation of the need for and the possibilities of establishing a sound and clear enemy picture took account of these, the latest, technological developments, but well-tried methods such as spies and light cavalry still formed the backbone of his military intelligence efforts.

While Sun Tzu taught that political aims should preferably be achieved without armed confrontation and, if that turned out to be unavoidable then with the least possible destruction, as far as the justification of the armed execution of political decisions was concerned Moltke differed in his philosophical outlook. Moltke regarded war, not as something to be avoided but as a natural manifestation of civilised societies' aims and prowess and an affair which ennobled those engaged in it.[65] Moreover, like Jomini he was at variance with Clausewitz as to war's subordination to politics. It was his firm conviction that for the duration of actual fighting – from the declaration of war and until negotiations for peace were initiated – politicians should mind their own business and leave the conduct of war to the professionals.[66] Moreover, as an addition to the enemy picture he introduced a division of the opposition not hitherto seen. While the "lawful enemy" was an opponent operating according to certain generally accepted rules, this did not apply to "the unorganised populace which resorts to the

---

[63] Helmuth Graf von Moltke (the elder), 1800-91, Prussian general, creator and first chief of the Prussian, later Imperial German *Großer Generalstab* [Great General Staff], 1858-88. Daniel J. Hughes, ed. *Moltke and the Art of War* (Novato: Presidio, 1993).

[64] Herman, *Intelligence Power*, p. 72.

[65] Hughes, *Moltke and the Art of War*, p. 23: "War is part of God's world order. War develops man's noblest virtues, which otherwise would slumber and die out: courage, self-denial, devotion to duty, and willingness to make sacrifices."

[66] Clausewitz, *On War*, p. 604-5 and Hughes, Moltke, pp. 21 and 36.

force of arms on its own initiative and from which his [the soldier's] life is not secure for a moment, day or night."[67] Moltke appears to have regarded this as an excuse for reprisals against communities suspected of harbouring partisans – or franctireurs in the vocabulary of the time.[68] His view on who should have the right to be called a "lawful enemy" has marked German martial law and behaviour in war for more than a hundred years. It has made itself unmistakably felt in countries occupied by Germany during both World Wars, and has been explicitly endorsed by, inter alii, the Second World War Nazi German Reichsbevollmächtigter (minister plenipotentiary) in Denmark, Dr. Werner Best.[69]

As mentioned above, in spite of obvious similarities in their thinking, the worlds of Jomini and Clausewitz on the one hand and that of Moltke on the other are far from being the same. Moltke noticed that:

> Modern wars call whole peoples to arms... The full financial power of the state comes to bear... Peace is endangered by the opinions of peoples, by desires for annexation and revenge...and by pressure of the parties (especially their spokesmen).[70]

Thus Moltke included the civilian population and the public martial fervour in his enemy portrait, and, ominously, he also put his finger on an evident precursor of the military industrial complexes of two world wars and, possibly, those of the Cold War too. He intimated that enmity might have no deep root in societies, but was artificially kindled by financial interests. "The money market also has today gained an influence that calls the armed forces into the field for its interests. European armies have occupied Mexico and Egypt to meet the demands of high finance." His prediction seems to have come true in July and August of 1914.[71]

Like Clausewitz, Moltke regarded the enemy as an animate entity with

---

[67] Cited from Hughes, *Moltke*, p. 23.

[68] Ibid., p. 32 with footnote 21.

[69] Werner Best and Siegfried Matlok, ed. *Dänemark in Hitlers Hand: Der Bericht des Reichsbevollmächtigten Werner Best über seine Besatzungspolitik in Dänemark mit Studien über Hitler, Himmler. Heydrich, Ribbentrop, Canaris u.a.* (Husum: Husum Verlag, 1988), pp. 38-39.

[70] Hughes, *Moltke*, p. 26.

[71] Ibid., p. 26

a will of its own. That will was an important part of his enemy image and a central object for intelligence to discover, as the strategic deployment of his own forces would have to provide adequate responses to it. "We can limit this [the enemy's will] only if we are prepared and decisive in taking the initiative. But we may not be able to break the enemy's will except with the means of tactics, with combat."[72] He was well aware, however, that in this respect the enemy would have a powerful say as to which kind of initiative would be needed; he realised that the military and moral consequences of every great engagement were far-reaching and would usually create a totally different situation. Such a new basis would therefore require renewed intelligence efforts and adjustments of the plans and the measures taken, because "no plan of operation extends with certainty beyond the first encounter with the enemy's main strength."[73]

Initiative is about acting first to render the other side's action futile, or – in the 20th century's terminology – to get inside the opponent's observation-orientation-decision-action cycle, his "OODA loop."

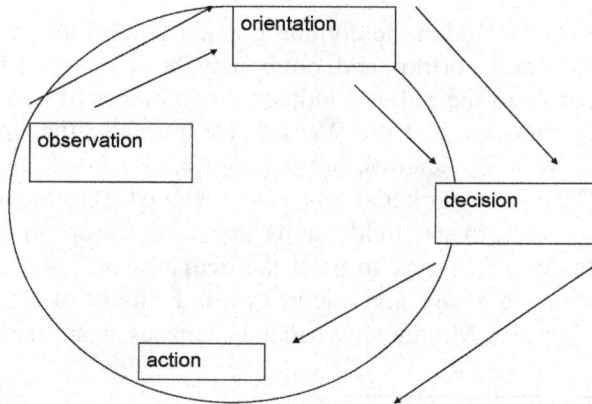

The ooda-loop

The OODA loop has to do with the relative speed of one's own and

---

[72] Ibid., p. 45.

[73] Ibid.

one's opponent's decision-action processes. In Nuclear Warriors, Richard Holmes explains that:

> The importance of tempo as a means of turning inside the opponent's OODA loop was demonstrated by retired USAF colonel John Boyd. Boyd started from a study of American aviators in air-to-air combat in the Korean War. They achieved a 10:1 kill ratio, despite the general superiority of the principal Communist fighter, the MiG-15, to the American F-86: it was only through observation through the F-86's bubble canopy and its ability to pass from one manœuvre to another because of his aircraft's exceptionally effective hydraulic controls that the American pilot enjoyed real advantage. Boyd maintained that these advantages proved decisive, because they allowed American pilots to force their opponents into a series of actions, assessing how the situation changed with each and steadily gaining a time advantage until a firing opportunity was offered.[74]

Although Moltke's observation applied to the army and formation levels, it covered in its essence the same as the "OODA loop" does today for the individual unit, combatant, or weapons platform. Maintaining the initiative necessitates a reliable image of the enemy including a certain insight or educated guess as to his intentions, and to a higher degree of perfection than that of the adversary's knowledge about oneself.

In Moltke's days the means available for intelligence gathering in the field were – apart from interrogation of prisoners – limited primarily to cavalry units: "Reconnaissance is intrinsically and almost exclusively the business of the cavalry... Cunning and ability, rapid judgement [*Blick*] and resolute action will be of worth."[75] While today it is commonly believed that leadership qualities can be acquired through training and education, in Moltke's days the general conviction was that you were either born to become a leader or you would never be one. Terms like *Blick, coup d'œil,* and *rapid judgement* were characteristics of a person born to command, and Clausewitz saw these qualities as hallmarks of the tactical commander that should be relied upon rather than meticulous intelligence work. Moltke agreed with Clausewitz in this respect, although he found that these gifts were not prerogatives of high command but were commonly found amongst the leaders of cavalry units, who were after all his era's intelligence collectors par excellence.

---

[74] Richard Holmes, *Nuclear Warriors.* (London, UK: Jonathan Cape, 1988), p. 113.

[75] Hughes, *Moltke*, p. 198.

When comparing the theoretical contributions to the perception of enmity and the creation of a portrait of the face of the foe we find a remarkable similarity of the views of Sun Tzu, Jomini, and Moltke. All three stressed the importance of thorough intelligence work prior to, as well as during, conflict, and agreed that spies were of essence in providing a basis for planning. Thus, we may add, they anticipated the present day notion of situational, battlefield, or battle-space awareness. Where they differed amongst themselves was in their aims. While Sun Tzu advocated the use of spies in order to avoid armed conflict if possible or else to confine it, Jomini merely observed their usefulness, accepting the fact that wars did occur and that fighting was necessary. Moltke was only concerned with actual combat and he saw spies – among various other means – as useful contributors to that end.

The Twentieth Century

The Second Boer War, 1899-1902, heralded yet another century of warfare and development in the fields of military technology, organisation and doctrines. This, the first major war of the 20th century, did not significantly add new methods to the well tried human intelligence addressed above, but the period did contribute important achievements to modernisation of its application.

The British and dominion forces addressed the need for systematic collection, processing and evaluation of information through formation of an intelligence staff of forty officers commanded by a brigadier who was nominated as the Director of Military Intelligence.[76] After the end of the War in South Africa, in most major European countries intelligence gathering at the strategic level intensified distinctly over the years of rising tension prior to the outbreak of the Great War, and public interest in the matter increased markedly at the appearance of espionage or spy literature like *The Riddle of the Sands*, *When William Came*, and *The Thirty-Nine Steps*.[77] The diplomatic services carried on the covert work they had been

---

[76] Robert Martyn, *Canadian Military Intelligence and the Revolution of Military Affairs of 1914-1918*. Queen's University. "http://members.shaw.ca/keepinga/smss/pdf/martyn_smss2001.pdf" (accessed 1 March 2003).

[77] Erskine Childers, *The Riddle of the Sands* (Virginia: IndyPublish.com McLean, no year); Hector Hugh Munro "When William Came" in The Complete Stories of Saki (Ware: Wordsworth Classics, 1993), pp. 487-575; John Buchan, The Thirty-Nine Steps, 1915.

doing for centuries, but now dedicated, professional, and well paid agents of espionage such as Sydney Reilly, Baron August von Schluga, and Colonel Alfred Redl reinforced these efforts. All three spies were active in the years prior to the Great War. Sydney Reilly, born 1874 (he is believed to have been shot by the Soviets; the year of his death is unknown), was a British-German-Russian triple-spy allegedly of Russian decent. August von Schluga, 1841-1916, was a Hungarian aristocrat spying for Prussia-Germany against Austria. Alfred Redl, born in Austrian Galizia in 1864 and committing suicide in Vienna in 1911, was the head of Austrian counter-intelligence, the Vienna based Evidenzbüro, who handed over the Austro-Hungarian deployment plans to Russia, Serbia, France, and Italy in exchange for huge amounts of money.

With the outbreak of war in August 1914, the diplomatic missions of the belligerent parties were withdrawn, and most diplomatic intelligence gathering and liaison work ceased except in neutral countries like the Scandinavian states, Switzerland and Portugal. The war further strengthened efforts of improving the gathering and analysis of information at the operational and tactical levels, and it also provided an opportunity for innovative thinking and experimentation in technology. The discovery in 1917 by British Naval Intelligence of the so-called Zimmermann Telegram was an example of a successful tapping and decryption of enemy correspondence as well as of clever deception. The Zimmermann Telegram was actually two coded messages sent by the German Foreign Secretary, Arthur Zimmermann, 1864-1940, in an attempt to persuading Mexico to invade the United States. The aims of this action was, primarily, to engage enough United States military forces at home so as to prevent them from being transferred to Europe and, secondly, to win over not only Mexico but also Japan for The Central Powers' cause.

A vast array of practical information gathering aids was employed at the battlefield or tactical level. Telephone, wireless, aerial photography, sound- and light-ranging, radio-intercept, and eavesdropping of trench telephone lines provided a glut of intelligence support opportunities to be developed and employed.[78] Harnessing modern technology for war entailed creation of army and naval signals units, flying corps, and intelligence collecting, processing, and analysing organisations. As technology gradually improved, and organisational patterns changed, parallel adaptation of tactical and operational doctrines saw the light of day. Along

---

[78] David Kahn, *Hitler's Spies: German Military Intelligence in the Second World War* (U.S.A.: Da Capo Press, 2000), pp. 34-35.

with this flurry of modification, the growing intelligence staffs collected and analysed the information gathered by the amazing new means and methods, and made sure that the products reached decision-makers in the shape of aerial photographs, intelligence summaries, reports, estimates, etc.[79] Intelligence pertinent to counter-battery fire would be delivered to target acquisition units by aircrews observing enemy gun positions.[80] In other words, as technology increasingly managed to facilitate timely transmission of information, the collection, analysis and use of intelligence became a consciously performed and indispensable element of the decision-action cycle.

Although light and flag signals were still used, the navies of 1914 mostly communicated by means of radio. Thus signals intelligence, communications intelligence and cryptography analysis materialised, facilitating fairly well updated knowledge of the location of enemy naval units and, in some cases, their commanders' missions. Throughout the Battle of Jutland, 31st May 1916, specialised teams at the German naval headquarters at Neumünster were able to monitor every movement of the British Grand Fleet in the North Sea. Similarly, the British Admiralty's 'Room 40' – the Royal Navy's intelligence establishment – was equally keen with respect to the German *Hochseeflotte* (the Imperial German North Sea Fleet).[81] Moreover, the intelligence organisations of the competing navies developed more or less in parallel. Thus, while the German *Kaiserliche Kriegsmarine* (Imperial Navy) had an intelligence branch at their admiralty staff comprising sections for Observation and Cryptanalysis, Military and Political Affairs, Foreign Navies, and Communications Intelligence, a similar development took place at the Royal Navy's intelligence headquarters in Room 40.[82]

---

[79] 1st (Canadian) Division introduced daily INTSUMs (intelligence summaries) in March 1915. Martyn, *Canadian Military Intelligence*, p. 10.

[80] Kahn, *Hitler's Spies*, pp. 34-37. The French author Antoine de Saint Exupéry in *Krigsflyver* [*Pilote de guerre*] (København: Jespersens og Pios Forlag, 1943) vividly describes the reverse side of aerial photo reconnaissance (viz. that the means of communications of French WW II photo reconnaissance had been outdated by the latest (German) developments in mechanised warfare). De Saint Exupéry was a captain and a pilot during the so-called Phoney War (1939-40) and during the German invasion of France in the spring of 1940.

[81] Ibid., p. 38.

[82] Kahn, *Hitler's Spies*, pp. 37-38.

However, although these organisations constituted major improvements in comparison with previous naval encounters, they did not guarantee full exploitation of intelligence. The late American military historian Michael Handel found that the Battle of Jutland was an example of how faulty decision-making might squander vital intelligence and opportunities. He opined that, in the case of "Jutland," thanks to the Royal Navy's excellent modern equipment, intelligence had the potential, if used properly, to bring the Entente an easy victory.[83] As we now know, the outcome was far from as clear cut as that.

In terms of insight into the opposing side's operational and tactical doctrines, the First World War started badly for the Central Powers as well as for the Entente with faulty and outdated knowledge of enemy doctrine. Basic intelligence was founded largely on observation of pre-war manœuvres as far back as the 1890's, and the experiences from the Russo-Japanese War of 1904-5 had not been taken seriously into account although most western powers had had military observers on the ground for the duration of that conflict. Old enemy images still existed, such as the notion widely extant in Britain that while the Germans were basically peaceful and noble creatures, the French were the real foe that the British forces ought to combat. For a millennium, France and Britain/England had competed for dominance on the continent of Europe and in the race for colonies, and it was not until the signing in 1904 of the Entente Cordiale that this enmity was put to rest. However, the change commenced as a high-level political process and the novel peaceful sentiments took years to percolate down through the tiers of society. Thus it took the First World War to ensure popular understanding for this new state of affairs.

On land though, at the operational and tactical levels increased emphasis was now placed on up-to-date information gathering by army formations. Thus, at the level of the fighting troops, where reliance on pre-war experience was less prominent, formations and units began to use observers and reconnaissance patrols, exploit prisoners along with their captured maps and documents, use aerial photography and chat with locals and refugees.[84] The trend was, thus, for formations and units to produce their own intelligence as opposed to waiting for higher headquarters to push

---

[83] Michael I. Handel, *Intelligence and Military Operations* (London: Frank Cass, 1990), p. 52.

[84] The Canadian Expeditionary Forces' Corps Headquarters created an observation section of one officer and forty other ranks to be employed along the entire corps front line. Martyn, *Canadian Military Intelligence*, p. 6.

their information forward.[85] In that respect, the fighting man displayed ingenuity and daring. Patrols and individuals at the lowest tactical levels carried messages, went across to ferret out enemy trenches, machinegun positions and barbed wire fences, and did all-in-all a remarkably successful job.[86] This happened on both sides, and the German author Ernst Jünger, at the time a subaltern of the German Imperial Army, told of the proceedings of one night patrol across to enemy lines: "In the night, thus, together with three companions I slid back amongst the trenches. We moved on the elbows and the tips of the toes to right in front of the English obstacles where we hid behind occasional shrubberies."[87]

New techniques however, did not make time honoured methods irrelevant. Interviews of prisoners of war employing shrewd exploitation of flattery, bribery and deceit rarely failed. As Handel pointed out:

> The best sources of information on Turkish strength and order of battle often proved to be prisoners of war, deserters, and captured documents. British officers often offered prisoners money or drink. They found that the Turk in contravention of his religious principles [was] usually a devoted adherent to the bottle.[88]

During the interwar years, 1919-1939, technological development continued, particularly in the field of signals intelligence. Spying thrived as always, and travellers, diplomats, and military attachés were free to go about their well-rehearsed liaison work amongst businessmen, politicians, Diasporas, disgruntled soldiers and left wing naïve political idealists; it was during this period that the Soviet Union managed to recruit the notorious "Cambridge Five," thus landing an impressive prize for the early Cold War years. Harold Adrian Russell Philby, 1912-1988, Guy Francis de Moncy Burgess, 1910-63, Donald Duart Maclean, 1913-1983, Anthony Blunt,

---

[85] Martyn, *Canadian Military Intelligence*, p. 7.

[86] For example, Gefreiter (lance corporal) Adolf Hitler throughout the war carried out a most dangerous job as *Meldegänger* (runner) carrying intelligence to and from his company commander's command post.

[87] Translated from: Ernst Jünger, *In Stahlgewittern* (Stuttgart: Klett-Cotta Verlag, 1990), p. 81. Original text: "In der Nacht schlich ich also mit drei Begleitern zwischen den Gräbern herum. Wir robbten auf den Fußspitzen und Ellenbogen bis dicht vor das englische Hindernis und verbargen uns dort hinter einzelstehenden Grasbüscheln."

[88] Handel, *Intelligence and Military Operations*, p. 145.

1907-1983, and John Cairncross, 1913-95, were named the "Cambridge Five" by their German born recruiter, Arnold Deutsch, after the Fünfergruppen (five members groups) – German communist resistance cells opposing the rising Nazi Party in Austria. Occasionally the term "The Magnificent Five" was seen, which alluded to an American Western from 1960 called *The Magnificent Seven*.

The inter-war period also revealed examples of the wider, partly non-military, study of potential enemies, their societies, ideologies, structural problems, and their possible war potentials. In *Calculations*, American Professors of military history Williamson Murray and Allan Millet have compared the governmental efforts of seven major Second World War belligerents to collect and process information on, inter alia, industrial and economic capacities of potentially hostile powers before that war.[89]

While at the outbreak of Second World War in September 1939 the British did well in the spheres of strategic and operational intelligence, the Germans largely outperformed them at the tactical level. However, the British grasped the importance of political and economic issues as well as of strategic signals intelligence and code breaking. Moreover, by a stroke of extraordinarily good luck the British Government Code and Cipher School at Bletchley Park managed to break the German codes. Thanks to pre-war Franco-Polish-British co-operation, the defection of some Polish engineers, who had worked in Germany on the encryption machine which later developed into the so-called Enigma ciphering device, the capture of a naval Enigma apparatus from a sinking German submarine, and the ingenuity of the mathematician Alan Turing, who was an unusually clever scientist developing a first generation computer, Bletchley Park was able to cope with German encrypted messages right from the beginning of the Second World War.[90] Also, the application of radar technology had enormous value on the defensive posture on the land, sea, and air environments.

Second World War intelligence was not only a matter of smart technology and effective collection of information. Equally as crucial to its optimal utilisation was the understanding at the highest political level of its importance. In his capacity as British Prime Minister from May 1940 until

---

[89] Williamson Murray and Allan R. Millet. *Calculations: Net Assessment and the Coming of the Second World War*. (Toronto: The Free Press, 1992).

[90] The UK's 'Government Code and Cipher School' at Bletchley Park was where the enemy secret codes were broken during the operation nicknamed "ULTRA." Handel, *Intelligence and Military Operations*, p. 295.

July 1945, Winston Churchill drew successfully on his scientific experiences with signals intelligence gained, primarily, from his tenures of previous offices as First Lord of the Admiralty and various other government posts during and after the Great War.[91] However, no less important was the priority which he gave to central co-ordination of the wartime intelligence efforts.[92] This harmonisation of requirements, collection, analysis, and results had no apparent parallel on the German side, where – because of competing semi-independent intelligence organisations – no co-ordination was carried out but on the highest political level, when intelligence reached the Führer.[93] By fragmenting the intelligence community and making the services compete for his favours, Hitler allotted a rôle to intelligence tailored to fit narrowly the ideological and political aims of the regime and the perceived enemy within the German Reich – the Jews, the Communists and the army generals doubting his genius – rather than the need for precise and timely information on the external foe. Therefore, as well as because of the unhealthy mistrust and failure to co-operate amongst such institutions as the *Oberkommando der Wehrmacht* (the joined supreme command of German armed forces), the armed services, the SS, the Foreign Office, and the Nazi Party, at the strategic level in Germany, chaos reigned supreme, and did so increasingly, as the war wore on.[94]

To be of any real value, the information gathered has to be processed and analysed quickly and correctly and subsequently disseminated in a timely fashion. Moreover, it has to be put in the correct context, which will include not only military hardware and plans but economic and industrial issues as well. This invariably happened with the Allies – not so on the German side. Noticing the unhappy course his country had chosen, the German architect and later Minister of Armaments Albert Speer observed that "one must be quite clear about the fact that those people, who plan the enemy bomber attacks on our economy, have an understanding of German

---

[91] Winston Spencer Churchill, British officer, author, and politician; 1874-1965.

[92] Michael I. Handel, *Leaders and Intelligence* (London: Frank Cass, 1989), p. 190.

[93] Handel, *Intelligence and Military Operations*, pp. 425-427.

[94] For a closer examination of the Byzantine German intelligence bureaucracy, see matrix in: Kahn, *Hitler's Spies*, pp. 44-45.

economic life; their planning is shrewd in contrast to that of our own."[95] Furthermore, strategic analysis, signals intelligence, and code breaking almost exclusively benefited the Allies, though not always perfectly. While the breaking of the Enigma encryption through Bletchley Park's "Operation Ultra" gradually improved and became close to perfect from 1944 onwards, some commanders did not fully understand that they would have to pose pertinent and precise questions in order to get useful and accurate intelligence. And even when one had been lucky enough to achieve correct information, there was no such thing as a guarantee that the enemy might not change his mind.

By penetrating the Italian naval codes through Ultra, Bletchley Park provided the intelligence which allowed an early maritime victory in the Mediterranean. This intelligence coup firmly established British naval supremacy in the eastern Mediterranean waters, and this became a pivotal factor in the battles for Greece and Crete that followed. At this early stage, Ultra had provided Royal Naval Admiral Cunningham's headquarters in Alexandria with advance warning of the Italian Admiral Iachino's intention of intercepting British convoys en route from Africa to Greece on the night of 31 March 1941. This insight enabled Cunningham to surprise the Italian naval task force, sink the cruisers *Zara* and *Fiume*, and seriously damage the battleship *Vittorio Veneto*.[96] Similarly in May 1942, naval signals intelligence provided the United States' Navy with almost complete and accurate knowledge of Japanese dispositions off Midway enabling the timely dispatch of carriers to intercept the Japanese force. In contrast, the Japanese had no knowledge whatsoever of the whereabouts of the US battle groups:

On 10 May 1942, Midway (referred to in Japanese signals as AF) was definitively identified [as a Japanese objective], while on 14 May it was learned that a Japanese invasion force would also be included in the imminent operation. The complete order of battle was obtained on 25th, and by 27th, Captain Layton was able to furnish Nimitz with the exact date of attack... The Japanese, whose plan depended on surprise, instead found themselves the victim of an unanticipated turn of events. In spite of their impressive numerical superiority, the Japanese fleet suffered a resounding defeat [3-7 June 1942].[97]

[95] Handel, *Intelligence and Military Operations*, p. 367.

[96] Handel, *Intelligence and Military Operations*, p. 40.

[97] Ibid., pp. 34ff.

Unlike the Allies' astonishingly successful strategic intelligence, the German efforts were mostly fruitless at that level. However, in the operational and the tactical spheres, the German Wehrmacht was efficient. Not surprisingly, time mattered more at the lower levels, making the value of communications intelligence with its time-consuming code breaking a rather doubtful affair. Conversely, practical combat intelligence had been highly developed and successfully put into practice by the Germans.

Acoustic intelligence, introduced in the First World War in the form of sound ranging as a target acquisition means for the artillery, was further developed in the Second World War. Additionally, sophisticated acoustic sensors were issued to German special engineer platoons to help give advance warning of approaching infantry. Imagery intelligence, based on aerial photography, was immensely improved and skilfully used by the Wehrmacht.[98] In combination with rather traditional methods such as scout car reconnaissance and prisoner of war interrogation as well as by means of thorough and highly meticulous appraisal of incoming information, collation, and expedient dissemination, these improvements allowed the Germans to achieve some very successful intelligence results, even when the war approached its concluding phase. "Operation Goodwood," for instance, was an encounter where the Germans attained a far more comprehensive picture of the British situation than the Twenty-First Army Group managed to build up on them. The intelligence staff with Field-Marshal Erwin Rommel, who, at the time, was responsible for the German invasion defence along the north and west coasts of Europe, the Atlantikwall (the Atlantic Wall), had worked hard, systematically, and effectively along such familiar lines as observation posts, prisoner interrogation, and aerial reconnaissance.[99] Apart from German diligence, Handel saw the Wehrmacht's success explained not only through the German efficiency but partly by General Bernard Law Montgomery's obsession with orderliness and his notion of a "tidy battlefield." This entailed numerous extra diligent measures which might have contributed to giving away the British intentions.[100] Second World War achievements

---

[98] Kahn, *Hitler's Spies*, p. 540.

[99] Montgomery's offensive with three armoured divisions east of Caen launched on 18th July 1944. Generalfeldmarschall (Field Marshal) Erwin Rommel (1891-1944). General Bernard Law Montgomery (later Field Marshal, 1st viscount of Alamein), (1887-1976).

[100] Handel, *Leaders and Intelligence*, p. 233.

in the intelligence field formed the point of departure for the endeavours to avoid surprise and inappropriate action in the dangerous and delicate milieu of the terror balance during the years of the Cold War. The technologies discovered and developed prior to and during the Second World War formed the basis for post war intelligence progress. Spies carried their trade into the Cold War, and names like Oleg Gordievskiy, Oleg Penkovskiy, Aldrich Ames, Robert Hansen and others were added to the history of the sordid profession of espionage.[101]

The development of intelligence means and methodology in the period of 1946-2003 gathered momentum following the demise of the Soviet Union and the subsequent conclusion of the Cold War. Advances in the fields of signals intelligence, communications intelligence, and decryption proceeded from Ultra to its Cold War and post-Cold War equivalents. Operation Venona, aimed at, and succeeded in, breaking the Soviet diplomatic and military codes. Aerospace[102]photography developed in the way of better platforms such as the U-2 spy plane, satellites, and unmanned aerial vehicles and the ordinary cameras were improved and partially exchanged for Infra-Red Line Scanners, Down Looking and Sideways Looking Airborne Radars, and thermal cameras. Radar technology and coverage made a quantum leap with the airborne early warning radars, the Synthetic Aperture Radar, and the establishment of continuous radar-chains overlooking entire continents and their airspaces.[103]

However, the most promising and decisive step forward was the ongoing development of Turing's computer and the subsequent improvement of communications and precision.[104]

Nonetheless, although the technology of the twentieth century has come to play a decisive rôle in intelligence, Liddell Hart reminds us that,

---

[101] Oleg Gordievskiy, KGB resident in London and double agent for the British from 1974 until defection in 1985. Oleg Penkovskyi, GRU employee recruited by the British in 1961, probably instrumental in the solution of the Cuba Crisis, arrested by the KGB in 1962. Aldrich Ames, American, Russian agent in the CIA, betrayed Gordievskyi in 1985. Robert Hansen, American, Soviet and Russian agent in U.S.A. arrested 2001.

[102] For fuller description of Venona see Nigel West, *Venona: The Greatest Secrets of the Cold War* (Glasgow: Harper Collins Publishers, 2000).

[103] Herman, *Intelligence Power*, pp. 73-76 and passim.

[104] For further details on precision see: Michael Russel Rip and James M. Hasik, *The Precision Revolution: GPS and the Future of Aerial Warfare* (Annapolis: Naval Institute Press, 2002).

It is wise in war not to underrate your opponent. It is equally important to understand his methods, and how his mind works. Such understanding is the necessary foundation of a successful effort to foresee and forestall his moves... A nation might profit a lot if the advisory organs of government included an 'enemy department' covering all spheres of war from the enemy's point of view – so that, in this state of detachment, it might succeed in predicting what he was likely to do next.[105]

To paint a portrait of a military opponent one should start with looking at the political aspirations of the hostile, or potentially hostile, society. Liddell Hart observes that, "the military objective should be governed by the political objective... The object in war is a better state of peace."[106] Consequently, the task making up the image of one's enemy must, first and foremost, be to delve into the question of the "state of peace" that might be more desirable for the enemy than the existing one. An obvious example would be the *Lebensraum* and resources which, in the 1930s, many Germans sincerely believed that they needed. The keen observer wanting to know the trend of German foreign policy might have studied Mein Kampf. There he or she would have found explicit information on what, at the time, would have been a better state of peace for Germany as perceived by the prospective German leader. The ardent student of that opus would then have become aware that, in the 1920s, Hitler's main concern was Germany's dearth of raw materials, which were insufficient to support the country's expanding population beyond a certain point in time. Hitler even went as far as to hint where these commodities might be found, thus pointing to the potential mission for the armed forces in the case of his accession to power.[107]

To proceed to the operational designs of the enemy, which must also be included in the portrait, Liddell Hart draws attention to his belief that the age-old insistence on "destruction of the enemy's main forces on the battlefield" leads to indecisive and exhausting results, as was, in his view, so clearly demonstrated by both world wars. He points to the moral objectives, achieved through decisive blows against "the Achilles' heel of

[105] B. H. Liddell Hart, *Strategy* (New York: Meridian, 1967), p. 207.

[106] Ibid., p. 338.

[107] Hugh R. Trevor-Roper, *The Mind of Adolf Hitler*, in introduction to Hugh R. Trevor-Roper, *Hitler's Table Talks 1941-1944: His Private Conversions* (New York City: Enigma Books, 1988), p. xii. Cf. Adolf Hitler, *Mein Kampf*, 626-630. *Auflage* (München: Verlag der NSDAP, Franz Ehers Nachfolger, 1941), p 154.

the enemy army," the headquarters and communications, and the hostile nation's "nerve-system," its "static civil centres of industry." Since movement and surprise are core elements of successful operations in war, an important detail of any enemy portrait will be the possibilities the enemy might exploit to find what Liddell Hart has called the "approach of least expectation." In his view, this is entirely a psychological phenomenon, and its usefulness depends on one's will and ability to see one's own limitations and weaknesses.[108] As the opponent will try to achieve his war aims, and their derived intermediate military objectives, as cheaply as possible, it can be assumed that logically such an approach will be one avoiding combat as long as possible. In this process, it is likely that he will try to split opposing forces or to cut them off from their bases, supplies, and reinforcements which will frequently be inadequately protected in order to be able to concentrate maximum effort with front line formations. In other words, if one looks for indications of enemy designs one is well advised studying one's own obvious vulnerabilities.

The Twenty-First Century

To be useful, intelligence should be precise and timely: two demands which both call for optimal precision. Seen in this perspective the wars in Iraq and Afghanistan confirm the importance to intelligence of what we may call 'the precision revolution'.[109] In a report on the Iraq invasion by the multinational coalition in 2003 prepared by Anthony H. Cordesman of the Washington based Centre for Strategic and International Studies, it is pointed out that the lessons learned in Iraq have demonstrated that the combination of imagery, electronics, signals, human intelligence, improved communications and command, and intelligence fusion at every level gave a near real-time day and night situational awareness:

> The US had vastly improved every aspect of its intelligence, targeting, and command and control capabilities since the last Gulf War, as well as spent some 12 years in surveillance of Iraqi operations and military developments. Its combination of imagery, electronic intelligence, signals intelligence, and

---

[108] Liddell Hart, *Strategy*, p. 327.

[109] Anthony H. Cordesman, *The Instant Lessons of the Iraq War: Main Report, Third Working Draft*. Report by the Center for Strategic and International Studies. Washington D.C., 2003.

human intelligence was honed in Afghanistan, and improved communications and command and intelligence fusion at every level gave a near real-time day and night situational awareness.[110]

The report stressed the importance of the connexion between highly sophisticated intelligence gathering and the application of ordnance. Such integration, the report claims, had entailed reduced ammunition consumption and minimal collateral damage. Moreover, intelligence had been sufficiently precise and timely and communications quick enough to allow that aircraft, whose bombing missions proved abortive, could be redirected onto new targets thus saving time as well as valuable fuel and ammunition resources. This rapid retargeting capability – ranging from few minutes to two hours – changed the ability to hit such targets as leadership compounds and suspected weapons of mass destruction facilities and to respond to active intelligence rather than bomb predetermined or fixed targets. This deprived Iraqi leaders of their 'sanctuary of slow response.'[111]

However, this report is also interesting for its omissions. Mention is made neither of the American "friendly fire" problems, responsible, for instance, for the killing of western journalists and Kurdish allies, nor of the faulty strategic intelligence on weapons of mass destruction.[112] Thus as of spring 2003, in spite of pervasive optimism battle-space awareness still was not complete and uncertainty had not been entirely overcome. This was partly due to the confusing and negative influence of skewed images of the enemy caused among other things by American hubris, propaganda, and manipulation of facts, partly caused by ignorance of one's own situation. The killing of four Canadian soldiers on exercise in Afghanistan in 2002 by US air force pilots may serve as an example of the latter, and it is a reminder of Sun Tzu's remark that one should be as cognisant of one's own forces as of those of the enemy.[113] In regards to the means, methods, and theory used in the creation of the image of an enemy, for over two thousand years the occasional adoption of new methods has primarily been due to invention of new technical means rather than decisive alteration of the

---

[110] Cordesman, *The Instant Lessons*, p. 5.

[111] Cordesman, *The Instant Lessons*, p. 10.

[112] The incidents were broadcast repeatedly on the British Broadcasting Corporation, BBC, as well as the Canadian Broadcasting Corporation, CBC, at the time of their occurrences.

[113] Griffith, *Sun Tzu*, p. 84.

basic ideas. Moreover, rather than simply being replaced, methods have been gradually adapted along with the ever changing technological realities. It seems obvious, for instance, that cavalry is gone, not because the tasks that it used to solve have become irrelevant, but because reconnaissance vehicles and unmanned aerial vehicles perform the same job more effectively. Likewise, while the methods of the new "vehicular cavalry" have been adjusted, the core concept of reconnaissance remains.

Although the technological aids have improved over time and methods and organisation have been developed along with this evolution, the object remains. The face of the foe should be multi-faceted and complete and, as we have briefly touched upon in the introduction, the depiction of one's foe should not be limited to his animate forces. It must encompass adversity in its potential entirety including a wide variety of other factors. These factors include, *inter alia*, weather, indications of imminent hostile action, bait, terrain, water obstacles, defiles, routes of advance, vegetation and possible traps, all of which remain matters to be probed.

Technological development has provided us with a more precise and increasingly timely portrait of the foe and left reconnaissance to progressively sophisticated collection platforms – sadly reducing highly merited institutions like cavalry to ceremonial functions; *sic transit gloria mundi*.[114] Nonetheless, remarkably many methods, such as patrols, topographic descriptions, maps, and interviews with human beings, still survive. The latest war in Iraq has proven that the fifth column's eyes and ears concept has not been totally forgotten. Eclectic exploitation of sources has been perpetuated and improved by the advent of dedicated intelligence staffs, computers, sophisticated sensors and the internet; and indeed by meta-systems like ISTAR, to which we shall grant a closer examination in Chapter VIII.[115] The decision-maker's informed intuition may still be precious, but technical innovations have provided adequate tools allowing substantial augmentation of level and scope of his or her awareness.

Today, it appears obviously relevant to include other threats in the image of enemy than what is strictly related to traditional war. The menace of

---

[114] "Thus perishes worldly glory."

[115] ISTAR is a NATO project aiming at establishing a "meta-system" fusing systems of Intelligence, Surveillance, Target Acquisition, and Reconnaissance to present to the end-user a comprehensive picture of the hostile environment. *Land Forces Information Operations. Canadian Forces, Field Manual, Intelligence (English)*, B-GL-357-001/FP001, 2001, p. 1-3.

international crime, threats to the environment, and natural disasters with
which humanity might be faced in the immediate or more distant future are
factors we cannot ignore with impudence. Moreover, we are well advised
to remember the consequences of the Balkan Wars in the last decade of the
20th century, which forced the European Union nations to come together to
agree at the EU Summit in June, 1999, that there was a need to develop a
European intelligence capacity. At that moment, many of the member states
of the Union did not possess substantial intelligence resources themselves.
However, since then a general consensus has emerged that a European
intelligence structure does present certain obvious advantages: it will
improve the European strategy for action against terrorism agreed upon in
2004, and it will prolong the strategies in this field adopted by the United
Kingdom and France in 2006. Moreover, it may provide the new players in
the common defence and foreign policy fields as well as the future
executives of common action with means, which will be more effective
than those already available in the modest Situation Centre with the High
Representative for Foreign Affairs. This may also enable the EU member
states to co-operate more effectively internationally with states sharing a
common interest in curbing transnational crime.

There may be good reason to see this in the light of the adjustment of
the French security system. As France has recently integrated her internal
security services and established a national security council accepting
parliamentary control of this institution, setting up a liaison cell between
this council and the president of the republic, France has realised the need
for and put into practice a policy addressing the challenges of the present.[116]
In a white paper presented by the French president on 17 June, 2006, and
adopted by the council of ministers the day after, intelligence has been
made the priority issue. The central co-ordinator of the National Security
Council had been subordinated directly to the president thus underpinning
the centrality of this function to the existence of the state.[117]

Thus, like Britain, France now possesses a central co-ordination of
intelligence matters, the *Comité interminnisteriel du renseignement* [the
interdepartmental intelligence committee], whose responsibilities comprise
the defence of the nation's political, military, societal, and economic
interests.

---

[116] http://www.iris-france.org/Tribunes-2008-06-18.php3, accessed 19 August 2009

[117]   http://www.lexpress.fr/actualite/politique/le-renseignement-nouvelle-priorite-
strategique_512498.html, accessed 19 August 2009

To many political and administrative French decision-makers the mere mentioning of a European intelligence service is utopia. They will hardly hesitate to remind us that the recent article 4-2 in the adapted Treaty of the Union states that security remains a responsibility of each member state.[118] Nonetheless, prior to the French EU chairmanship in 2008 President Nicolas Sarkozy declared that the occupation with knowledge and prediction of issues influencing security must be a matter of priority which should be developed to benefit the defence of Europe. Although European intelligence would hardly be in a position to solve all security deficits it would be necessary to think creatively and audaciously.[119]

With the final implementation of the Lisbon Treaty in December 2009 – which introduced a permanent President of the European Council elected for 2½ year terms and a High Representative for Foreign Affairs, while the EU presidency carried on rotating every six months – continuity in policy-making and the scope of military reach-out might have been decisively strengthened. Reality has proven otherwise. Theoretically, the fields of foreign policy, diplomacy, defence and security would now all be centrally co-ordinated under the auspices of the office of the High Representative for Foreign Affairs, although so far this has not materialised.

---

[118] B. Mignot, "Le renseignement stratégique" in *Penser les ailes françaises*, No. 10, June 2006, pp. 82-85. «Pour de nombreux responsables politiques et administratifs français, l'évocation même d'un renseignement européen relève de l'utopie. Ceux-ci ne manquent pas de rappeler que le récent article 4-2 du Traité rénové de l'Union européenne indique que «la sécurité nationale reste de la seule responsabilité de chaque État membre.»

[119] Ibid., No. 10, June 2006, pp. 82-85. « Présentant les conclusions du Livre blanc sur la défense et la sécurité nationale, le Président de la République vient d'annoncer que «la fonction connaissance et anticipation serait prioritaire» et que «nous devons faire davantage pour la défense de l'Europe». Au moment où notre pays engage, après l'Espagne, l'Italie ou le Royaume-Uni, une réforme de sa communauté nationale du renseignement, il peut être utile de tenter de comprendre pourquoi il est peu probable que la politique du renseignement fasse partie des sujets que la France aborde avec ses partenaires à l'occasion de sa toute prochaine présidence de l'Union européenne. Demeurant impensable pour beaucoup d'esprits, le renseignement européen ne peut à l'évidence apporter une réponse immédiate aux défis de sécurité mais il mérite dès maintenant une réflexion plus audacieuse. »

Chapter II: Actors on the Intelligence Stage

*Fear them not therefore; for there is nothing covered
that shall not be revealed; and hid, that shall not be known*[1]

APART FROM ALL the official agencies that we discussed in Chapter I
and the host of real, imagined or potential enemies amongst competing
players on the international stage, there are additional collectors of
information as well as many more objectives such as terrorists, subversive
elements, industrial conglomerates and a host of other individuals and
organisations on which the nation state and those claiming to protect it wish
to keep a watchful eye. In theory, thus, there is nothing covered that we
should not be able to reveal.

Cold War Private Intelligence Initiatives

The Cold War was a period when two opposing blocs continuously
maintained images of each other as potential enemies and where evil
intentioned foreign agents as well as local traitors were perceived to be
hiding in every shadow. Thus intelligence services did not limit their
activity to what lay beyond the national borders, but closely followed
domestic politics, popular movements, students' manifestos, and

---

[1] Matthew: 10, 26.

manifestations of sympathy with foreign countries and organisations.

Moreover, here and there the state's official counter-intelligence services were supplemented by private organisations feeling free and obliged to watch particular groups of citizens. In many countries, which had been occupied by Nazi Germany during the Second World War, such agencies sprouted up from the wartime resistance movements, such as the Danish Firmaet (the firm) which was a bourgeois, pro-western group of people keeping an eye on the Communist Party, and the AIC or *Arbejdernes Informationscentral* (Workers' Information Centre), a Labour Party affiliate monitoring, inter alia, Socialist and Communist influence with and subversion of the trade unions. AIC had a network of around 6,000 informers, who had contacts to at least 100,000 persons countrywide. To put this in the proper perspective it should be mentioned that the total number of Danish inhabitants at the time was a mere four millions. In a report from 1956, the AIC analysed the Communist infiltration of Danish industry concluding among other things that "We must acknowledge that the Communists are like a Fifth Column."[2]

In the period between the end of the Second World War and the signing of the North Atlantic Treaty, in most western countries leading politicians were acutely aware of the dangers emerging from the growing east-west disagreement. In Denmark the trend towards painting menacing faces of the potential foe was reinforced when, in 1948, the Danish Prime Minister received a number of warnings that the Soviet Union was preparing an invasion of Scandinavia. The Danish ambassador to Washington, Henrik Kaufmann, added to the general commotion by sending his associate Poul Bang-Jensen to Copenhagen with a confidential report, in which he concluded that only unequivocal Danish indications that the country would be inclined to join the prospective Atlantic Alliance would dissipate the imminent threat of Soviet aggression. Confidential or not; Bang-Jensen felt that the government was not sufficiently attentive. Thus he shared the report's content with a number of persons with close ties to former bourgeois as well as Labour freedom fighter organisations, who quickly went about consolidating private intelligence gathering. Although in most democratic countries private intelligence initiatives would hardly be lawful, in Denmark these organisations were known to the changing governments, which kept them under their wings benefiting from their unofficial intelligence collection. In Denmark, this slightly irregular practice became publicly known as, in 1975, the Prime Minister Jens Otto Krag, apparently

---

[2] Bo Lidegaard, *Jens Otto Krag 1914-61* (Copenhagen: Gyldendal, 2001), p. 201

faintly intoxicated, became excessively talkative during a party at the American Embassy. An inquisitive journalist happened to be present and soon managed to relate this to a wider audience. However, the opposition had been as engaged in the establishment of and acquiescence with these 'alternative intelligence agencies' as had the government, and therefore did not want to exploit this minor faux pas. High-level politicians of both sides in Parliament had accepted the existence of these private watch-keepers, the American Central Intelligence Agency was supportive, and the issue was quickly laid to rest.

The activities of Firmaet included spreading of pro-western propaganda, registering of Communists, and year-long monitoring of the flat of the deputy chairman of the Communist Party, Mr. Alfred Jensen and his wife. Mr. Kjeld Olesen, later to become an MP and Minister for Defence in a Labour government, was one of those conducting the monitoring of Jensen. As he was later confronted with the doubtful legality of this activity he declared that "when we recall the atmosphere at the time, I had no qualms. We all regarded the Communists as traitors – pure and simple."[3]

Stay Behind Networks

In the period from 1998 to 2008, it was disclosed that shortly after the end of the Second World War a number of former freedom fighters agreed to re-activate their wartime organisations to counter the obvious Soviet threat and to help prepare Denmark better than when the Germans invaded in April 1940. They created a dormant resistance movement, or a stay behind network as it has been termed later, parallel to the 'Gladio' complex organised and sponsored by NATO and the United States. Many believed that a Soviet invasion was likely, and that the Danish Communists would betray their county just as the Danish Nazis had done in 1940. The Communists were to be countered through psychological warfare, disinformation, tapping of telephones, and registering. The contributors to the stay behind network, the Firmaet, which existed from 1948 to the mid 70s, through clever psychological warfare managed to create confusion and disagreement within the Communist Party. Using material gleaned from the tapping of Alfred Jensen's telephone conversations the Firmaet produced

---

[3] Charlotte Aagaard, "Kold Krig i Blikkenslagerbanden" (Cold War amongst the Plumbers' Gang), *Information*, 21 November 2005.

so-called 'black letters' combining internal knowledge with intrigue and disinformation. These letters were sent to individual members of the party. None of these suspected outsiders, because the letters contained information given to no one external. Within the party incrimination and disunity resulted.

It was obvious that the feeling of being threatened was widespread, and in 1962 the government issued a pamphlet called Hvis krigen kommer (If War Comes) indicating that the nuclear stand-off between the United States and the Soviet Union might soon turn into a genuine military confrontation on Danish soil.

It seems reasonable to claim that all those who were engaged in these activities saw a host of demons threatening war and renewed alien occupation of the country, and that they divided the world into two distinct groups, "them and us." However, as soon as this dichotomy leading to demonisation of the opponent started applying to fellow citizens of one's own country this became a liability to the democratic rule of law society. The heyday of semi-official intelligence was 1948-63. Since then, society's acceptance of non-state actors of this kind has slowly dissipated, not least because the old cross-party fraternity between former members of the Resistance Movement ceased to influence politics, and eventually ceased to exist.

Whistleblowers

The end of Cold War and the dawn of the War on Terror have to some extent changed the creation of enemy images, but not fundamentally the way they are conceived.

In many countries we have witnessed attempts to pinpoint the evildoers, the traitors, the agents of influence, and those who have lined their pockets giving assistance to foreign states. The archives of the STASI (*Ministerium für Staatssicherheit* [East German Espionage and Security Service]), have been opened, US and British archives are by and large accessible to the public, and for a short while even the Russians let inquisitive researchers have a glance into some of their secrets.

The curiosity as to the secret dealings of the War on Terror is immense. However, while intelligence services do their best to disclose and dismantle terror plans, potentials and networks, lots of organisations and individuals busy themselves with finding out whether the true enemy may perhaps be found amongst their own political leaderships. Whistleblowers, as these individuals have come to be known, abound all over the western world, and cases like Valerie Plame in the USA, Frank Grevil in Denmark, and Catherine Gun in the UK are but a few. However, while the need for disclosing 'the enemy within' quickly and fully seems to be urgent as well as justified, some of the commotion, in the guise of whistle blowing, simply serves the commercial interests of the tabloids amongst whose readers the appetite for public scandal appears insatiable.

The whistleblowers are not alone. In 2006 a so-called public and independent intelligence service, called "WikiLeaks," saw the light of day, and its founder, Australian Julian Assange, became a much publicised target of attention – not least of which to the US authorities whose secrets were no longer as safe as they would prefer. This service is dedicated to finding out and making public the secret dealings by economic criminals – Iceland bankers for instance – manipulated facts, and governments who send their soldiers fighting on the basis of fabricated intelligence. WikiLeaks has received rewards for its achievements from Amnesty International and The Economist. The aim of the organisation is to deprive people in powerful positions the possibility of exploiting their sway by providing all interested citizens around the world with correct and sufficient information on which to base their opinions, arguments, and decisions. In 2009, WikiLeaks revealed – from an American confidential report received from a source that remains anonymous to the wider world – that intelligence services of the countries fighting in combined operations in Afghanistan did not co-operate adequately. The point WikiLeaks tried to make was that because of incomplete intelligence the officers and soldiers engaged in these operations received less than optimum protection and that the public in the home countries was not informed. Likewise, this open intelligence service helps keep an eye on troop behaviour in combat. Thus, in April 2010, WikiLeaks uploaded video footage shot from a US gunship depicting American soldiers' killing of eight Iraqi civilians. The soundtrack recorded their roaring "hurray" as the Iraqis fell.[4]

In 2012, an employee with the US National Security Agency (NSA), Edward Snowden, commenced a fruitful co-operation with journalist Glen Greenwald leading – in the following year – to major leaks of highly sensitive information, which his position had allowed him to glean from material collected by the agency. His aim appeared to be merely to trigger an international debate on the dangers of state secret mass surveillance. One of his rather colourful early revelations was that of American General

---

[4] *The Times*, 6 April 2010, "Leaked video footage shows Iraqi journalists killed by US gunships," http://www.timesonline.co.uk/tol/news/world/iraq/article7088548.ece

David Petraeus' extramarital activities. The two of them plus documentary filmmaker Laura Poitras then started to work together to inform the public of what was actually being done by United States authorities to tap private electronic communication as a means to combating terrorism. A central item on Snowden's long list of disclosures concerned the programme called "Prism," which allowed the NSA to monitor private exchanges at internet platforms like Google, Facebook, Yahoo and Skype. Greenwald managed to persuade the British newspaper The Guardian to publish his subsequent articles with what he might find relevant during his collaboration with Snowden, who he had agreed to meet in Hong Kong to take over his glut of appropriated documents. In 2013, Greenwald published his views in his book *No Place to Hide*.[5]

The Rare Intelligence Co-operation

As the difficulties agreeing on EU intelligence initiatives show, it is a well established fact that by tradition intelligence is a closely guarded national matter and results are shared with partners only by a quid pro quo basis. Nations generally are, more often than not, reluctant to co-operate unless they get something of equal importance in return, and even then friends and allies do not necessarily share all available information. Even amongst the NATO countries no official, central co-ordination takes place. However, within a coalition or alliance intelligence collaboration is imperative. The more information we get from disparate sources the closer we are at dissolving some of the uncertainties, which are unavoidable in war.

One rare example of fairly effective collaboration in this field is The Falklands War of 1982. During this conflict the United Kingdom received extensive support from France and the United States and co-operated successfully with various other countries, which were not themselves parties to the conflict. For a number of years prior to Argentina's invasion of the crown dependency, the UK Joint Intelligence Committee had believed that, although it was obvious that sooner or later Argentina would wish to claim sovereignty over the islands, only peaceful means would be employed. British intelligence collection on Latin America had been starved of resources for some years, and their knowledge of Argentine military, navel, and air capabilities was scarce. Moreover, the lack of intelligence stations in the area made insight into Argentine political aims

---

[5] Glen Greenwald, *No Place to Hide* (New York: Metropolitan Books Henry Holt, 2014).

and bellicosity and the various services' and agencies' intentions almost impossible, because this would have required intensive human intelligence (HUMINT) activity. However, while HUMINT and code-breaking remained sole British responsibilities, the US provided maritime reconnaissance and extended image coverage of the area. France's support was equally important because of the French Exocet missiles and the French fighter aircraft employed by the Argentine air force, the Mirage III and the *Super Étandart*. These weapons systems were seen as the main threat to the Royal Naval fleet approaching the operations area. Moreover, it appears likely that France helped actively to prevent Argentina from buying additional Exocets on the black market.

Conversely, the atrocities in New York and Washington D.C. on 11 September 2001 might have been avoided but for the lack of co-operation amongst the American intelligence and security services. The perpetrators' backgrounds and their entry into the United States were known to the CIA which, however, did not adequately engage the FBI, which was empowered to act upon that intelligence. Thus the terrorists were allowed to take flying lessons and to prepare their sordid activity undisturbed by US police and security services.

Big Brother Society

When, in 2013, American journalist Glen Greenwald went to Hong Kong to receive what had been collected by Edward Snowden, he was amazed by the sheer size and scope of the material. Much of it revealed that surveillance had taken place not only of potential opponents, but of American citizens as well as friendly and allied powers such as Germany and France. There were many thousands of documents – many of them classified as 'top secret' and 'FVEY' – produced by not only almost every sub-unit of the NSA, but also by allied intelligence services.[6]

The methods used by the NSA included tapping directly into fibre-optic lines and underwater cables, redirecting messages traversing US territory and co-operating with allied intelligence services. Moreover, at the time of the revelations agreements existed between the NSA and various telecom,

---

[6] 'FVEY' meaning releasable to the UK, Canada, Australia and New Zealand, the four collaborating countries with which the US have close intelligence sharing ties. Glen Greenwald, *No Place to Hide* (New York: Metropolitan Books Henry Holt, 2014), pp. 90-1.

technology, and internet companies, such as IBM, Microsoft and Motorola, to hand over information on customers kept by these corporations. The 'Prism' programme would allow NSA apparently unlimited access to communication data passing through internet platforms like Facebook, Yahoo and Google.[7]

The 'Five Eyes' co-operation – including the UK, Canada, Australia, New Zealand and the United States – was (and remains) an incisive surveillance system, allowing monitoring telecommunication and internet use by citizens of the five member countries: individuals who are believed – rightly or wrongly – to be up to no good viewed primarily from a terrorism perspective. However, another tier of collaborators exists including, among others, countries like Denmark, Austria, France, Turkey, Saudi Arabia and Germany; all of them partners with more limited affiliation and not excluded from being targets themselves. The latter fact was notably illustrated by the revelation that the US had tapped the mobile phone of one of their closest allies, German chancellor Angela Merkel.

However, although the Five Eyes collaboration is on a quid-pro-quo basis, it also happens that the NSA pays its partner services for developing the technical means to serve the agency's purposes. Not surprisingly, this espionage goes both ways, making NSA partners spy on the USA as well.

---

[7] Greenwald, *No Place to Hide*, pp. 105-8.

Chapter III: Thoughts, Beliefs and Emotions

I think therefore I am.

THINKING ABOUT THE great issues of temporal life is one of the core concerns of human beings, and René Descartes suggested in the mid-17th century that if man wonders if he exists this is in and of itself proof that he does.[1] This seminal axiom has since been a pillar of western philosophy, and it wields a considerable influence on how we see the face of our foe. Thinking is closely linked with experience, and although much understanding is acquired through conscious endeavours, a huge part of our mental activity is influenced by thinking, beliefs, subconscious material, social norms, emotions, history, religion, tradition, and the philosophical basis of our cognition. Our insight and intuition are products of the processing of sensory information, including perception, awareness and judgement all harking back to this basis.

---

[1] The Latin version of his dictum, "cogito ergo sum," is known from the *Principles of Philosophy* published in 1644. Descarte published *Principles of Philosophy* in Latin, but the point of departure was his earlier work from 1637, *Discourse on Method*, in which the dictum was stated in French "je pense donc je suis."

Societal Reality

The portrait of the foe is formed by shrewd espionage and interpretation of information gathered by tapping telephones, exploiting satellite images, and a wide variety of other relatively accurate means of collection. However, fractions of the enemy image, which are not direct derivatives of our intelligence efforts, materialise out of the conscious and subconscious intellectual baggage hidden in all human beings. History, national ethos, geography, economy, religious beliefs, and moral creed of one's society, contribute important – and more or less conscious – drives to enmification and thus add an unpredictable human touch to the rigorous endeavour to achieve objectivity.

On the emotional side many feelings with roots in our past may contribute to prompt hostile attitudes. A people's common notions of having been split, united, or reunited, having overcome national disasters, lost a province or two, enduring sufferings, having limited access to natural resources, perceiving oneself as chivalrous or being the chosen people all are motives which have influenced enemy perceptions of groups, states, and nations from Antiquity up until today. On the one hand, these and similar semi-conscious emotions have exercised that influence because any entity of like-minded human beings will see itself as being positively distinguished from everybody else by one or more of these characteristics, thus perceiving their enemy as their negative complement. However, on the other hand, subconscious drives appear as well. Our mental preparedness is shaped and many of our reactions are prompted by the subconscious residue of traumata from and conditioning through our upbringing and early life. Even history is not to be relied unconditionally upon, since it is rarely a precise depiction of all available facts. It depends on the style, sympathies, and outlook of the chronicler or historian who has researched it, the style and attitudes of its time of composition, as well as the context in which it is being read. History was not always, and it is not everywhere researched and written to depict – as demanded by German historian Leopold von Ranke – *wie es eigentlich gewesen.*[2] The works of Homer, William Shakespeare and Arthur Bryant, to mention but a few, are

---

[2] "How it really happened." Leopold von Ranke, is assumed to be the founder of modern evidence-based historical research. The above dictum is a break away from history for the sole purpose of glorifying monarch and country. The very late release of the "ULTRA secret," decades after the end of the Second World War, may serve as an example that history must of necessity be incomplete when access to sources is prohibited, thus allowing the true sequence of events to be, at least temporarily, blurred.

examples of history with a more or less obvious bias. They are glorifying epics of their heroes.

The quest for accurate explanations of events has not always been the sole motivator to historians, nor is this necessarily the case in contemporary cultures where hidden assumptions may dictate otherwise. The American war correspondent Chris Hedges observed how, in Yugoslavia, history was created to fit immediate and narrow partisan interests:

> The competing nationalistic propaganda in Yugoslavia created a conflict in the country best equipped of all Eastern European states to integrate with the West after the collapse of Communism. Because there was no real reason to fight, there was an urgent need to swiftly turn a senseless fratricide, one organised by criminals and third-rate political leaders for power and wealth, into an orgy of killing, torture, and mass execution. This indiscriminate murder, these campaigns of ethnic cleansing were used to create facts, as it were. The slaughter was carried out to give to these wars the justification they lacked when they began, to fuel mutual hatred and paranoia as well as to enrich the militias...[3]

Politicians, political advisers, spin doctors, news paper editors, and similar key opinion makers rarely create images of the opponent which are one hundred percent objective and free of intended manipulation. After all, they have a political aim, which goes beyond simply winning the war or the battle on hand. Thus, as the current public enemy picture is formed, the available information is sifted through a filter of biased political and historical preconceptions, and, as Hedges suggests, bias exist in any society and in any person.

Largely, all decision-makers judge events and developments against a background of their particular country's interests, history, economy, moral values, and ethnic and political outlook. For Napoléon the defining assumptions seem to have concerned territorial and economic survival of the new, post-revolutionary, First French Empire behind secure borders, a cordon sanitaire of his allies in the Confederation of the Rhine, and treaties with competing great powers. For Churchill the aims appear to have been the British Empire's integrity and the assumed historical obligation to balance continental powers, not to mention his sense of the common interests of the English Speaking Peoples. To George W. Bush and Donald

---

[3] Hedges, *War Is a Force*, p. 27. Far from being mainstream among war correspondents, Hedges presents some very personal observations. Biased, as some of the observations may be, they are first hand accounts and among the primary sources of the events addressed.

Rumsfeld the agenda was probably about shaping the new century into one dominated by the United States.

Feelings of moral superiority and great power prerogatives as well as historical preconceptions are very often prominent in political rhetoric, and they contribute decisively to distorting reality. This in turn leads to skewed interpretations of events and faulty conclusions. To avoid this pitfall it is of imperative importance to interpret a potential opponent's attitude, rhetoric, and actions on the background of thorough knowledge of his actual economic and societal circumstances and his recent as well as more distant historical track record.

Examples abound of misinterpretations of information due to absence of ability or will to see the full context. Among those of the first half of the twentieth century is the French and British governments' failure to understand the reasons for and the implications of German rearmament and reintroduction of conscription from 1934 onwards. German needs, interests, and bellicosity in the late 1930s were governed by geography, economy, demography, and recent history – not least the territorial cessions and the reparations instalments forces upon the country by the Treaty of Versailles. These motivators were not understood correctly, or at all, because political leaders in Britain, France and elsewhere did not appreciate the societal and historical factors featuring below as well as on the surface of German society.[4] Thus, dismissing as rhetoric what was actually open declarations of intent, Britain and France stumbled into faulty appraisals, making late and insufficient preparations for the upcoming challenge. With hindsight the dangers are obvious – as early as the publication of *Mein Kampf* in 1925, Adolf Hitler claimed a need for German living space, not by means of re-conquering Germany's colonies, but by expansion of the homeland towards the east: "Dann mußte sich das neue Reich wieder auf der Straße der einstigen Ordensritter in Marsch setzen" ("Then, the new Reich would have to proceed in the footsteps of the Teutonic Knights").[5]

This declaration we now interpret as meaning that Germany would simply have to invade Poland, Lithuania, Latvia, Estonia and the Soviet Union (Russia) in order to fulfil her needs for raw materials and space for growth.

---

[4] Azar Gat, *Fascist and Liberal Visions of War* (Oxford: Clarenden Press, 1998), pp. 43-80.

[5] Hitler, *Mein Kampf*, pp. 149-153.

Erkenne deine Zeichen,
Es lösen sich die Fesseln
schwerer Not —
Der Freiheits-Sonne
Muß die Knechtschaft weichen. —
Ein neues Deutschland
Grüßt das Morgenrot!

Reichskanzler Adolf Hitler

H.K.24

Hitler gazing firmly towards the east (German postcard)

Prominent among thenorms for decent behaviour is the traditional distinction between killings organised by a state, which is acceptable and honourable, and murder, which is not. This distinction is neither particularly old, nor is it universal. While unlawful, duels as a gentlemanly obligation were socially accepted, and indeed expected, in the Austro-Hungarian Empire right up to the eve of the First World War.[6] Similarly, contemporary societies with a recent tribal tradition still regard extra-judicial killing as an acceptable way of protecting family honour.[7]

A lot of unconscious mental baggage influences the painter of an enemy portrait while painting. Few of us can suppress the enemy perception totally, which tradition, religion, and rhetoric have called forth in our minds. One might venture to suggest that most of it belongs in the cerebral dustbin, but reality shows otherwise. The political leader or newspaper editor creating a compelling image of the foe may take pride in having done so consciously, sustaining his or her self-image as an opinion maker. He may have vilified and dehumanised the foe and distorted the true representation. He may even have got widespread public support in return, but when it comes to actual fighting his picture of the opposition may turn out to divert focus from what really matters. The usefulness of such public-consumption-enemy portraits depends on the chain of persons and authorities processing and exploiting the information.

Sir Basil Henry Liddell Hart interviewed a number of German generals shortly after the end of the Second World War. During one of these conversations, General Günther Blumentritt lamented the pervasive ideological bias of Nazi German intelligence as he told him that, "very little reliable news came out of England... All that side of intelligence was directed by OKW under Hitler...carried out by a special branch of the SD.

---

[6] „Der Offizier war gemäß dem Standesethos sogar zum Duell verpflichtet. Denn wer die Ehre des einzelnen verletzte, beleidigte gleichzeitig den ganzen Offiziersstand und damit auch den Kaiser als obersten Kriegsherrn...„ "The officer had an obligation to duelling because of his professional ethos. As one who offended the honour of an individual offended the entire officer corps and, thus, the Emperor as the Supreme Commander..." Georg Markus, *Der Fall Redl* (Frankfurt am Main: Ullstein, 1986), p. 30.

[7] An article in the Danish newspaper *Politiken*, 15 September 2003, brought contemporary evidence of murderers being acquitted because their "honourable killings" had been committed in "righteous and understandable affect." From internet: http://politiken/VisArtikel.iasp accessed 15 September 2003. The article reports incidents in 2003 amongst the Palestinians in the Gaza Strip, where brothers had killed sisters, who had "brought shame upon the families."

We were dependent on them for our information."[8] Other sources seem to confirm Blumentritt's implication that intelligence collected and processed by the SD was insufficient and imprecise as a basis for fulfilling the Wehrmacht's operational needs because it was tailored to fit the Nazi party's dogma and preconceptions. Moreover, since the British were extremely successful in breaking spy rings, catching individual spies directly upon their arrival, as well as in feeding false information into the German intelligence services, the little that did come out of Britain was mostly misleading. Hitler was disinclined to accept intelligence which did not fit his prejudices and political aims and, to a large extend, he directed the war on the basis of ideology rather than reality.

The American author Robert Kaplan draws attention to an upside-down version of this problem that is found in the United States, namely having pertinent information but refusing to use it. In the U.S. there is a centre for army analysis tasked with establishing meticulous files on what may be perceived as potentially unstable countries. These states are carefully rated based on, for instance, their demography, economy, and history. However, the usefulness of this endeavour depends on the officers analysing and utilising the information, and although that office warned the American administration of the break-up of Yugoslavia a year in advance – according to Kaplan – no one took any particular notice of the warning.[9] It appears justified therefore to observe that in both these cases – the German and the American – professional intelligence efforts have been in vain, to the extent that political agendas seem better served by parameters consciously introduced and less task-oriented but politically or ideologically convenient.

Hostile feelings do not spread simply by contact or through contagious viruses like the flu. Language, spoken, written or illustrated, is the means. Enmity is always strongly reflected in rhetoric – propaganda and ordinary political debate alike – and the values and trends of society forcefully influence its martial vocabulary. It is obvious, therefore, that American presidents Woodrow Wilson and George W. Bush expressed themselves differently around 90 years apart, as did Prime Ministers Lloyd George and

---

[8] Liddell Hart, *The German Generals Talk*, pp. 234-35. OKW or *Oberkommando der Wehrmacht* was the Nazi German tri-service supreme command during WW II. From 1942 onwards all foreign intelligence was directed by the SD, the intelligence department of the SS.

[9] Robert D. Kaplan, *Warrior Politics: Why Leadership Demands a Pagan Ethos* (New York: Vintage Books, 2003), p. 75.

Churchill; each epoch has its own phraseology.

Changes in usage is not only a consequence of the well-known modification of language over time, it also signify intended alterations of style, policy and ethos. In an article published in 1996, the American author Paul Belbutowsky provides a striking example of this dynamic, pointing to the recent inflation in the use of the term "warrior":

> The increasing use of 'warrior', which more adequately describes the 'fighter' at the primal level, is pre-military and, as such, belongs to the archaic world. Warrior is therefore an appropriate description of group or clan members whose end is combat in support of their leader. Terms such as 'tribal' and 'primitive' also are used in an attempt to describe warfare in places like Somalia. While problematic, this language attempts to define and clarify that intangible quality of conflict embedded in the culture itself, where fluidity reigns and where there is no order of battle in the conventional Western sense.[10]

Such a change might be interpreted as a reflection of the impact of the post-Cold War era's many low-scale conflicts among tribal clans or political factions, but it also conveys the notion of "a just war." The combatant – "warrior" – is no longer society's unreflective "killing-machine" but a conscientious individual, who is fighting for an idea, his leader, and the sake of good; not for evil or profit. Similarly, expressions of 2003 vintage like "the Axis of Evil," "the Axis of Weasel," "the Old Europe," and "the Usual Cohort" accompanying American efforts to make other powers sign up for the Iraqi enterprise characterise recent rhetorical attempts to highlight good-evil, willing-unwilling, progressive-reactionary and democratic-authoritarian distinctions."[11] These expressions were employed consciously by the George W. Bush administration along with the Old Testament dictum of: "He, who is not with me, is against me" turned into "those who are not with us – i.e. the US – are with the

---

[10] Paul Belbutowsky, "Strategy and Culture." *Parameters* (Spring 1996): pp. 32-42.

[11] Vocabulary used by, respectively, U.S. President George W. Bush (State of the Union Speech, 2002 (from http://www.salon.com/news/feature/2002/02/07/tehran/index_np.html, accessed 6 November 2003)); U.S. Secretary for Defence Donald Rumsfeld (who apologised for his "weasel-remark") on 22 January 2003 (http://www.scrappleface.com/MT/archives/000608.html accessed 6 November 2003)) and made the "Old Europe-statement" also on 22 January 2003 (http://www.rferl.org/nca/features/2003/01/24012003172118.asp accessed 6 November 2003), and U.S. Secretary of State Colin Powel in address to the UN Security Council prior to coalition engagement in the war on Iraq 2003.

terrorists." The verbal culture, which permeates society's daily life, is decisive of the way its politicians and other influential people describe the situation, the problems ahead, the potential or actual adversaries, and the notions of hostility.

Although, for the most part, politics and public debate are supposed to lie within the realm of straightforward tangible affairs – such as dealing with the economy, communications, and living space – emotional parts of the rhetoric frequently employ references to matters belonging to the metaphysical sphere. While overtly these issues play minor rôles at the rhetorical level, subconsciously their influence might be a lot more pervasive than is immediately apparent. The German early twentieth century author, Oswald Spengler, addressed this phenomenon in Der Untergang des Abendlandes (The Decline of the West), first published in 1917. Spengler warned against the trend of letting metaphysics take the place of rationality, which to him seemed to be a possible, or even a likely, though deplorable development:

> Consider that the well-being of the soul will play a bigger rôle for future generations than all might of this world, and that under the impression of metaphysics and mysticism, which now seem to substitute Rationalism... This strive seizes exactly the best brains, then nothing can stop the decline of this big theatre (the Western civilisation).[12]

Oswald Spengler may have been more accurate in his prognostications than was actually acknowledged in his own time. Metaphysical arguments did in fact play a rôle in a great number of the conflicts of the twentieth century, and there is little to indicate that those of the twenty-first should be markedly different in that respect.

However, Spengler's effect on German society between the world wars went beyond the mere metaphysics. His most notorious contribution to enmification through a them-and-us approach took its point of departure in Nietzsche's concept of culture as opposed to civilisation. In Spengler's view civilisation was the inescapable fate of any culture, it was the deflowering following blossom, a spiritual old-age, demise. He sees this dialectical pair – culture and civilisation – in the context of the age of

---

[12] (My translation) Oswald Spengler, *Der Untergang des Abendlandes* (München: Verlag C.H. Beck, 1990), p. 1191. Original text: „Gesetz den Fall, daß das Heil der Seele den begabtesten künftiger Generationen näher liegt als aller Macht dieser Welt, daß unter dem Eindruck der Metaphysik und Mystik die heute den Rationalismus ablösen...gerade die Auslese des Geistes ergreift...so wird nichts das Ende dieses großen Schauspiels aufhalten..."

various peoples. While in his perception Britain and France were old peoples already in decline and having reached the phase of civilisation, the Germans constituted a young people – a forceful and growing cultural entity. When Germany lost the First World War, it was only because, in the nick of time, the entente powers managed to cajole the USA into joining them by tempting it with liberalism, democracy and human rights.[13] In spite of Spengler's warnings against metaphysics and mysticism, pseudo- or semi-religious feelings may be also kindled and maintained. Throughout the 1920s and 1930s, and with references to a Germano-Nordic mythology and folkloristic national romanticism, Germans were reminded of other – more national – deities than the one which Judaic-Christian tradition had to offer.

As so many other Germanic romantic nationalists, Adolf Hitler was influenced by a number of pseudo-scientific turn-of-the-century writers. Particularly during his Vienna period, he had access to and, according to some of his Viennese acquaintances, took a remarkable interest in the pseudo-religious, Germano-chauvinistic and folkloristic thoughts offered by authors like Guido von List, Adolf Georg Lanz von Liebenfels, Hans Goldzier, Hans Hörbiger, Otto Weininger and Arthur Trebitsch. None of these had any scholarly background, and Hitler took their messages as and where he found them in magazines, popular science periodicals, and newspapers but rarely from primary sources.[14] Although not in the case of the Al Qaeda-Islam nexus, which we shall examine below, it is not uncommon that metaphysics merge with secular legend, as with Nazism: "Himmler himself was from his youth on very emotionally engaged and read plenty of esoteric and mythological literature, which was closely linked with early anti-Semitic and ethnocentric tendencies. He believed, e.g., in an Atlantic primordial culture, which he ascribed to Greenland."[15]

---

[13] Adam Paulsen, *Overvindelsen af Første Verdenskrig: Historiepolitik hos Ernst Troeltsch, Oswald Spengler og Thomas Mann* [*Overcoming the First World War: History Politics with Ernst Troeltsch, Oswald Spengler og Thomas Mann*], (Copenhagen: Museum Tusculanum Publishers, 2014), pp. 82-3.

[14] Brigitte Hamann, *Hitlers Wien: Lehrjahre eines Diktators* (München: R. Piper, 1996), pp. 293, 309, 319, 323, 325, 329 and 333.

[15] (My translation) Original text: „Himmler selbst war seit seiner Jugend an Übersinnlichem interessiert und las reichlich esoterische und mythologische Literatur, die früh mit antisemitischen und völkischen Tendenzen verbunden war. Er glaubte z. B. an eine atlantische Urzivilisation, die er im Norden bei Grönland verortete." From internet, http://ns-edenkstaetten.de/nrw/de/wewelsburg/thema_3/ss_esoterik.html and http://www.wewelsburg.de/startscreen/startframes.html accessed 30 November 2003.

As a further example one might take a look at the castle Wewelsburg, where Heinrich Himmler in his capacity as Reichsführer SS founded a shrine for the "SS knights," complete with cathedral like halls of worship, tombs laid out for use by the twelve most conspicuous SS-heroes and grounds, and where, during WW II, the chosen few celebrated winter solstice in lieu of Christmas.

As if explaining Adolf Hitler's sentiments, Hedges opines that "national myths ignite a collective amnesia in war."[16] They give the past generations nobility and greatness they never possessed in their own right and, as in the case of Himmler's Wewelsburg, they prepared the nations' warriors for heroic demigod status that they did not deserve. Almost every group, and especially every nation, has such myths contributing to creating the martial fervour the nationalists use to kindle a conflict. Hedges provides a recent historical example:

In the former Yugoslavia, it was the nationalist propaganda pumped out over television, far more than ancient hatreds that did the most to provoke rivalry and finally war between the ethnic groups. "The nationalist governments...used the absolute power they wielded over the media to play and replay images that provoked outrage and anger. They told stories, many of them fabricated, about alleged atrocities committed by the enemy."[17] In the 1990s, that kind of myth building spiralled into a vicious circle. The enemy was vilified and demonised so that he no longer appeared human.[18]

The Israeli historian Omer Bartov, in his *Hitler's Army*, also identified this phenomenon. Amongst the soldiers of the Nazi German army in the East there was "no doubt in the existence of a mythical Jew... Quite on the contrary: reality did not disprove myth, but was rather moulded so as to fit it."[19]

Similarly, Hitler's view of the eastern enemy was one of brutes and slaves who needed a master – a view that, apparently, was shared by many of his Volksgenossen.[20] Richard Holmes has phrased this phenomenon with

---

[16] Hedges, *War is a Force*, p. 46.

[17] Ibid., p. 46.

[18] Ibid., p. 21.

[19] Omer Bartov, *Hitler's Army* (New York: Oxford University Press, 1992), p. 127.

[20] Trevor-Roper, *Hitler's Table Talks 1941-1944*, pp. 33, 40 (table talks of the night of 17/18 and midday of 24 September 1941).

striking clarity:

> Bartov is right that the conditions, moral and material, of war on the Eastern Front made it a 'unique phenomenon in human history'. One of the dark strengths of Nazism was its ability to feed on German culture, and it brought to the fighting on the Eastern Front a blend of history and mythology, geopolitics and philosophy, which helped sustain the soldiers in surroundings of almost unimaginable barbarity.[21]

These attitudes led to inhuman behaviour towards the enemy, who in turn fulfilled the expectations and behaved with primordial cruelty. At the same time, the Germans saw their own people as the embodiment of absolute goodness. Although this might have had a positive effect on the will to fight and consequently increased the number of enemy personnel killed, it is doubtful whether it has optimised the final outcome of the struggle. During the Second World War in the Soviet Union and East Asia and the more recent wars in the former Yugoslavia each side has often reduced the other to a mere object of derision.

Der Untermensch [the subhuman], Nazi-propaganda deriding the Slavs

---

[21] Holmes, *Nuclear Warriors*, p. 209

However, not everyone believes in the need for enemy images depicting savages and infidels. Richard Holmes informs us that, German author and First World War infantry officer "Ernst Jünger strove to maintain professional standards. "It has always been my ideal in war," he wrote, "to eliminate all feelings of hatred and to treat my enemy only as an enemy in battle and honour him as a man according to his courage."[22] We may assume – and hope – that in this respect Jünger was not unique.

As late as in the last decade of the nineteenth century, Helmuth von Moltke hailed war as being "a part of God's world order," comprising qualities that ennobled the societies that fought. He was not alone. Particularly on the European continent, a medieval legacy of perceived chivalrous obligation permeated the officer corps and to some extent also the societies surrounding them. Though Moltke, no doubt, held his view out of sincere and honest conviction, little did he suspect of what lay ahead. The chivalrous attitude, however, persisted. In 1937 the French film *La Grande Illusion*[23] lamented the demise of the aristocratic officer and his noble, white gloved slaying; Ernst Jünger described in *In Stahlgewittern* (*In Storms of Steel*) and in *Kampf als inneres Erlebniß* (*Combat as an Inner Experience*) his sentiments of respect and lack of hostility towards the opposing fighting man of the Great War;[24] and the apologetic and appreciative platitudes, possibly, reached a climax with Himmler's speech to the SS in 1943.[25]

Lots of officers in lots of wars have fought with decency and distinction just as Moltke, and it is tantamount to sacrilege when Himmler aligns himself and other of Germany's most ruthless thugs with that tradition. Nonetheless, it points to the absurdity of the distinction between killing and murder. Killing for "high finance," as Moltke put it, is hardly more reasonable than killing for individual subsistence. However, tradition and cultural heritage, which make us accept the dogma of an impersonal enemy, are age-old; because as Holmes tells us: "without the creation of abstract images of the enemy, and without depersonalisation of the enemy

---

[22] Holmes, *Firing Line*, p. 370.

[23] D: Jean Renoir, S: Jean Gabin.

[24] Holmes, *Firing Line*, p. 370.

[25] See also the paragraph on religious aspects. Joachim Fest, 1963, pp. 162 and 166, quoted in Miller, Am Anfang, pp. 99-100.

through training, battle would become impossible to sustain."[26] For this reason most societies maintain armed forces, and the soldiers, sailors and airmen of these must be conditioned to kill should the need arise.

However necessary as it may appear, there is one serious problem with conditioning or programming of citizens: the resultant brutalisation of the entire society.

Those who lend themselves most easily to conditioning are people who have never themselves had the opportunity of building a robust and sound ego; who were, so far, the under-dogs and therefore need someone else to step on. Such people abound in societies with structural problems like great numbers of laid off workers, hyperinflation, and unequal distribution of the niceties of civilised life – such as Germany in the 1930s and Iraq in the last decades of the twentieth century. The Austrian psychiatrist Viktor Frankl spent some important years of his life as a prisoner in German concentration-camps and made some very apt observations with respect to the enmity demonstrated by SS guards and Kapos, most of them possibly recruited amongst the outcasts of German pre-war society.

Frankl was already a medical doctor and a psychiatrist before entering the German camp system. To understand his book fully one must recall the notion that in the conduct of their lives all men aim at realising certain personal idols – or guiding images. Thus the neurotic personality is chiefly distinguished by the asocial or unrealistic quality of the image he or she has adopted. While another individual might wish to be a father, or a judge, the neurotic wants to be king or queen.[27] Enmification in this context is a kind of self-inflation. Whether defined in terms of Adler's fictions, Jung's persona, or Freud's identification with the father, the inflated self wants to know only its virtues; its vices are relegated to some nether world. There they readily form the raw material for projections onto the image of one's enemies, real or imagined.[28] Frankl experienced the self-inflation of guards and Kapos personally on his body as daily beatings, scorn and arbitrariness. First of all, it was important for the tormentors to see themselves as miles above the prisoners – their enemies. "[Leaving the railway carriage in Auschwitz] we had to pass a high ranking SS-officer... Now standing before him, tall, slim, handsome, dressed in an immaculate dashing uniform – an

---

[26] Holmes, *Firing Line*, p. 361.

[27] "The Neurotic Constitution" (1917) quoted in Rieber et al., *The Psychology of War and Peace*, p. 8.

[28] Rieber et al., *The Psychology of War and Peace*, p. 11.

elegant, well groomed man..."[29] They would want to demonstrate their ultimate power, even though in some cases they themselves were hardly more than elite prisoners:

> The senior prisoner of the barrack made a short speech of reception and said that – on his 'word of honour' – he would, personally, hang any one who had had dollars or precious metals sewn into their belts, and 'it is going to be from that beam' (he pointed); he explained proudly that the camp regulations gave him that prerogative.[30]

In Frankl's experience, haughtiness, distance, contempt, and arbitrary violence were the tools provided by the Nazi society's conditioning machinery right from family upbringing, through school, Hitler Jugend, and Bund deutscher Mädel – the Nazi versions of boy scouts and girl guides orgaisations – to the SS training facilities, and eventually the concentration-camps. Remarkably, Frankl does not say anything about enemy images being created by and in himself being the prisoner, only about an almost silent anguish.[31]

Machiavelli and Clausewitz agree that policy and arms cannot be appraised independently of each other. Keegan wants us to see this compound differently and begins his book – as we shall see when dealing with propaganda – stating that "war is not the continuation of policy by other means."[32] But, it may be claimed, this is precisely the reason why enmification starts within society at peace. All human interaction may be characterised as social activity (social from Latin *socius* = citizen), thus also policy, commerce, religious worship, and enmity.

---

[29] Viktor E. Frankl, *Psykologi og eksistens* (*Psychology and Existance*) (Copenhagen: Gyldendal 2002) p. 18.

[30] Frankl, *Psykologi og eksistens*, p. 21.

[31] Frankl, *Psykologi og eksistens*, p. 29: "it is not the physical pain, which is most important, but the mental anguish being unfairly punished". P. 25: "a man in his sixties implored the concentration camp doctor M to save his son from the gas chamber, and Dr. M. had curtly and correctly refused". p. 31: "The overseer comes, square jawed, rosy cheeked, his face reminds me definitely of a hog's head". p. 66: "In the night [after the International Red Cross take-over of the concentration camp] SS-men with trucks arrived [collecting the patients (inmates)]... [I saw photos from] a small camp. Thence my patients had been taken, the barrack doors locked and the camp set on fire."

[32] John Keegan, *A History of War* (New York, U.S.A.: First Vintage Book Edition, 1994) p. 3.

Stressing the primary importance of policy, Clausewitz regards war as a part of man's social existence, which leads us back to asking: who is creating the enemy image?[33] Well, society is – the society which believes to have found an aim worth fighting for and which has at its disposal a military machine likely to be capable of fulfilling that aim. To shoot at each other to get one's way is no new method within the context of social exchange, and we can hardly deny that it is social in the sense that it is perpetrated by one society against another, whose politicians have decided so by mandates more or less willingly provided by the citizens.

A society feeling under stress will look for potential adversaries not only beyond the borders but frequently within. Most countries have intelligence and security services whose main task is to guard the state's internal security by keeping an eye on subversive elements, suspicious activities, and the influence wielded by foreign powers through their embassies, sympathisers or covert intelligence gathering.

Homosexuality is probably the one proclivity which, over the years, has caused the most trouble for some intelligence services, but at the same time one which has been exploited extremely skilfully by others. As was briefly touched upon in a previous chapter, the Austro-Hungarian Colonel Alfred Redl, who sold his country's war plans to Russia during the period 1909-13, is a prime example. During a language course in Russia in the early years of his career, Redl's sexual inclination had been discovered by the *Okhrana*, the Russian intelligence service. When, after a few years, Redl took up a post at the Austro-Hungarian embassy in St. Petersburg, the Russians were keen to exploit their knowledge. Promising to keep quiet about it, they asked him, in due course, to respond positively to their summons, and as, after finishing his staff course some years hence, he took up a position at the *Evidenzbüro* – the Austro-Hungarian counterintelligence service – the Russians did indeed resume contact. Hence Redl began handing over increasingly important documents, for which he was generously remunerated. He kept a male lover, whom he furnished with an expensive car and equally valuable horses; and his own lifestyle became overtly extravagant. All the time his knowledge that exposure of his homosexuality would lead to immediate dismissal and loss of income led him to ever graver treason.

As for many years gays might be coerced into co-operation by threats of disclosing their sexual proclivity, they were easy targets for foreign intelligence services, and for this reason they were seen by many as

---

[33] Ibid., p. 149.

potential enemies within. In late modern Europe and the United States homosexuality has been tabooed, and probably here and there it has remained so right up till the end of the Cold War. Moreover, as demonstrated by such trials as those against the author Oscar Wilde and the computer mathematician Alan Turing, a key member of Britain's Operation Ultra, until the 1960s homosexuality remained a criminal offence in many, otherwise tolerant, societies. In Britain, imprisonment was the usual punishment for male homosexuality until 1948, when medical treatment was introduced as an alternative remedy. British legislation in this field goes as far back as the "Buggery Act" of 1533 criminalising homosexuality. This act was sharpened in 1861 and it remained in force, mutatis mutandis, until 1967. The British intelligence historian Richard Deacon has made the very apt observation that, while post Second World War Soviet intelligence has had trouble finding ideological sympathisers in Britain; they have resorted to blackmailing or compromising homosexuals as they had done successfully during the interwar period. However, he intimates that Cold War Soviet recruiting efforts have been hampered by the fact that British Secret Intelligence Service (SIS/MI6) actually employed gays knowingly, because they were useful in attracting foreign male agents who were not susceptible to female enticement.[34]

As mentioned above, the mathematician Alan Turing was indicted for having had unsavoury relations to another man and sentenced with reference to the same paragraph as was Oscar Wilde 50 years earlier. He was given the choice of prison or medical treatment with an oestrogen concoction to assuage his libido. He chose the latter but was nonetheless stripped of the security clearance which had so far allowed him to work with cipher material. On 8 June 1954 he was found dead. Beside him lay a half eaten apple and it was widely speculated that he had committed suicide. His mother, however, believed his death to be a consequence of his haphazard way of keeping chemicals at home. The computer company Apple adopted the half eaten apple as its logo, paying homage to the deceased genius.

Religious Aspects

Most societies have – and have always had – their basis in religion, and

---

[34] Richard Deacon, *A History of the British Secret Service* (London: Panther Books, 1984), p. 475-76.

enmity and conflict are phenomena which are possibly as old as humanity itself, cf. Genesis 3 and 4. They can be substantiated at least as far back as written history goes, described by Thucydides amongst others, and it is therefore not surprising that these two phenomena cover a lot of common ground in any society's cultural heritage. An important premise for the concept formation in almost any language is the use of religious justification of enmity. Expressions like "righteousness," "covenant," "fight the Lord's battle," "let thine enemies perish," etc., all convey the concept of a group standing together confronting someone else, someone who it is acceptable to demonise and to beat into submission. Most societies, however, do not limit their belligerent vocabulary to religious phrases. Notions like territory, blood, liberty, equality, and fraternity, defensible borders, living space, and access to harbours play significant rôles as well. Although some expressions seem to disappear while others emerge, the basic cultural background for enmity remains. While catch phrases of yesteryear like "The White Man's Burden" make little sense in the 21st century, today's hot issues like "indirect security" and "Islamic terror" do. Change in vocabulary happens all the time, and normally it signifies an intended modification in style, policy or ethos, but it does not necessarily erode the cultural preparedness for changing gear smoothly into a more bellicose rhetoric.

Apart from the ill-fated Soviet attempt to create an atheist state, most societies have national myths rooted in religion. Since enmity and conflict are as old as humanity itself and can be substantiated as far back as written history goes, it is not surprising that these phenomena cover a lot of common ground in most societies' cultural heritage.[35] In almost any language, religious phraseology forms an important part of the concept for enmity, and religious arguments are frequently used for justification of aggression. In a quest for approval of organised killing Holy Scriptures often appear helpful. The most central written heritage of the Judaic-Christian world, the Bible and the Torah, both speak of Eve's partaking of the fruits from the "Tree of Knowledge of Good and Evil."[36] Allegedly, one consequence of this knowledge materialised as Cain's sudden impulse to

---

[35] cf. Genesis 3 and 4. As far as written military history is concerned Thucydides is assumed to be responsible for the oldest existing account.

[36] Genesis 3: 1-5.

kill his brother, Abel.[37]

Although religion has hardly ever been the only, let alone the real, cause for war, it has frequently been used by those wanting war for purposes like power and wealth. Scriptures of many religions have presented pretexts for wars like the Islamic conquests in the seventh through the seventeenth centuries, the Crusades from the eleventh through the thirteenth centuries, and the Thirty Years War, and they still deliver plenty of fuel for the martial fervour of "holy warriors" such as the Taliban and Al Qaeda terrorists.[38]

Additionally, an age-old, if feeble, excuse for enmity, persecution, and genocide as "a lesser evil" than the alternative on hand may be attributed to religious leaders. The Jewish high priest Caiphas figures notoriously amongst them with his preposterous attempt at a vindication of the execution of Jesus. It was a national necessity he claimed, because: "it is expedient for us, that one man should die for the people, and the whole nation perish not."[39] The Romans had not threatened annihilation of anybody at the moment, but the priesthood used this threat because they wished to get rid of Jesus, who, they believed, menaced their position.

It will hardly be seen as unreasonably harsh to judge such arguments, conjured up for the occasion, as an unholy fusion – and confusion – of

---

[37] Genesis 4: 8. Dave Grossmann, *On Killing: The psychological Cost of Learning to Kill in War and Society* (Boston: Little, Brown and Company, 1996), pp. 132-33.

[38] Muhammed and his caliphs waged Jihad converting infidels as they went, and, thus conquered Syria, Palestine, Egypt, and North Africa in the seventh century; Spain, Portugal, parts of France, and Sicily in the eighth, invaded the Italian mainland in the ninth and reached Vienna in 1683. Bernard Lewis, *What Went Wrong? The Clash Between Islam and Modernity in the Middle East* (New York: Oxford University Press, 2003), p. 4.

Jihad has been used, further, for the spread of Islam outside the heartlands, e.g., into sub-Saharan Africa, India and Indonesia. Religious motivation increased during the period of the Crusades, notably under Saladin (1174-93) who re-conquered Jerusalem. Richard Holmes, Ed., *The Oxford Companion to Military History* (Oxford: Oxford University Press, 2001), pp. 466-7 and 242.

The Crusades (1095-c. 1300) encouraged by the changing Popes with promises of release from the burden of sin and, in the case of the crusaders' death, direct entry into the kingdom of Heaven. They served the re-conquest of the Holy Land from the Muslim infidels and, in the thirteenth century, the Christianisation of the Baltic by the Teutonic Order. Ibid., pp.242-4.

The 30 Years War, though having its roots in dynastic-imperial ambitions, served primarily the "Counter Reformation." The religious motives were pretext rather than cause. Ibid., pp. 909-10.

[39] John 11: 50.

religious duties with the temporally opportune. Opportunism like this lends itself to any governmental, doubtful but expedient, attempt to get rid of inconvenient groups or individuals. With similar arguments, ruling majorities and powerful institutions have endeavoured to justify the Inquisition, the pacification of the Indians and other infidels, as well as the Holocaust, the Nazi onslaughts on the Poles, Ukrainians, Russians, and other civilian populations, and the genocide in Bosnia in the 1990s.

Taken out of context, scriptures can be exploited to benefit almost any cause, and this has been done repeatedly by people claiming to be Jews or Christians and by many others as well. As Hedges points out, in the former Yugoslavia in the 1990s, not only the political, military, and criminal warmongers propagated hatred and confrontation in order to advance national causes unknown a few years previously, "the principal religious institutions – the Serbian Orthodox Church and the Catholic Church in Croatia – were willing accomplices. They were national churches and worked as propagandists for the states."[40]

It is a pervasive belief that Christianity has facilitated western secularism, among other things because of the Reformation that detached temporal power from matters eternal. Conversely, Islam has never had a reformation and many – but certainly far from all – Muslim states still combine government and religion. The primary religious justification for Islamic terror acts of recent years have been that the "infidels" must be driven out from the holy soil of the believers – including the tiny peace of land constituting Israel.

While Islam contains many different views on violence and Jihad, there are some amongst its scribes who vehemently urge their fellow Muslims to fight against the "apostate peoples," i.e. the rest of the world. As an example, one might consider the religiously martial fervour of the Ayatollah Khomeini in his address in 1983 on the anniversary of the Prophet Mohamed's birth:

> If one permits an infidel to continue in his rôle as a corrupter of the earth, his moral suffering will be all the worse. If one kills an infidel, and this stops him from perpetrating his misdeeds, his death will be a blessing to him. For if he remains alive he will become more and more corrupt. War is a blessing for the world and for all the nations.[41]

---

[40] Hedges, *War is a Force*, p. 46.

[41] Robert W. Rieber and Robert J. Kelly, "Substance and Shadow: Images of the Enemy" in Rieber, *The Psychology of War and Peace*, p. 15.

Likewise, through the *Al Qaeda Manual* the terrorist network informs us in a politico-religious statement opposing Islamic values to what they call the Greco-Western civilisation that:

> The confrontation that we are calling for with the apostate regimes does not know Socratic debates, Platonic ideals, or Aristotelian diplomacy. However, it knows the dialogue of bullets, the ideals of assassination, bombing, and destruction, and the diplomacy of the cannon and machine-gun.[42]

The Qur'anic style, though not the precise wording, strikes chords similar to those of Caiphas. In both cases, infidels and martyrs will have to die for the sake of the many, the holy soil, and the believers. Also, the aversion against Western cultural influence in the Islamic world seems to drive their quest for religious vindication of confrontation.[43]

With the exception of a number of fundamentalist Islamic states, nation and religion go hand in hand; and as one creates an image of the enemy, religion frequently joins with national myths to produce the required justification for the killing. This denudes the opponent of precisely the human qualities that would otherwise have permitted a rational resolution of the conflict short of military combat.[44]

Democratic governance rests on secular perceptions of statecraft, but most western states are mired, nevertheless, in the residue from the mixture of temporal and divine power which for centuries was a key feature in European monarchies. Since the introduction of absolutism, European monarchs have been the embodiment of their states' national identity and, at the same time, since they have been ruling through divine mercy, they have linked religious beliefs with nation, moral values and history. Thus in many cases, in a strange and obscure manner the metaphysical elements in bellicose rhetoric have combined religion and national myth.

Today, an additional aspect of this conundrum materialises in pugnacious Islamist oratory. Since nation matters less in Islam than in most

---

[42] Al Qaeda. *The Al Qaeda Manual.* Computer file impounded by British Police in Manchester. From internet, accessed 1 November 2002. www.disastercenter.com/terror, "Presentation."

[43] Bernard Lewis, *What Went Wrong? The Clash Between Islam and Modernity in the Middle East* (New York: Oxford University Press, 2003) pp. 158-60.

[44] Rieber et al., *The Psychology of War and Peace*, p. 37.

other creeds, religion proper seems to dominate completely over secular politics in the metaphysical contribution to confrontational rhetoric.

From recent literature, such as the *Al Qaeda Manual*, it appears that even today metaphysical values can promote feelings of unity and righteousness – more radical perhaps, but in many respects not very different from those of Christian, secular, or atheist societies of bygone eras – and this influences the way the images of the enemy are brought about.

The British author Robert Graves, relating his experiences as a First World War British infantry officer – he was a captain of the Royal Welch Fusiliers – described the fervour of a Roman Catholic padre giving his "blessing and told them [the soldiers] that if they died fighting for a good cause they would go straight to Heaven or, at any rate, be excused a great many years in Purgatory."[45] This appears a flagrant confusion of the padre's loyalties: the one to his temporal master with that to his revered vocation. Moreover, it strikes a chord of superstition, but if it was, we may assume that superstition still exists, influencing political attitudes and martial fervour even today.

While some politicians state their intentions in a direct manner, as did Adolf Hitler, religious persons and idealists talk in a kind of coded language. You should not slay, or want, or steal, but you are a good Christian if you love your neighbours – but not their spouses, of course – help the poor and preach the gospel of peace. In Islam there are similar, although not absolutely identical, norms of good and evil.

Whether we like it or not, religion, more often than not, pervade the rhetoric of a bellicose party claiming to wage a righteous war. According to Rousseau, the community cannot demand any religious belief from its citizens, as it has no authority in the world to come and therefore also no influence on its members' afterlife. But temporal authorities can demand decent behaviour in this world. This notion is in sharp contradiction of what has happened in recent years, when Islamic fundamentalists and terror organisations demand religious devotion and martial fervour of their followers and promise them reward in Heaven in return. Thus, we see a strange substitution of the codified jus ad bellum, the legal right to wage war for a righteous cause, with a claimed religious justification for war – fas ad bellum.

In a quest for approval of organised killing holy scripts are often

---

[45] Robert Graves, *Goodbye to All That* (London: The Folio Society, 1981), p. 170. Graves, the son of an Irish father and a German mother, strongly claimed an Irish origin, though at the time up until the writing and publishing of *Goodbye to All That* he lived in England.

helpful. The Bible tells us that Cain fell to the temptation of killing his brother.[46] Though Cain was punished by God's curse, the Lord also "set a mark upon him, lest any finding him should kill him."[47] Thus, tolerated on Earth despite his sin, Cain reproduced himself leaving his sin, his curse, and his mark as legacies to posterity. This alone does not make killing and enmity pardonable; it merely constitutes a religious explanation of the origin. Since the Scriptures – Jewish, Christian, Muslim and others – have presented the pretexts for so many wars, and still deliver plenty of fuel for bellicose enthusiasm, it seems opportune to examine the justification thus embedded.

It lies beyond the scope of this book to undertake a comprehensive study of the world's religious texts. However, some examples from the Bible, in its capacity as a generic scripture, are useful for finding possible explanations for religiously motivated bellicosity, because such findings may be used as building blocks in the further scrutinising of the composition of the face of the foe.

The Jews' view of their enemies – and the Christians' view as their spiritual heirs – may be understood through their notion of being chosen. The land of Canaan was given to them by God, and those who threatened this, their rightful possession, must be their enemies: "And the Lord God of Israel delivered Sihon and all his people into the hand of Israel, and they smote them: so Israel possessed all the land of the Amorites, the inhabitants of that country."[48] The fact that Israel, and Judah,[49] are the Lord's chosen people gives them a religiously unique position: "For from the top of the rock I see him, and from the hills I behold him; lo, the people shall dwell alone, and shall not be reckoned among the nations."[50] Israel is the Lord's people: "They that are delivered from the noise of the archers in the places of drawing water, there they shall rehearse the righteous acts of the Lord,

---

[46] Genesis 4: 8, and Dave Grossmann, *On Killing: The psychological Cost of Learning to Kill in War and Society* (Boston: Little, Brown and Company, (paperback) 1996) pp. 132-33.

[47] Genesis 4: 11-15.

[48] Judges 11: 21.

[49] The fact that the Israelites split and from ca. 925 – 539 BC were two separate kingdoms is noted. For practical purposes the term Israel hereinafter refers to the whole people as well as the whole country before, during and after the dichotomy.

[50] Numbers 23: 9.

even the righteous acts toward the inhabitants of this village in Israel: then shall the people of the Lord go down to the gates."[51] The wars waged by Israel are the Lord's wars, as we see it expressed by Saul telling David, "behold my elder daughter Merab, her will I give thee to wife: only be thou valiant for me, and fight the Lord's battles."[52] Thus, the enemies of Israel were enemies of the Lord, "and when David came to Ziklag, he sent of the spoil to the elders of Judah, even to his friends, saying, 'behold a present for you of the spoil of the enemies of the Lord'."[53] The Israelites allowed themselves to let a first glimpse of "righteous enmity" slip into their religious language praying, "so let all thine enemies perish, oh Lord: but let them that love him be as the sun when he goeth forth in his might."[54]

Although these Scriptures are very old, the notion of "selection" – and thus the basis for enmity towards those not being chosen – is not coined until the writing of the Deuteronomy and the Deuteronomic Historical Work. Israel is holy, consecrated to the Lord who has chosen this people amongst many. The reason was not that Israel was a better people – on the contrary, the Israelites had been living in deprivation and serfdom for about a century in Egypt[55] – it lay exclusively in God's love and devotion:

> For thou art an holy people unto the Lord thy God: the Lord thy God hath chosen thee to be a special people unto himself, above all people that are on the face of the earth. The Lord did not set his love upon you, nor choose you, because ye were more in number than any people; for ye were the fewest of all people: But because the Lord loved you, and because he would keep the oath, which he has sworn unto your fathers, has the Lord brought you out with a mighty hand, and redeemed you out of the land of bondmen, from the hand of Pharaoh king of Egypt.[56]

When God freed Israel from the Egyptian yoke Israel materialised as a nation and, by this divine intervention, became God's chosen people:

---

[51] Judges: 5, 11.

[52] 1 Samuel 18: 17.

[53] 1 Samuel 30: 26.

[54] Judges 5: 31.

[55] Parts of 14th and 13th Centuries BC.

[56] Deuteronomy 7: 6-8.

"And because He loved thy fathers, therefore He chose their seed after them, and brought thee out in his sight with his mighty power out of Egypt."[57] Being chosen implied responsibility: "Now, therefore, if ye will obey my voice indeed, and keep my covenant, then ye shall be a peculiar treasure onto me above all people."

Isaiah emphasises the vast scope of implications of God's choice of Israel:

> I the Lord have called thee in righteousness, and will hold thy hand, and will keep thee, and give thee for a covenant of the people, for a light of the Gentiles; To open the blind eyes, to bring out prisoners of prison and them that sit in darkness out of the prison house.[58]

Thus, if one sees oneself as chosen by God wanting to get something positive out of the promised land, then everyone endangering that endeavour will become one's enemy and God may be assumed to be supportive of one's struggle against him.

In the Biblical sense, of course, only Israel is chosen. However, amongst the Gentiles, in this profane world of political strife, the Holy Scriptures have been seen rather as a generic manuscript for any ruler to adjust to fit his particular need. Definitely, it takes some "poetic licence" to fit these Scriptures to the purposes of the Crusades, the Thirty Years War, or the two world wars. But over the years the precise tally of religious texts with actual political needs has become less important, and the incongruence has been frequently compensated by the broader notion of Christian tradition and the belief in a righteous cause blessed by the Lord for its noble intent.

Moreover, the age-old excuse for enmity, persecution, and genocide as 'a lesser evil' has been provided by Caiphas.[59] As previously intimated, this kind of opportunism may vindicate any doubtful, but convenient, governmental act of violence perpetrated in order to get rid of undesirable groups or individuals. We might read into this a justification of the Thirty-Years War and the crimes against humanity in The Balkans in the 1990s as well as the atrocities in New York and Washington in 2001. Taken out of

---

[57] Deuteronomy 4: 37. and Hosea 11: 1. "When Israel was a child, then I loved him, and called my son out of Egypt."

[58] Isaiah: 42, 6-7.

[59] St. John 11: 50.

their contexts, Scriptures can be exploited to benefit almost any cause, and this has been done not only by Jews and Christians.

Islam – like most religions – has its persuasive power in the essential mystery of the religious experience. Generally speaking, Muslim fundamentalists worldwide express solidarity with Islamic regimes, even where these are of an obvious oppressive nature. To miss this point and simply assess the order-of-battle of Islamic militants, not understanding the modus operandi of Muslim-oriented terrorist groups, is to underestimate the diverse influence of this faith. The primary targets for Islamic terror acts of recent years have been "infidels," who allegedly profaned the soil of Islam, prominent among which are the citizens of the United States of America.

Although Islam, as far as the Qur'an goes, is not a cantankerous religion, there are among its scribes those, who vehemently urge fight against what they call "the apostate peoples." Thus, the Ayatollah Khomeini in his address on the anniversary of the prophet Mohamed's birthday in 1983, which we mentioned above, stated that "war is a blessing for the world and for all the nations."[60]

Also, in the politico-religious statement – opposing Islamic ideals to Western civilisation – the *Al Qaeda Manual* recommends "the dialogue of bullets, the ideals of assassination, bombing, and destruction, and the diplomacy of the cannon and machine-gun."[61] This Qur'anic style encouragement to kill, though not the precise words, is akin to Caiphas' pathetic excuse. The real meaning obviously is that although so many infidels, and quite a few martyrs as well, will have to die, this happens for the sake of the many, i.e. the ummah of Islam and the believers.[62] Thus, religion joins with psychology to produce the required justification for the killing.

That image of the enemy, which religion contributes to creating, is one that denudes him of precisely the human and moral attributes and characteristics that might permit a rational resolution of the conflict short of military combat. The preliminary work of enmity that occurs before and during armed struggle is usually a two-sided venture. One builds up the

---

[60] Robert W. Rieber, ed., *The Psychology of War and Peace: The Image of the Enemy* (New York and London: Plenum Press, 1991) p. 15.

[61] Al Qaeda. *The Al Qaeda Manual.* Computer file impounded by British Police in Manchester. From internet, accessed 1 November 2002. www.disastercenter.com/terror, "Presentation."

[62] Ummah = community.

justice of one's own cause, while simultaneously vilifying the opponent. In Saddam Husein's Iraq, from 1991 onwards, the regime personified the United Stated as an enemy through depiction of its leadership as utterly corrupt and evil; the president was portrayed as an individual heading a belligerent empire seeking to dominate the Middle East and the Arab world by intimidating Muslim countries.[63]

Moreover, it is not only genuine religion which provides feeble excuses for war and praises the killing of non-believers. Pseudo-religious speech goes a long way doing similarly. Glorification of killing under the aegis of war, though not necessarily of war proper, possibly reached a climax with Himmler's infamous speech to the SS in 1943, in which he expressed his anticipation that History would know how to appreciate the unselfish and honourable commitment with which they were carrying out their task under severe mental and physical stress, and "yet remained decent."[64] One might suggest that, while the general argument that war has had a chivalrous element is a fair one, Himmler was talking about activities that went well beyond what a traditionalist would call war.

Those brought up with a Judeo-Christian, or a Clausewitzian, world view might argue that men engaged in war did not cease to be rational human beings with a responsibility to one another and to God. Thus, the SS-men are difficult to fit into the usually accepted definitions of war-fighters, just like the Al Qaeda warriors, who do not simply fight their foe asymmetrically: they have an asymmetric view of conflict. Logically, the SS's genocidal activities were murder, not war, but as they were an integral part of the bellicose regime's policy of conquest it seems understandable

---

[63] Rieber et al., *The Psychology of War and Peace*, p. 37.

[64] „Unter uns soll es einmal ganz offen ausgesprochen sein, und trotzdem werden wir darüber nie in der Öffentlichkeit reden... Es gehört zu de Dingen, die man leicht ausspricht „Das Jüdische Volk wird ausgerottet", sagt jeder Parteigenosse, „ganz klar, Steht in unser Programm. Ausschaltung der Juden. Ausrottung, machen wir."... Von euch werden die meisten wissen, was es heißt, wenn 100 Leichen beisammenliegen, wenn 500 daliegen oder wenn 1000 daliegen. Dies durchgehalten zu haben, und dabei...anständig geblieben zu sein, das hat uns hartgemacht. Dies ist ein nie geschriebenes und nie zu schreibenes Ruhmesblatt unserer Geschichte..." [My translation] "Among ourselves we will, sooner or later, be able freely to express this, though publicly we must remain silent... It is among the things that one easily mentions, "The Jewish people is being exterminated," says all party comrades, "of course, it's written in out programme. Removal of the Jews. Eradication, we will do it... Most of you will know what it means when 100 bodies lie there together, when 500 lie there or when 1000 lie there. To have coped with that and still remaining decent, that has made us hard." Joachim Fest, 1963, pp. 162 and 166, quoted in Alice Miller, *Am Anfang war Erziehung* (Frankfurt am Main: Suhrkamp Taschenbuch, 1983), pp. 99-100.

that many observers judge German warfare as also including this aspect. The half-religious half-temporal myths of Destiny, racial purity, and Germany's obligation to lead might have tempted many Germans to accept Himmler's words as a well-deserved praise. These myths pervaded the German society at the conscious level, but the reason this could happen is to be found in realm of the subconscious.

Cultural Aspects

Culture, which permeates our daily life, determines the way we describe our enemy and establish the image of hostility. During the First World War, German and Western descriptions of their respective opponents were different in language as well as focus, and so was the nature of Warsaw Pact and NATO Cold War rhetoric. The coalition-of-the-willing which fought in Afghanistan until 2014, did not fight in order to eradicate the infidels or to conquer land, but in a "comprehensive approach" to rebuild society and introduce security, democratic standards, and the rule of law. Their opponents are the Taliban and Al Qaeda, who are commonly termed terrorists rather than enemies. Their sins are drug dealing, oppression of women and non-believers as well as world terrorism. The coalition – whose official designation is International Stabilisation Force (ISAF), from 2003 onwards led by NATO – makes an effort not to use the terminology of bygone eras, such as crusade, barbarians or any kind of racial stereotypes. This coalition insists on being in the country by invitation by President Karzai – who they had themselves installed in 2001 – and being there to make a difference. Moreover, it claims it will be leaving as soon as the Afghan forces can take care of the citizens' security.[65] Thus the individual coalition officer and soldier sees herself or himself, not as a killer, but as a worthy representative of modern, peace loving, democratic society providing security for her or his home country simultaneously with shaping the conditions for a better life for the Afghans. The vocabulary has changed along with the changing political context and the new tasks thus derived.

---

[65] In 1991, Hamid Karzai was installed as leader of a transitional government for Afghanistan by the US. June 1992 the Loya Jirga appointed him president, but it was not until October 1994 that with slightly more than 50% of the votes cast that he was elected president by the Afghan people.

History

Our enemy images materialise out of our conscious and unconscious intellectual baggage, of which the officially recognised history – the one we were taught at school and told about by our veteran grandparents – is an important element. Thus, we all "know" that the Crusades were necessary to rid the holy city of Jerusalem of the occupation by the infidels, that the Boers treated immigrants badly, and that NATO was established "to keep the Americans in, to keep the Russians out and to keep the Germans down." It is common knowledge that the Holocaust was perpetrated by the Nazis and that the Soviet Union's Gulag made millions of their own citizens disappear. However, military commanders, political leaders, and policymakers generally do not always realise that history is not, everywhere, researched and written the way it happens in their own society.

When emotions run high, history cannot free itself from bias. One example is that – in the years following the German occupation of Denmark, 1940-45 – Danish official history cast those who had worked for the Germans as "vermin" and their liquidation by freedom fighters as "tidying up."[66] Conversely, today's Danish Second World War historians describe the same events in an attempted matter-of-fact fashion where the reasons for each individual killing are explained.

Today's quest for the most accurate communication and explanation of events has not always been the sole motivation of historians, nor is this necessarily the case in contemporary cultures outside the western Judaic-Christian sphere. Seen through the eyes of William Shakespeare, King Henry V and his longbow men did a brilliant job at Agincourt (French: Azincourt), while scant attention is paid the French armoured knights and the *Connétable de France* Charles d'Albret, who commanded on behalf of King Charles VI. A recent example might be the way President Robert Mugabe and his regime blame Rhodesia's colonial power, the United Kingdom, for all the trouble in today's Zimbabwe, while a more realistic description would be that the country was the best functioning entity in Africa until Mugabe's forced redistribution of land in 1999 and the conviction of him for breach of human rights in 2002.

Rational and credible theories on political history originate with the

---

[66] Examples of such early and biased accounts are: Vilhelm la Cour, *Danmark under Besættelsen I-II* [*Denmark During the Occupation I-II*] (Copenhagen: Westermanns Forlag, 1945-47) and Børge Outze & Ebbe Munck, *Danmarks Frihedskamp: Skrevet af danske Journalister I-II* [*Denmark's Fight for Freedom: Written by Danish Journalists I-II*] (Copenhagen: Bogforlaget Nutiden, 1948-49).

Greeks, who pioneered logical thought and a view of history based on the latest available insight and facts. Thucydides' history of the Peloponnesian War is an early endeavour to achieve a relevant and fairly unbiased account of what actually happened and why it did.

One must be aware of differing cultural approaches to the place of man in relation to Cosmos and individuals vis-à-vis commonality. We are not alone, and even Napoleon did not win his battles solely because of his own genius. Similarly, the adversity we encounter does not lie exclusively with the enemy commander. He has subordinate commanders, he may have allies, partisans or terrorists may be around, and weather, terrain and chance play important rôles as well. Montgomery knew that Rommel's Afrika Korps was not the only object against which to turn his attention prior to El Alamein, in the autumn of 1942. The Italian allies, the Axis minefields, the delimitation of the battlefield by the Mediterranean Sea and the Qattara Depression, and the channelling effects of the El Tada Plateau and the Ruweisat and Miteiriya Ridges were elements of immense importance to his planning and the sequencing of the operation. Without such an appreciation, accurate evaluations of the intelligence sources' reporting will be hampered considerably, and the resulting image will be a distorted one, as we saw in Operation Market Garden in 1944, where Lieutenant-General Browning dismissed last minute intelligence from the Dutch resistance movement because, allegedly, he did not want to upset Montgomery by changing the agreed plan. Omitting vital information and turning the blind eye to unpleasant facts is bound to lead to faulty conclusions, and policy makers thus get a skewed interpretation of events.

The exposure of modern man to an overwhelming presentation of symbols requires a discriminating study of human culture so as to understand the meaning of history.[67] The backdrop for our enemy image is the history per se as well as the history of thoughts, emotions and religion as integral parts of our culture and that of the opponent. The failure to do that with sufficient incisiveness and diligence are among the reasons that so much went wrong in the western attempt to democratise and westernise Afghanistan during the first decade and a half of the twenty-first century.

Operation Enduring Freedom, the US invasion that started in November 2001, differed from both the British (1839, 1878 and 1919) and Soviet (1979) invasions of central Afghanistan in its narrow military naïveté by making very limited use of earlier experience in that country, thus not considering any significant post invasion deployment that would be

---

[67] Belbutowsky, "Strategy and Culture," pp. 32-42.

essential, or at least relevant, for the regular military forces. The very name of the operation highlighted the roots and depth of the pre-invasion strategic analysis – a 'light footprint' would be sufficient. This was years before the crisis that led to the successful bureaucratic rebellion of senior officers of the American army and Marine light infantry against the paradigm of winning by quick manœuvre plus accurate strike and the introduction of a new counter-insurgency doctrine.[68] According to the Pentagon's understanding at the time, its armed forces should smash the enemy military quickly with overwhelming, scientifically distributed, accurate firepower, and then redeploy to bases ready for the next operation, leaving allies and civilian agencies to pick up the pieces and maybe providing some Special Force elements for a time to train the locals.[69] This economically attractive modus operandi was made dependent on the use of air power very similar in concept and motive to Royal Air Force's 'air policing' policy for the border zone in the 1920-30s. Due to the failure until 2011 to capture Osama bin Laden and continued low level problems on the border, a light division size army force remained, and most of the large country was left to the re emerging warlords.

In 2005, following years of retraining and expansion from their bases in Pakistan, the different – mainly Pashtu – militant units under the 'Taliban umbrella' stepped up operations in southern and eastern Afghanistan. Many of the insurgent organisations were not religiously motivated Taliban and Al Qaeda warriors, but a new generation of tribal fighters striving to achieve control of territory, poppy production, mineral wealth, and smuggling routes, and a better use of history – on the part of the western coalition – might have allowed responses more adequately tailored to the situation on hand.

The US chose to send armed unmanned aerial vehicles into Pakistan's Federally Administered Tribal Areas' airspace on cadre assassination missions, but the Taliban has managed to continue its attacks, including the bombing of the Indian Kabul embassy in July 2008, along with the rather limited facilities supporting US and other western operations. Considering that all along the Pakistani Inter-Services Intelligence agency (ISI in daily

---

[68] It seems fair to suggest that this crisis was a direct consequence of the Bush-Rumsfeld administration's illogical defence policy of worldwide military engagement running parallel with cuts in budgets and personnel numbers.

[69] Moreover, nation-building, which would have been a logical follow-up on destroying an allegedly hostile regime and a country's infrastructure, was not on the US agenda during the first decade of the 2000s.

parlance) has conducted a massive co-operation with the Taliban Islamists in order to kindle anti-Indian sentiments and prop up all possible Islamist groupings in the whole Afghanistan-Pakistan-Kashmir wider area, a more shrewd use of historic knowledge in combination with a massive human intelligence effort might have provided a quicker, cheaper and more humane conclusion to the fighting.

Art

In the world of intelligence collection and analysis art as a category of culture influencing everyone's comprehension is often dismissed. Art is mostly seen only in the context of the decorative arts. In the story of mankind, however, art reveals the unfolding of the symbol in graphic form, often indicating the values of a people. In creating a work of culture, the artist becomes an instrument of a transcendent power.

For those studying Northern Ireland, an inquiry into the history of the murals and slogans on the walls of the city of Belfast reveals much relevant information on the story of the political struggle which has happened there. In Latin America, too, paintings display the feelings of groups in conflict with authorities. Here, the god figure is often portrayed as an Indian or a peasant, symbolic of the inner struggle felt by the group. Similarly, the images of the *Sendero Luminoso* [the Shining Path] symbolise all that, which is showing the proper course. Likewise, Goya's painting of a French firing squad executing Spanish partisans, who have rebelled against the French occupation of their country, is part of a national heritage that emphasise the sufferings which loyal citizens must take upon them to uphold their freedom and independence. While the firing squad – the enemy – is depicted dark, cruel and impersonal, and shown from behind, the partisans' faces are illuminated by the muskets' muzzle flashes making them appear noble in their agony.[70] Art, thus, is precisely the element, which most obviously demonstrates the psychological aspect of enmity which, mostly, is either hidden or embedded in grandiose speeches.

Art helps us to realise that the enmity, which is a key mental factor in the process of establishing an enemy portrait, is a multi-faceted quantity based on national affiliation and historical heritage as well as cultural, religious and emotional dispositions. Moreover, although most citizens of

---

[70] "The Third of May 1808" is a painting completed in 1814 by the Spanish painter Francisco Goya (1746-1828), now in the Museo del Prado, Madrid.

western secular societies will be reluctant to admit it, metaphysical and chauvinist elements, present in wartime propaganda and frequently supported by heroic art, are difficult to avoid totally.

"The Third of May 1808"

Art, however, is not necessarily sheer propaganda, but it does mostly have to fulfil political requirements. Paintings of battle scenes must satisfy the need of the institution that pays the artist, and recent examples are the paintings commissioned by the Danish Armed Forces to be hung at the Danish Museum of National History. Dead civilians had to be left out of the paintings, and co-operation between the Danish Army and the local security forces must play a key rôle.[71] It is evident that the influence of the mental, cultural, historical and other peripheral elements is often conveyed to the public through outstanding works of art, but the face of the foe comprises many, and a lot more pertinent, aspects such as forces, weather, terrain, logistics and popular sympathy that remain central to creating an image of the opponent that is militarily useful.

---

[71] E.g. Mathilde Fenger's battle painting "Transition" finished 2013 and Peter Carlsen's painting canvas depicting the air battle in "Libya 2011" hung in April 2014.

Chapter IV: Psychological Forces and Effects

Military action is intertwined with psychological forces and effects.[1]

Upbringing and Behaviour

MOST PSYCHOLOGICAL ASPECTS of hostility are indeed hidden and need to be scrupulously uncovered to be understood. Enmity is a key characteristic of adult life, but as far as the individual grown-up is concerned its origin may be traced back to early childhood and the religious, cultural, societal, and political norms enforced upon him/her throughout the process of upbringing. The universe created through eighteen years of education permeates all conscious and unconscious mental activity and forms the mental scales on which new impressions are weighed. The ways of bringing up children, the creativity and societal norms, humiliation and dignity, freedom and limitations marking them for life bear a heavy responsibility for later enmification of entire societies. The anthology entitled *The Psychology of War and Peace*, first published in 1991 and edited by American psychologist Robert W. Rieber, induces us to realise that:

> While no subject deserves closer attention than that of war, an important component phenomenon of the mentality needed to wage war has gone largely

---

[1] Clausewitz, *On War*, p. 136, quoted in Handel, *Masters of War*, p. 27.

undiscussed – enmification. Though it is possible to think of war in purely objective aims...war is inconceivable without a clearly defined image of the enemy.[2]

That image, however, is a mosaic composed of unconscious as well as conscious elements supplied by sources as diverse as family, school, tradition, church, political organisations and politicians, media, and society per se. In the first chapter of *The Psychology of War and Peace*, Robert W. Rieber and his co-author Robert J. Kelly opines that: "Enmification is a basic human tendency" and "a process which goes beyond objective and historical conditions. It entails psychological processes that run very deep and which rapidly acquire their own momentum."[3]

Behaviour has three phenomenologically distinct features. It may be single and situation determined, like opinion and decision behaviour – behaviour based on conscious decision – or behaviour within a crowded environment. It may be relatively durable, but still situation-determined, such as habits (in a non-technical sense), or it may be relatively durable and situation-detached, as life-style is. There are three different subsystems of functions in the structure of human information processing: belief systems, rôles and rôle systems, and self. Within the belief systems we discern two ideal typical types of behaviour. Single purposeful behaviour is preponderantly the outcome of patterns of thought, whereas single accidental behaviour is the effect of more attitudinal – principally emotional – processes. Both these forms of behaviour are dependent on perceptions organised in a definition of the situation and culminating in behavioural intentions. Habits depend on a dynamic tissue of attitudes, expectations, and perceptions, which one may call a rôle definition. Some authors describe them as rôle enactment. Life styles depend on specific kinds of rôles, which we may call the self, wherein personality traits (or basic attitudes), values, personality characteristics and self definition cluster together.[4]

While behaviour based on thought is assumed to vary with the situation, habits and life styles are forms of behaviour that have roots in the past, ultimately to be found in childhood and upbringing.

---

[2] Rieber et al., *The Psychology of War and Peace*, p. 4.

[3] Rieber et al., *The Psychology of War and Peace*, p. 6.

[4] Hendrick J.C. Rebel, "Fearing the Army and the Enemy: Psychological Explanation of the Dutch Sociopolitical Reality" in Rieber et al., *The Psychology of War and Peace*, p. 174.

The Swiss psychologist Alice Miller has conducted a vast research in the causes and sources of violence perpetrated by persons who have committed serious crimes.[5] She has found that, without exception, they have all been subjected to extreme violence during their upbringing. Miller studied the childhood of Adolf Hitler which has given her ample opportunity to draw some interesting parallels between authoritarianism and certain paranoid trends towards groups. These trends lend themselves all too easily to enmification or demonisation, partly because such groups are perceived as substitutes for the violent father, partially because the target communities are generally accepted as scapegoats.

Amongst the persons surveyed, Miller found a general penchant towards expressing repressed feelings in the form of destructive acts against others, like crime and genocide, or against themselves, like alcoholism, drug addiction, psychic illness and suicide.[6] She, further, noticed that electronic measuring on infants has shown that *"tenderness as well as cruelty is felt and acquired right from the beginning* (emphasis in the original)."[7] Moreover, Miller attaches considerable importance to the negative influence of authoritarian upbringing, and she believes that:

> ...helped by the analytical knowledge of repression and projection mechanisms it becomes easier to understand the Holocaust, and the history of the Third Reich makes us see the consequences of the "black pedagogy" more clearly. Seen against the backdrop of rejection of everything childish, accumulated during upbringing, it becomes almost understandable that men and women led a million children to the gas chambers. They were brought up to kill everything childish or lively in themselves. They had – in this way – to pass on the cruelty

---

[5] i.e. murderers, drug addicts, and top-Nazis (Hitler, Himmler).

[6] Miller, *Am Anfang*, p. 13. [my translation from:] „Die nun von ihrem eigentlichen Grund abgespalteten Gefühle von Zorn, Ohnmacht, Verzweiflung, Sehnsucht, Angst und Schmerz verschaffen sich dennoch Ausdruck in zerstörerischen Akten gegen andere (Kriminalität, Völkermord) oder gegen sich selbst (Drogensucht, Alkoholismus, Prostitution, psychische Krankheiten, Suizid)."

[7] Miller, *Am Anfang*, p.14 f. [my translation from:] „Ferner haben elektronische Messungen an noch ungeborenen Kindern enthüllt, die von den meisten Erwachsenen bisher noch nicht wahrgenommen wurde, nämlich daß *das Kind sowohl Zärtlichkeit als auch Grausamkeit von Anfang an fühlt und lernt.*"

of their own childhoods, the killings of their own souls.[8]

Similarly, in 1956 Fromm (1900-80) proposed that an urge to die arose from what he called "negative transcendence." When an individual could not find meaning in his life, indeed when he no longer sought such meaning, then the capacity for transcendence, which is inherent to mankind, turned into a malevolent psychological force which sought death and which could readily be turned outward as a sadistic destructiveness: "Certainly, such an evil psychological turn could be detected in the phenomenon of Nazism, with which Fromm was familiar, just as it can be found today, in a somewhat different form, amongst a certain group of psychopaths."[9]

The authoritarian upbringing, which Miller found prevalent not only in Germany but in all German speaking societies, apparently brings about such negative transcendence as an outlet for frustrations. These are caused by a sense of guilt that people accumulate when not being able to find an acceptable object for the anger and hatred heaped up on the bottom of their souls because of the social taboo attached to hating one's parents for their abuse of the child. Such tabooing raises a demand for someone else as an acceptable object for hatred, and:

> ...it may have been Hitler's most 'brilliant idea' to give the German youth, that so early in life had had to learn to harshness, obedience, and suppressing their feelings, the possibility of projection onto the Jews. This was no new idea, it had been seen before in most wars of conquest, in the Crusades, and by the Inquisition. But it is interesting that here the concept is used within the realm of narcissism; *a part of 'self'* is being fought, though not anything dangerous

---

[8] Miller, *Am Anfang*, p.107-108. [my translation from:] „Wie uns die analytischen Kenntnis der Abspaltungs- und Projektionsmechanismen helfen kann, das Phänomen Holocaust zu verstehen, so hilft uns die Geschichte des Dritten Reiches, die Folgen der „Schwarzen Pädagogik" deutlicher zu sehen: Auf dem Hintergrund der aufgestauten Ablehnung des Kindlichen in unserer Erziehung läßt es sich beinahe leicht begreifen, daß Männer und Frauen ohne auffallende Schwierigkeiten eine Million Kinder als Träger der gefürchteten eigenen Seelenanteile in die Gaskammer geleitet haben... Ihre Erziehung war von Anfang an darauf ausgerichtet, alles Kindliche, Spielerische, Lebendige in sich abzutöten. Die Grausamkeit, die ihnen zugefügt wurde, der seelische Mord am Kind, das sie einst waren, mußten sie in der gleichen Weise weitergeben..."

[9] Rieber et al., *The Psychology of War and Peace*, p. 9. The psychologist Erich Seligmann Fromm was born in Frankfurt, Germany, in 1900 and died in Switzerland in 1980.

like a threat to existence (emphasis in the original).[10]

As it is known from Dave Grossman's research of the preconditions for effective military combat (see below), there is an obvious necessity that a well defined image of the actual or potential enemy permeates the brains of soldiers to condition them to the act of killing other human beings. Apart from the dedicated military training, conditioning takes place by the everyday influence of society through television, video games and the general societal attitude towards strangers. There is a direct connexion of this manipulation with similar conditioning of entire societies to animosity against nations, ethnic groups and individuals with certain characteristics (deficiencies).

This all leads Miller to claim that "if psychoanalysis might for once turn away from its obsession with 'death drives,' ample evidence is available to substantiate a *conditioning* starting in early childhood allowing significant contributions to peace research (emphasis added)."[11]

Miller's point of departure is the social milieu of the child. The Austro-Hungarian provincial society in which Adolf Hitler grew up tolerated no opposition towards parents and supported education by a rigorous interpretation of Catholicism and extensive use of corporal punishment:

> The child Adolf had no chance of ever escaping his father's daily chastisement, because it had very little to do with the boy's offences but emanated from the father's own unsolved problems. The racial legislation of the Third Reich placed the Jew in exactly that position vis-à-vis the ordinary German... Because Adolf Hitler's relationship with his father did not imply any kind of affection (in *Mein Kampf* he calls him Mr. Father) his hatred of him was continuous and

---

[10] Miller, *Am Anfang*, p.110-111. [my translation from:] „Es mag als Hitlers „genialer Wurf" gelten, den so früh zur Härte, zum Gehorsam, zur Unterdrückung der Gefühle erzogenen Deutschen die Juden für ihre Projektion angeboten zu haben. Doch der Gebrauch dieses Mechanismus ist keineswegs neu. Er ist in den meisten Eroberungskriegen, in der Geschichte der Kreuzzüge, der Inquisition, auch in der neusten Geschichte zu beobachten. Das bezeichnende für diese Verfolgung ist, daß es sich hier um einen Narzißtischen Bereich handelt. *Ein Teil des Selbst* wird bekämpft, nicht ein wirklich gefährlicher Feind, wie z.B. bei realer Existenzbedrohung.

[11] Ibid., pp.172-73, [my translation from:] „Wenn sich die Psychoanalyse einmal von ihrer Bindung an die Annahme des Todestriebe befreien würde, könnte sie dank dem vorhandene Material über die frühkindliche *Konditionierung* sehr viel wesentliches zur Friedensforschung beitragen."

unequivocal.[12]

Consequently, repressed hatred would have to be projected onto someone and the Jews were always there readily available for that purpose.

Excerpt from front page of the SA weekly *Der Stürmer*, No 22, 1938.

Heading of the article: *Meister des Betrugs* [Master of Fraud] Caption of the drawing: Der Kurgast [the sanatorium patient] Below the drawing: Der Jude wirkt wie des Teufels Schatten in der sonnigen Welt [the Jew works as the Devil's shadow in the sunlit world

That part of the conditioning of the Germans, which was about seeing in the image of their enemy the picture of a Jew, was a simple and an almost obscure process. At the time – amongst most European peoples – the Jews were recognised as an acceptable object for common disdain.[13] In Nazi Germany as everywhere today, the youths were easy targets for such

---

[12] Ibid., pp.191-92. [my translation from:] „Zugleich bedeutete das Rassengesetz die Wiederholung der eigene Kindheitsdramas. So wie der Jude jetzt keine Chance hatte, konnte einst das Kind Adolf den Schlägen seines Vaters nicht entgehen, denn die Ursache der Schläge waren ja die ungelösten Probleme des Vaters, die Abwehr seiner Trauer um die eigene Kindheit... Solche Väter pflegen...wenn sie mit einer Stimmung nicht fertig werden...ihr Kind zu verprügeln, um sich ihr narzißtisches Gleichgewicht wieder zu verschaffen. Diese Funktion hatte der Jude im Dritten Reich... Weil Adolf mit seinem Vater keine Zärtlichkeit verband (en nennt ihn in *Mein Kampf* bezeichnenderweise „Herr Vater"), war der aufsteigende Haß in ihm kontinuierlich und eindeutig." Cf. Clausewitz *On War*, pp. 137-38, concerning hatred, hostile feelings.

[13] Miller, *Am Anfang*, pp.195-96.

conditioning, because they had learned from their parents who it was acceptable to hate.[14] Alice Miller mentions a lady, who told her that she had actually never met a Jew, but as she entered the BDM (Bund deutscher Mädel, i.e. the League for German (Nazi) Girls) she realised, much to her relief, that now, for once, she was actually given an opportunity to stigmatise somebody else as being an enemy and to hate that person without being reproached.[15] We may call this upbringing or brainwashing, but the crux of the matter is that this woman was conditioned and that she did not herself realise that her attitude had been acquired involuntarily and unknowingly. Obviously this was exactly what the Nazi regime intended, and Hitler, in one of his conversations with Hermann Rauschning (1887-1982) the pre-Second World War president of the Free City of Danzig, made the point openly admitting that, "it is an extraordinary pleasure for us to see how people around us do not realise what really happens to them."[16]

Nazi Germany was singular in many respects but, as far as conditioning to enmity of the youth was concerned, she was not. Other nations master that task too and, in Dave Grossman's view, modern media have taken over much of the negative rôle of the past's authoritarian upbringing. In many societies enemy perceptions – which ought to be reserved for military personnel – are conveyed in a subtle and obscure manner through films, videos and games, which it is impossible for a child or an adolescent to see through. Fiction alone is hardly sufficient, but, intertwined with the glut of semi-factual or simplified information poured out by television documentaries, video-shows and tabloid press, hidden messages will sink in with many of those of the children and youngsters who have no recourse to parental guidance.

---

[14] Ibid., pp. 201-02. „Jugendliche können von ihren Eltern ableiten, wenn sie ein eindeutiges Feindbild bekommen, das sie dann frei und erlaubtermaßen hassen dürfen (emphasis in the original)".

[15] Miller, *Am Anfang*, p. 220. [my translation from:] „Ich kenne eine Frau, die zufällig nie mit einem Juden in Berührung gekommen war, bis sie in dem „Bund Deutscher Mädel" eintrat. In ihrer Kindheit wurde sie sehr streng erzogen... Sie erzählte mir später, mit welschen Begeisterung sie „von den Verbrechen der Juden" in *Mein Kampf* gelesen und welsche Erleichterung es in ihr ausgelöst hatte, zu wissen, daß man da jemanden so eindeutig hassen durfte (emphasis in the original)."

[16] Adolf Hitler in Hermann Rauschning „Gespräche mit Hitler [Hitler Speaks]" (Europa, Wien: 1973) p. 181 in Miller, *Am Anfang*, p. 82. [my translation from:] „Dann gewährt es uns aber auch einen ganz besonderen heimlichen Genuß, zu sehen, wie die Leute um uns nicht gewahr werden, was mit ihnen wirklich geschieht."

As Grossman writes, if such:

> ...manipulation of the minds of impressionable teenagers is a necessary evil, one which only reluctantly and with reservations may be accepted for combat soldiers, how should we feel about its indiscriminate application to civilian teenagers of this nation [the USA]? For that is what we are doing through the rôle models being provided by the entertainment industry today.[17]

Consequently, the results are not at all very different from the atrocities perpetrated by the Nazis, e.g. the SS action on 10 June 1944 in Oradour sur Glane. "Holmes concludes that 'the road to My Lai was paved, first and foremost, by the dehumanisation of the Vietnamese and the "mere gook rule" which declared that killing a Vietnamese civilian did not really count."[18]

What we do while conditioning our soldiers – and many a modern society unconsciously do this to its civilian youth as well – is providing them with a necessary a priori psychological excuse for hating and, subsequently, for killing. Being conditioned they do not have to be ashamed of themselves for doing so. They acquire the psychological ability to kill and to control their feelings whilst they are doing so – as well as ever after: "When man first picked up a club or a rock and killed his fellow man, he gained more than mechanical energy and mechanical leverage. He also gained psychological energy and psychological leverage that was every bit as necessary in the killing process."[19]

It may be sad to acknowledge this necessity, but that does not make go away the need for programming human beings with a view to their and their fellow-warriors' survival in war. Grossman relates that "Jerry...an officer with Special Forces (the US Green Berets), when asked how he was able to do the things he did, acknowledged simply that he had been "programmed" to kill, and he accepted it as a necessary for his survival and success..." and that:

> Duane...had conducted a remarkable number of successful interrogations during his lifetime, and he considered himself to be an expert of the process popularly known as brainwashing. He felt that he had been "to some extent

---

[17] Grossman, *On Killing*, p. 319.

[18] Ibid., p. 190.

[19] Ibid., p. 132.

brainwashed" and that soldiers receiving modern combat training were being similarly brainwashed. Like every other veteran whom I have discussed the matter with, he had no objection to this, understanding that psychological conditioning was essential to his survival and an effective method of mission accomplishment.[20]

Again, it appears that the face of the foe is not an objective representation of his actual looks to provide simple recognition, but rather a somewhat distorted picture serving, also, to install the right emotions in the person seeing it. Thus, "most Vietnam veterans did not necessarily exercise personal kill in Vietnam. But they had participated in dehumanising the enemy in training... (emphasis added)"[21] The nexus with ordinary life is present, if not obvious, in this need for combat self-assurance.

When an individual is under great stress, particularly the kind of stress that arises from social disorder, this is felt as a diffuse anxiety. A sense arises of being threatened, but it is a vague, undifferentiated threat at least initially.

Having a clear-cut enemy is obviously preferable – one can channel one's emotional energies – much the way anger or even a well-focused fear is preferable to a diffuse sense of panic. And so, at times, even the best of us resort to the creation of a personal bogey-man, someone whom we can hate, and feel better for it.[22]

The Frogs, the Huns, the Jews, the Gooks and lots of other stereotypes will serve this purpose. Similarly, in his analysis of *Massenpsychologie* [mass psychology], the Austrian psychoanalyst Sigmund Freud (1856-1939) sought to reinterpret the processes of emotional contagion in terms of the centrality of the Oedipus complex. The key issue was, he believed, that people tended to find in the leader of their group a father-substitute providing common identification. Aggression against the leader, the other side of the oedipal ambivalence towards the father, became taboo and had to find an outlet elsewhere.[23] This way, the leader became a demigod, a person whose status was above that of ordinary human beings. Serving a

---

[20] Ibid., p. 257.

[21] Ibid, p. 259.

[22] Rieber et al., *The Psychology of War and Peace*, p. 7.

[23] Ibid., p. 11.

purpose in armed struggle though it may, elevating the leader to sacrosanct status is a dangerous path to tread. Empires have vanished because of it, and Napoleonic France and Nazi Germany may serve as examples.

From Thucydides to Lewis F. Richardson, from ancient historians to modern psychiatrists, a long line of scholars have elaborated on how fear distorts images, how distorted images promote fear, and how this dangerous spiral has led nations to mutual destruction and endless suffering and misery and moral depredation throughout the history of mankind.

The face that we see is a twisted one, and while one side of the image distortion is the intentional supply of emotional fuel, another is the misapprehension materialising out of the military commander's or the political leadership's incompetence. And here, too, the authoritarian personality plays a significant rôle, because, facing grim realities, such persons are prone to suffering from cognitive dissonance.[24] British psychologist Norman F. Dixon has examined this aspect in *On the Psychology of Military Incompetence*:

> Authoritarians will be less likely to understand enemy intentions, and act upon information regarding such intentions as conflict with the beliefs and preconceptions which the commander might hold. The events following the Cambrai tank offensive in the First World War and, in the Second World War, the repeated inability of senior commanders to accept the possibility of an enemy offensive in the Ardennes, are the cases in point.[25]

Another side of the authoritarian personality is its needs for support and approval. Dixon finds that:

> ...commanders with weak egos, with over-strong needs for approval and the most closed minds will be the very ones least able to tolerate the nagging doubts of cognitive dissonance. In other words it will be the least rational who are the most likely to reduce dissonance by ignoring unpalatable intelligence (my emphasis). Research on individual differences in cognitive dissonance suggests that its effects are likely to be strongest in those afflicted by chronic low self-esteem and general passivity.[26]

---

[24] "Cognitive dissonance" is a psychological conflict materialising every time incompatible beliefs and/or perceptions collide in a person's mind.

[25] Dixon, *On the Psychology* p. 264.

[26] Dixon, *On the Psychology*, p. 166.

Bent on not to discover too much that might risk disclosing that dissonance, i.e. the discrepancy between reality and internalised norms, a commander will find compelling reasons for not undertaking the actions momentarily needed,[27] or as Dixon puts it, "in brief, then, military incompetence involves: ...A failure to make adequate reconnaissance... [and] a suppression or distortion of news from the front, usually rationalised as necessary for morale or security..."[28]

This kind of unwillingness to see is not limited to the military sphere of warfare. At the political level and in expert advice to that level convenience or incompetence or both also make themselves felt. Donald Rumsfeld's conduct of the war in Iraq is one example. Other sad proofs of this perilous mechanism are the British political decision-making efforts between the world wars:

- Field-Marshal Montgomery-Massingberd, Chief of the Imperial General Staff 1926-33: 'There are certain critics in the press who say we organise the Army again for a war in Europe...the Army is not likely to be used for a great war in Europe for many years to come.'
- Sir Ronald Charles, Master-General of Ordnance, 1933: 'There is no likelihood of war in our lifetime.'
- Sir Hugh Elles, Director of Military Training, 1938: 'The Japanese are no danger to us and eager for our friendship.'[29]
- Prime Minister Neville Chamberlain, "Peace in our time..."

The image of a menace from potentially hostile Germany was, thus, ignored for many years. In Britain, apart from Churchill, only very few realised what was coming and nobody really wanted an enemy, Central Europe was conveniently remote, and "it is much more difficult to feel spontaneously hostile towards an enemy you cannot see."[30] This was one way of deceiving oneself as to the willpower and the courses open to the future foe. Another would have been ignoring his capabilities through disrespect or outright contempt, as it was the case in the German pre-war

---

[27] As it was the case with the staff of 21st Army Group abstaining from renewed intelligence efforts in order not to "rock the boat" in Montgomery's plan for Operation 'Market Garden', autumn 1944.

[28] Dixon, *On the Psychology*, p. 153.

[29] Ibid., p. 164.

[30] Ibid., p. 171.

administration: "From his [Hitler's] extreme ethnocentrism came another well-known form of military incompetence: that which comes from gross underestimation of the enemy and in particular the ability of a civilian population to withstand the effects of war."[31]

Thus we see a trend amongst politicians and officers alike to adapt their images of the enemy to suit short term goals. Consequently, this accepted picture becomes the point of departure for the practitioners of the military, naval, and air force professions, whose task it is to do the actual fighting. Parts of this clutter may be filtered away, but much of the distortion is so deeply ingrained in everyone's mental baggage that many of us will never realise that it is there. The crux of the matter is that any society, in order to keep up the will to fight – and this is assumed to be a key necessity in war – has to conceive a myth that can be commonly accepted, a national ethos, which no segment of society can seriously challenge without risk of upsetting the entire war effort – not even those who so desperately need precision, exactitude and truth.

Hence the influence of society on the enemy image cannot be ignored. Having an enemy is a general – a collective – phenomenon.

In December 1916 Jung wrote:

> The psychological concomitants of the present war – above all the incredible brutalisation of public opinion, the mutual slandering, the unprecedented fury of destruction, the monstrous flood of lies, and man's incapacity to call a halt to the blood demon – are uniquely fitted to force upon the attention of every thinking person the problem of the chaotic unconscious which slumbers uneasily beneath the ordered world of consciousness. This war has pitilessly revealed to civilised man that he is still a barbarian, and has at the same time shown what an iron scourge lies in store for him if he ever again should be tempted to make his neighbour responsible for his own evil qualities.[32]

To the vast majority of citizens it is obvious, apparently, that our neighbour is responsible because the "us-and-them-dichotomy" lies deep in all of us. It is an integral part of daily life; it applies to ordinary neighbours, to national neighbours and to neighbouring creeds alike.

For many years it has been "politically correct" to deny the existence of any difference between them and us, especially if this distinction has

---

[31] Ibid., p. 322.

[32] Jung, "Two lessons in Analytical Psychology", 1972, p 4 in .Rieber et al., *The Psychology of War and Peace*, p. 10.

ethnic or religious undertones. However, this political correctness is a superficial phenomenon, and although the human inclination to distinguish may not be universal it is certainly frequent. The so-called "cartoon crisis" of recent years, which occurred when a Danish newspaper – the JyllandsPosten – published a number of caricatures of the Muslim prophet Mohamed, was indeed an eye-opener in this respect. While western secular norm includes freedom of expression, equality amongst religious creeds and practices and the notion that the law applies uniformly to all citizens, apparently this is not the rule in Islamic societies. As the crisis broke out, fundamentalists immediately demanded prosecution of the newspaper editor and the artist and craved that the Qur'anic scriptures and symbols be given privileged status and exemption from the legislation applying to other religions. Within weeks, violence against Danish embassies and boycott of Danish products spread from Denmark to large parts of the Middle East. Therefore the general feeling of being something apart from any other culture may not be politically correct, but undeniably it lies latent in many societies, Christian, Moslem or atheist. However well suppressed, it will surface every time clashes of opinion, let alone war, occur.

Striking much the same chord, it appears that the general British animosity during the Napoleonic Wars against the French is an example of the 'them-against-us-dichotomy' which, during The Great War, let many Britons believe that his country was actually fighting the wrong enemy. Similarly, the view that Sweden was evil personified materialising amongst the Danes during the calamities in the last part of the 17th century did not alter until, in the middle of the 19th century, Prussia took over the place as the closest and most obvious menace.

Additional fuel for the 'them-and-us-animosity' is supplied by the Nazi German onslaught on the Soviet Union. As mentioned by Bartov, the Germans cultivated an image of themselves, "us," depicting the Germanic race's heroic combat for survival against the barbaric hordes of Slavs. "Them" were the barbarians, whose ground might in future provide living space for the civilised westerners; they were Jewish Bolshevists and Untermenschen [sub-humans]. Nothing indicates that the "them-and-us-dichotomy" is merely a phenomenon of the past. On the contrary, there is reason to believe that similar subconscious mental baggage was at large in the Vietnam War, and the Abu Ghraib Prison incidents goes some way to suggest that at least some US soldiers and NCOs have held similar views on the Iraqis.

The Subconscious

Not every human thought or deed is a result of conscious determination. Lots of patterns of reaction are held ready beneath the surface and leap into action when they are prompted.[33] This is possible because, psychologically, the face of the foe is a synecdoche comprising in one portrayal all the enmity, adversity and trouble that upbringing and conditioning have supplied allowing us to project them onto the foe.

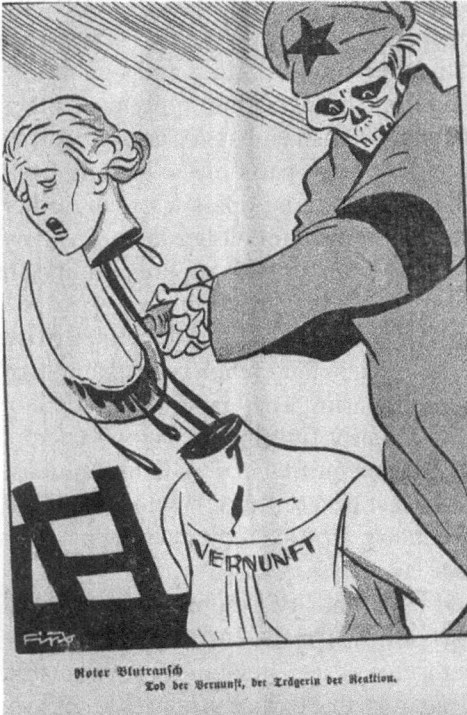

Excerpt from the
SA weekly *Der Stürmer*,
No 22, 1938.

"Vernunft" [Reason]
Subtitle: "Roter Blutrausch.
Tod der Vernunft, der Trägerin
des Reaktion" [Red blood frenzy:
the death of reason,
reaction personified]

The primary function of this synecdoche is to dehumanise the enemy so that the image ceases to be a personal one, but one which fits into them-and-us dichotomies like those mentioned above. This helps the subconscious self to establish a stereotype which boosts the enmity, though it does not contribute to creating a credible and precise representation of the foe. Standardised language is used to demonise the opponent and cast

---

[33] The author is indebted to the psychologist Maria Buhl for guidance into the following insights in the psychological aspects of enmity.

him in the rôle of the aggressor and oppressor. Demonisation blurs the face of the foe even more, and when clashing with reality it entails cognitive dissonance with citizens generally and, in particular, with the soldiers who have been conditioned to adopt this hostile attitude to another group or nation. As long as the individual soldier accepts that he or she is not slaying a fellow human being but an unknown quantity representing the hostile entity, he or she will probably more willingly violate the commandment that "thou shalt not kill."[34] The cognitive dissonance trouble does not materialise until the moment when he or she realises that reality does not tally with the skewed "face of the foe."

Possibly, we all suffer from of being to some degree conditioned, and beyond a certain point we might relapse into the preconceived stereotypes forced upon us by upbringing, propaganda and official rhetoric.

One of the most level-headed and apparently unbiased war accounts ever to be written by a combatant is probably that of Sergeant Adrien-Jean-Baptiste-François Bourgogne (1785-1867).[35] Although during his service with Napoleon's colours in Russia, he must have been under severe stress, he mostly describes the enemy precisely and without much hostile emotion. Nevertheless, even this highly composed soldier has not managed to free himself completely of the clichés of the accepted vocabulary acquired during his upbringing in revolutionary and imperial France as well as during active service on the battlefields of Europe. Thus during the retreat from Moscow, apparently he gives way to subconscious habits of reaction stating among other things that the Emperor was annoyed by "seeing himself followed by this horde of barbarians [the Cossacks]... They howled like wolves to excite each other, but did not dare to attack."[36]

Many psychological aspects of the enemy image are indeed subconscious foundations for habits, preferences and life styles, and these must be uncovered and made conscious to be understood. Seeing combat in this light, one may look upon enmity and aversion as rather normal characteristics of adult life whose origin can be traced back to early

---

[34] Exodus: 20, 13.

[35] Sergeant [later second-lieutenant] Bourgogne joined the Imperial French Army in 1805 and saw active service 1806-15. Original title of his memoirs: *Mémoires du sergent Bourgogne.*

[36] Adrien-Jean-Baptiste-François Bourgogne, *The Retreat from Moscow: the Memoirs of Sergeant Bourgogne* [*Mémoires du sergent Bourgogne*] (London: The Folio Society, 1985), pp. 84-85.

childhood and the religious, cultural, societal and political attitudes of society in general and the parents in particular. They are predominantly repressed but internalised, and they remain present beneath the surface of the well behaved citizen's calm appearance. If the process of creating such a universe proceeds throughout a person's formative years, it will permeate subconsciously much of his or her mental activity, emotions and whole demeanour, and it will provide the scales on which new impressions are weighed. Thus, the value systems generally accepted by society and underpinning the education of its children will accompany most of them for life bearing in them the seeds of later attitudes. American psychologist Robert W. Rieber noticed that:

> While no subject deserves closer attention than that of war, an important component phenomenon of the mentality needed to wage war has gone largely undiscussed – enmification. Though it is possible to think of war in purely objective aims...war is inconceivable without a clearly defined image of the enemy.[37]

To vilify, demonise, dehumanise or otherwise make efforts to turn a fellow human being into an adversary is what the process of enmification is all about. However, this conversion from friend to foe is no straightforward or simple process; it appears to be one of creating a mosaic composed of subconscious as well as conscious elements supplied by sources as diverse as family, school, tradition, church, political organisations and influential personalities, media and society in general. To put together such a montage is an ongoing and time consuming process, but it need not be anything dramatic. We all, now and then, attribute negative traits to fellow citizens, with whom – for lesser or graver reasons – we have fallen out. This is the root of the enmification process and it is a basic human inclination. Rieber argues:

> It goes beneath the surface of objective historical conditions, and it involves deeply rooted psychological processes that might acquire their own momentum. Having an 'enemy' goes far deeper than merely having a competitor or an adversary. To have an enemy' is in a sense to be possessed. One no longer feels in command of one's own destiny: there is an enemy out there, and one's own fate is tied to his... In an important psychological sense, one is out of control... Ultimately, the enemy comes to dominate one's thoughts and feelings to the point where one is virtually bewitched by that combination

---

[37] Rieber et al., *The Psychology of War and Peace*, p. 4.

of fear and hatred...[38]

Alice Miller's research into the causes and sources of violence leads her to believe that "being possessed" to the point of not being "in control of one's own destiny" has obvious roots in traumatic childhood experiences. As these experiences will always lie hidden somewhere amongst the individual's subconscious material, they is important to our understanding of the unclear image of the foe occurring as a result of the enmification process, and we shall take yet another look at them in the following.

While one side of the subconscious image is provided intentionally by society supplying emotional fuel, another comprises the misapprehensions of biased political leaders, military commanders and intelligence personnel. Because subconscious enmity and national myths combine to influence decision-makers just as much as they influence anybody else, bias in evaluation of information is a ubiquitous and serious risk. It leads to more or less distorted images and, hence, to misinterpretations and dysfunctional decision-making.

The minds of the fighting men and women are torn between two incommensurable imperatives. On the one hand they need clarity, but if the concrete and timely information, which is available, is misinterpreted the picture will be an unclear and untrue representation of reality. On the other, if the perceived reality contradicts the norms and values of the individual fighter cognitive dissonance materialises. This typically happens in war because the demand to kill in action contradicts the commandment that "thou shalt not kill," which is internalised in the minds of most soldiers, or at least combatants brought up in Christian societies. We are used to believe that killing is cardinal sin. Now as war is the soldiers' milieu, killing is sanctioned and expected, and this presents a dilemma. Some killings are mandatory; others are inadmissible, even in war. If we cannot get a clear image of the enemy, our efforts will be ineffective; but if we do, we shall be killing and maiming contrary to our beliefs – unless we have been effectively conditioned.

It seems strange that the distinction between murder and acceptable killing is maintained in wartime, but the theory on cognitive dissonance goes some way to explain this. There is a difference between personal conviction and official behaviour, and it is remarkable that soldiers in their official capacity do frequently display behaviour which runs counter to

[38] Ibid., p. 6.

their personal belief. This conundrum causes stress and cognitive dissonance, and it remains to be researched to what extent it may also influence the occurrence of post traumatic stress disorder (PTSD) amongst veterans.

Another remarkable effect of cognitive dissonance appears when there is a clash between reality and the inbred deference to authority subconsciously accumulated through childhood and youth. In the context of cognitive dissonance the authoritarian personality plays a deplorable but important rôle. Norman F. Dixon has argued convincingly that authoritarians are less likely than are freer personalities to grasp the motives and intentions of their opponents. Moreover, they are less willing to act upon the information they receive regarding such intentions if this conflicts with the beliefs and preconceptions which they know that their superiors hold. This aspect of cognitive dissonance is a key element in Dixons' theory on the authoritarian personality and an important part of the explanation of our problem with incomplete cognisance or misinterpretation of information on the opponent.[39] Cognitive dissonance was probably exactly the trouble when, in the autumn of 1944, Lieutenant-General Frederick "Boy" Browning, commanding the allied airborne corps, abstained from renewed intelligence efforts allegedly on the ground of not wanting to jeopardise Montgomery's plan for "Operation Market Garden," – the allied joint and combined advance in the autumn of 1944 though the northern parts of the Netherlands. The available information, on which he declined to act, represented a true picture of reality and, as he ignored it, a false enemy portrait materialised, from which he could draw but inadequate conclusions and give out only inappropriate orders.[40] In the end, although Montgomery claimed that Market Garden was a 90% success, as far as allied casualties were concerned, the operation was a disaster.

War leaders try their best to combat the evils, which they perceive as threatening their respective countries, and being the supreme authorities within their spheres they impose on their military executives enemy perceptions which will invariably expose many of their subordinates to the risk of cognitive dissonance.

There seems to be a trend amongst politicians – and some officers – to seek public support through adopting an image of the enemy which suits

---

[39] Norman F. Dixon, *On the Psychology of Military Incompetence* (London: Futura, 1988) p. 264.

[40] Richard Holmes et al. *The Oxford Companion to Military History* (Oxford: Oxford University Press 2001), pp. 83-84.

short term emotional goals that are, in many respects, not too different from those which appear prominently during electoral campaigns.[41] An interesting example of this trend surfaced during interviews with senior US armed forces officials conducted by this author at various American military institutions in the spring of 2003. Several interviewees claimed that they were well aware that in early 2003, when invasion of Iraq was imminent, government agencies, knowing the incorrectness of the contention, had propagated a link between Al Qaeda and Saddam Hussein simply in order to boost public support for the engagement in what was expected to be a short and sharp conflict.

The face of the foe materialising out of such distorted impressions will mostly be a rather blurred picture, which then becomes the point of departure for the professionals whose task it is to do the actual fighting. The enemy image, the basis for action, gets murky from meaningless, irrelevant and confusing details. Parts of the clutter may be filtered away, but because of conditioning, culture, religion and other societal phenomena much of the distortion is brought about by material ingrained in everyone's mental baggage. Thus, frequently, it will not be realised that the picture used has been only partially true. But the fighting forces need a precise, timely and comprehensive picture, which under these conditions cannot be guaranteed.

The kernel of this predicament is that in order to keep up the will to fight – and this is axiomatically desirable – any society has to conceive a commonly accepted enemy notion, a myth, a national ethos, and a good cause. No segment of society can be allowed seriously to challenge this mental point of departure, because that would constitute a severe risk of upsetting the entire war effort. This seems to be true not only for politicians and other opinion leaders, but up to a point for those as well who so desperately need precision, exactitude and truth.[42] Liddell Hart gives a striking example illustrating that even highly professional officers may fall victim to society's preconceptions. He quotes a former Nazi general who suggested that the Germans "counted on the British advance to be deliberate and that of the Americans to be clumsy."[43] This appears to go at least some way towards demonstrating that the military decision-makers'

---

[41] Interviews in the spring of 2003 with senior US armed forces officials conducted at American military institutions by the author.

[42] Liddell Hart, *The German Generals Talk*, passim, and Bartov, *Hitler's Army*, passim.

[43] Ibid., p. 252.

enemy images are indeed influenced by the belligerent society's myths.

Wars, possibly, would not occur if no envy, fear and prejudice existed. Envy may have its natural background in the fact that some places on earth yield higher profits than others. Fears and prejudices, however, are sentiments which we kindle and keep alive by myths, religion and repressed frustrations that we are not as privileged as we believe others to be. War is a matter of clashes amongst societies whose historic antagonisms have thrived over decades or centuries rather than years. The underlying sentiments of the peoples involved are not like whims causing school children to fight; rather they are carefully nurtured attitudes approximating habits and life styles – e.g. can any Israeli settler today imagine what it would be like not to live with enemies right on his or her doorstep? However, what is founded on fears and prejudices, myths, religion and repressed frustrations is not the objective truth, but rather constitutes subjective views on societies that we assume to be hostile. These prejudiced views blur the clear image of the objective reality, which the fighting man or woman, whether civilian or military, needs and tries to perfect.

Therefore, and because the subjective, imprecise and mythical image is frequently the point of departure for much of the political propaganda, the conditioning and the indoctrination, such endeavours are counter-productive towards the objective depiction of reality that is required as soon as serious clashes of interests materialise, be they armed or not.

Like anybody else, and based on the conditioning they have undergone, decision-makers carry with them the remnants of the "mythical enmity" into their professional duties in politics and war influencing their, presumed, sound judgement. A few years ago, the world learned of a striking example of this as the shock of realism suddenly dawned upon American Lieutenant-General William Wallace when he was confronted with the realities of the War in Iraq in March 2003. In an interview during actual combat he admitted – much to the consternation of his superiors – that the fighting the troops saw was not the kind of war their training had allowed them to expect. On Sunday 30 March 2003, the British newspaper The Observer reported:

> The shape and scale of the dilemma facing the coalition was mapped out by the US Army's senior ground commander in Iraq, Lieutenant-General William S. Wallace. 'The enemy we're fighting is different from the one we'd war-gamed against,' 'I'm appalled by the inhumanity of it all... The attacks we're seeing are bizarre – technical vehicles [pick-ups] with .50 calibres and every kind of weapon charging tanks and Bradleys.' What Wallace was complaining of,

again in military shorthand, was the fact that the Iraqis had the audacity to destroy his armoured fighting vehicles with heavy-calibre machine guns jerry-rigged on the flat beds of pick-up trucks. It was not only a brutal enemy, but an imaginative one, too. As US officers in the field discovered, the defenders of Saddam's regime were using all possible means at their disposal, no matter how low-tech, to repel the US forces. In the fighting around Najaf last week, US commanders were shocked to encounter a well-orchestrated barrage of small arms and machinegun fire...

Moreover, on Saturday 29 March 2003 The Guardian, another British newspaper, told its readers:

General Sir Mike Jackson, head of Britain's army, declined to predict how long the war would last. He acknowledged that the invading troops had not seen 'displays of a welcoming population'." The American net news The State: "The enemy we're fighting against is different from the one we'd war-gamed against," said Wallace, commander of V Corps.

As demonstrated through the above examples, the enemy images produced partly by preconceptions and ignorance, and partly by outdated information from the Iraqi Diaspora in the United States, were not too helpful when it came to creating reliable situational awareness, though they may have been useful as far as initial public support was concerned. However, the troops on the ground needed precision, clarity and objectivity to form a sound basis for their dispositions. This was true for the War in Iraq, and it will be as important in any future conflict.

Over centuries past, the kind of preconceptions that led Germans including their generals to trust official myths and made General Wallace and his subordinates stumble into combat have entailed many an unhealthy troop allocation. It is the armed forces themselves, then, who must make an effort to filter unnecessary societal prejudices and official rhetoric to allow their minds to establish a "clean" enemy picture, sufficiently sober and incisive to be acted upon – and the closer to the sharp end the more pressing the need. The graph opposite illustrates this nexus.

The fighting forces need as their enemy image a "naturalistic" depiction close to that of photography. "Expressionist" or cartoon-like portrayals of tormentors, sloppy Americans and primitive Iraqis as referred to above do more harm than good in this field, although they may serve other purposes satisfactorily. The fighting men and women need the three dimensional photographic clarity, which can be provided by present day state-of-the-art technology, and that they will get, probably sooner or later. Nevertheless, it remains to be seen how good it will be and if it will be able to filter or suppress the various more or less subjective images.

The fervour-incisiveness nexus

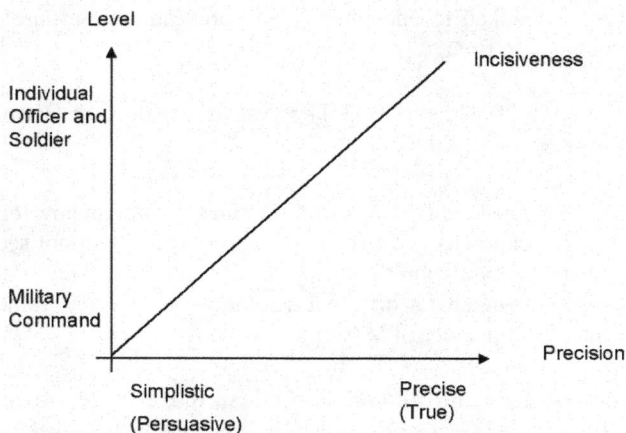

Level

Individual
Officer and
Soldier

Incisiveness

Military
Command

Precision

Simplistic
(Persuasive)

Precise
(True)

As discussed above, subconscious and intangible matters as well as internalised mythical notions influence the comprehensive enemy awareness. They are tied to each individual's perception and contain elements of experiences and beliefs divorced from the actual or prospective hostility. Amongst the sources of bias are the individual's conscious as well as subconscious enemy images, as these may have developed over the years under the influence of official rhetoric, press and commonly accepted assumptions on good and evil. The unavoidable subjectivity necessarily limits the perfection and certainty of any enemy appraisal created by human beings, technology not being in a position to provide it alone. On the one hand, while too much subjectivity distorts images it is obvious that distorted images promote unnecessary insecurity and fear. On the other, war is impracticable without an image of the enemy which is convincingly threatening even if, to some extent, this includes these intangible aspects as well. Warring parties, states and non-state actors alike, wish to boost the motivation of their populations and their warriors by skewed enemy images, but they will be well advised to notice that this practice may produce severe drawbacks with respect to situational awareness.

It may be true for any country, what Norman Mailer has said about the United States in his contemplative volume Why Are We at War, "When you have a great country, it is your duty to be critical so it can become even greater. But culturally, emotionally, we are becoming more arrogant, more vain."[44] This seems to be exactly the dichotomy that has made so many images hazier than strictly necessary: the lack of capacity to be critical of one's own causes and motives, and the absence of will to see one's own shortcomings.

---

[44] Norman Mailer, *Why are we at War* (New York: Random House, 2003), p. 15.

Chapter V: Hitler Has Forgotten Harrow – The Use of Propaganda

> *Hitler...declared that the fight was between those who have been through the Adolf Hitler Schools and those who have been at Eton. Hitler has forgotten Harrow, and he has also overlooked the vast majority of youth in this country who have never had the advantage of attending such schools, but who have by their skill and prowess won the admiration of the whole world.*[1]

THE FACE OF the foe has been the centre of attention to warring societies for centuries, and increasingly technology and objectivity have come to play crucial parts in the process of creating the enemy images. While we shall address the approaching possibilities of clear and concise images of the opponent in a later chapter, some confusing factors pull it in the opposite direction.

Seen in the context of our wish to understand and get a clear depiction of the enemy, the rôle of the individual's perception is no less important than the sophisticated modern means of intelligence collection, analysis and interpretation. Soldiers on patrol watching enemy movements at close quarter, radar operators tracking hostile aeroplanes and intelligence officers trying to collect and analyse information and deduct enemy intentions, or at least enemy options, from the information they have received play each their individual part in creating the face of the foe.

There is much evidence to suggest that in addition to objects, persons and activities – which can be registered by high-tech sensor systems – to a certain extent less tangible matters influence the overall enemy awareness as well. This is tied to each individual's perception, and it contains a considerable number of elements of personal attitude accumulated

---

[1] Speech by Winston Spencer Churchill at his old school, Harrow, on 18 December 1940.

throughout upbringing, education, conditioning and experiences that are divorced from the concrete and genuine characteristics of an actual or prospective adversary. Such elements unavoidably contribute to introducing a certain prejudice in the individual's estimates, and this psychological twist of our minds is unfortunate because biased enemy images lead to miscalculations and inadequate decisions. However, if the sources of bias can be found, we may be able to do something to minimise the damage. If a person's attitude is biased by the unavoidable subjectivity, inevitably this will reduce the perfection and certainty of his or her enemy portrayal regardless of the sophistication of the equipment used.

Righteous War

Any war is propagated as being a righteous one by the government leading its country into it. Since the acceptance of norms for civilised warfare codified at the end of the Thirty Years War (1618-48) by the Peace Treaty of Westphalia of 1648, it is essential that hostilities are not opened without provocation serious enough to claim that national interests, or at least national honour, have been challenged. Nonetheless, history and prejudices of ancient origin are frequently parts of the rhetoric aiming at gaining public support for the war. Therefore, the party wanting war will make sure that the prospective opponent delivers the apparent cause for opening hostilities.

We will mention but two examples.

In 1870, the Prussian Ministerpräsident [Prime Minister] and Reichskanzler [Chancellor] of the North German Confederation, Count Otto von Bismarck (1815-98), challenged French honour to such an extent that the French Emperor Napoléon III felt obliged to declare war on Prussia. In 1868 Spain had sought a candidate for her vacant throne and approached, among others, Prince Leopold von Hohenzollern-Sigmaringen (1835-1905) a Catholic kinsman of the Prussian king. The French government perceived this as a Prussian attempt to envelop France and protested. Bismarck saw in this development an opportunity, not only to displease France, but to persuade the Catholic south German states that the Hohenzollern family were indeed the right dynasty for a future German Reich. In May 1870, with King Wilhelm I's approbation, Bismarck announced that the prince would be pleased to accept the offer, and on 6 July the French government declared this completely unacceptable. Consequently, on 12 July Prince Leopold renounced his candidature, but Napoléon III now saw fit to demand that Prussia should obligate herself never again to submit candidates for the Spanish throne. On 13 July, the French Ambassador, Benedetti, laid this demand before King Wilhelm in the spa town of Bad Ems, and now the king resolutely declined. In the evening he sent a telegram to his government in Berlin informing about the state of affairs so far. Seeing the enormous potential of its content, Bismarck, now publicised the telegram in an abridged form, which actually made it look like a royal Prussian insult to the Emperor. Thus offended, France, on 14 July, mobilised and appropriated the fiscal means to wage a war; and on 19 July she declared war on Prussia. In this way, Bismarck not only made the war look like one of self-defence, he also achieved the support of the South German states.

Likewise, in 1939 Nazi Germany ascertained that concentration-camp inmates, who were forced to attack a German border post, were clad in Polish uniforms. Having swallowed Austria, Sudentenland, Moravia and Bohemia, the latter three forming today's Czech Republic, Hitler wished to link up with East Prussia, which, since the signature on 28 June 1919 of the Versailles Treaty, had been separated from the German main territory by the "Polish Corridor" and Danzig (today Gdansk). Hoping that, as so often before, the world would accept what would formally be a war of self-defence, he made prisoners dressed up in Polish uniforms attack a German border installation, and as in the early hours of 1 September 1939 his formations crossed the border, German news broadcast that "as of four o'clock this morning, we [the Germans] are returning the fire." This was meant to look like a Polish aggression vindicating German armed reaction, but for once it was not believed by any others than the Nazis themselves.

Jean Jacque Rousseau, 1712-78, in his treatise *Contrat Social (Social Contract)*, of 1762, stated that there is a connexion between justice and the individual person's membership of the community. The community is supported voluntarily by its members, who are therefore willing to defend it. Justice means freedom, and freedom is the key precondition for the community. This implies that the community has the right to wage war – it has the jus ad bellum – when matters vital to its existence are at stake, and in that case the war is righteous. This justification will be part of the warring party's propaganda effort which, invariably, will depict the foe as the aggressor who threatens the community's existence. The Prussian Prime Minister [Ministerpräsident] Otto von Bismarck's keenness, in 1870, to achieve a French declaration of war, though the war was sincerely wished for by himself, serves as one archetypical example; Austria's ultimatum to Serbia in the summer of 1914 is another. Thus, paradoxically both parties will claim to wage a just and therefore a defensive war, which is illogical, as if both were entirely on the defensive there would be no armed clashes.

Enmification and Propaganda

Conscious and internalised norms, traditions and accepted myths, as well as subconscious or repressed impulses accumulated since birth, constitute the fertile soil for breeding enmity. When a nation deems it necessary to prepare its citizens for the possibility of war, the foundation is already cast and a burgeoning hostility has only to be cultivated to come to fruition. At that moment, tradition, myth, national necessity and cultural heritage increasingly dominate the channels for official rhetoric, and grievances – real or conjured up for the occasion – start to manifest themselves in the press. And patriotic thinkers and authors are frequent suppliers of arguments in favour of war.

In the late modern era, any war must be vindicated by being defensive – a response to the ill intentions of a hostile force. If this is not obviously the case, the public opinion must be manipulated into believing that it is. Like many other German intellectuals, the theology professor and author Ernst Troeltsch did what he could to justify the cause of the Central Powers – and in particular imperial Germany – by propagating the view that up to the outbreak of the First World War the Entente had been leading a long war of culture claiming that Germany was a society of oppression, reaction and militarism. While the West was for democracy and high moral standards, Germany was not. Troeltsch opposed this view claiming that freedom simply was not identical notions in Germany and in Western democracies like France and Britain. The Germans were the epitome of free popular individualism, demanding access to the seas, colonies of their own and opportunities to further their worldwide national ambitions without interference by a 'moral world police.' Because the western powers were waging a cultural war against all things German, Germany had to redefine the relationship between German and Western tradition. The war had led to revitalisation of spirit and belief, and to a simultaneous decline of materialism, philistinism, and scepticism. The war had brought Germany back to its idealistic inheritance and marked Germany's victory over hedonism, plutocracy and dull acceptance of nature's regularity. Germany was Kultur [Culture], the West merely civilisation. Thus, authors like Troeltsch actively promoted the notion of different sets of values setting Germany apart from the rest of the Western world and paving the way for a them-and-us dichotomy making war the logical outcome.[2]

Another German author, and later Nobel laureate, Thomas Mann, agrees as to the opposition of culture to civilisation. This pair of 19th century notions – originating with Nietzsche – achieves its propagandistic function in an identity context by emphasising Germany as a haven of culture and stigmatising her enemies as the epitomes of civilisation. While culture is an authentic way of life borne by a unique world view, civilisation is its negative opposite characterised by reason, scepticism, enlightenment, dissolution and decency. Mann sees culture personified by characters like the Prussian King Friedrich II (Frederick the Great, 1712-40-86), civilisation by the French philosopher François-Marie Arouet Voltaire (1694-1778).[3]

The unique quality of the German tradition – central to Troeltsch and Mann as well as to Oswald Spengler – does not appear until the era of Romanticism, which, in Germany, materialises as a revolt against all Western European notions of science, morality, utilitarianism and the abstract idea of the equality of all human kind.

Instead, German Romanticism develops into a conservative revolution leading to mystic and contemplative visions of a large and rich cosmos of individual spirituality as opposed to western utilitarianism and logic; thoughts that are not that different from what Spengler prophesised in *Der Untergang des Abendlandes* [*The Decline of the West*].[4]

Also prominent amongst the obvious examples of conscious enmification, are the German press campaigns leading up to the crises over Czechoslovakia in 1938 and the invasion of Poland in 1939; and the behaviour of considerable segments of the Anglo-American press in connexion with the overtures to the war on Iraq in 2002-3. A few examples of the latter may be illustrative. In early 2003, Fox News and the Murdoch paper press in various countries in Europe and America propagated the just

---

[2] Adam Paulsen, *Overvindelsen af Første Verdenskrig: Historiepolitik hos Ernst Troeltsch, Oswald Spengler og Thomas Mann* [*Overcoming the First World War: History Politics with Ernst Troeltsch, Oswald Spengler and Thomas Mann*], (Copenhagen: Museum Tusculanum Publishers, 2014), pp. 21-26.

[3] Paulsen, *Overvindelsen af Første Verdenskrig*, pp. 142-3.

[4] Paulsen, *Overvindelsen af Første Verdenskrig*, p. 62. See also Spengler, *Der Untergang des Abendlandes* (München: Verlag C.H. Beck, 1990), p. 1191.

American war.[5] The *New York Post* called France and Germany "the axis of weasel" as they did not support the martial effort of the United States, and a French Murdoch paper called President Jacques Chirac "a worm." Moreover, Michael Savage of the MSNBC telecast his opinion that "We need racist stereotypes right now for our enemy in order to encourage our warriors to kill the enemy."[6]

Rhetoric that creates abject images of the enemy is employed because it is believed, rightly or wrongly, that without them and without depersonalisation of the enemy through public and military conditioning of society the coming war will receive insufficient support.[7] This aspect of the enmification process is called propaganda. In this the political will and the glorification of the nation's military instrument merge into a synthesis of public martial fervour harking back to Machiavelli's and Clausewitz's shared belief that policy and arms cannot be appraised independently of each other.

Claiming in the 1990s that war is not, as Clausewitz has claimed, a continuation of policy by other means, British military historian John Keegan drew attention to war as a cultural phenomenon. He substantiated the argument through the assertion that war antedates state, diplomacy, and strategy by many millennia "and reaches into the human heart, places where self dissolves rational purpose."[8] If this is true, it helps explain why enmification seems to start within society at peace. Clausewitz too regarded war as part of man's social existence.[9] Who, then, creates the enemy image? It follows logically that society as a whole does. The society which believes to have found an aim worth fighting for, and which has at its disposal a military machine likely to be capable of fulfilling that aim, will try to make sure that the overwhelming majority of the citizenry supports the scheme. This is of necessity to democratic societies where war is unthinkable without reference to the public will. However, the amount of

---

[5] Roy Greenlade, "Their Masters Voice" in *The Guardian* 17 February 2003.

[6] "GE., Microsoft bring Bigotry to Life, " from *FAIR Action Alert* quoted in Rampton, Sheldon and John Stauber. *Weapons of Mass Deception: The Uses of Propaganda in Bush's War on Iraq*. New York: Jeremy P, Tarcher/Penguin, 2003, pp 169-70.

[7] Holmes, *Firing Line*, p. 361.

[8] John Keegan, *A History of Warfare* (New York, U.S.A.: First Vintage Book Edition, 1994) p. 3.

[9] Ibid., p. 149.

propaganda produced by dictatorships to convince their own subjects of the righteousness of their cause indicates that authoritarian rulers feel much the same need.

In 2003, the American authors Sheldon Rampton and John Stauber published a book called *Weapons of Mass Deception: the Uses of Propaganda in Bush's War on Iraq*, a partisan but well annotated description of the marketing of the early 2000s wars in Afghanistan and Iraq. They claimed that, in 2001, the Pentagon awarded a $397,000 (US) four-month contract to the Rendon Group to handle public relations aspects of the United States' engagement in Afghanistan.[10]

Public relations work is necessary to ascertain that the citizens know and understand their government's policy. Then, is it not reasonable to assume that public relations and propaganda are two faces of the very same coin? Possibly, and it may be a matter of judgment which of the terms should be applied in each individual case. However, it seems to be generally accepted that the more one-sided or biased the material gets the more it merits the term "propaganda." The Anglo-American governmental efforts to persuade the UK and US electorates as well as world opinion of the wisdom of engaging in a war in Iraq in 2003 may serve as the most recent example. The heavy focus on the assertion of a link between the terrorist network of al Qaeda and the Iraqi dictator Saddam Hussein, the Iraqi weapons of mass destruction, the claimed ability to deploy and employ these within a timeframe of forty-five minutes, and the insistence on being threatened at home along with the absence of emphasis on moral aspects and human rights violations by the opposing regime may be interpreted as a rather one-sided approach with clear-cut propagandistic aims.[11]

Prior to conflicts, it can be observed how governments, loyal media, and individual politicians endeavour to ram home their message through whatever method they find adequate. Not only the more trashy tabloids but also numerous media that boast more serious journalism yield to

---

[10] Sheldon Rampton and John Stauber, *Weapons of Mass Deception: The Uses of Propaganda in Bush's War on Iraq*. (New York: Jeremy P, Tarcher/Penguin, 2003), p. 49. The authors are editors of the quarterly *PR Watch: Public Interest Reporting on the PR/Public Affairs Industry*. They have received the George Orwell Award for "exposing the American use of 'double speak'."

[11] Further corroborated by Elisabeth Bumiller in "Bush Aides Set Strategy to Sell Policy on Iraq" in *New York Times*, 7 September 2002, p. A1, quoted in Rampton and Stauber, *Weapons of Mass Deception*, p. 37.

government or public pressure – or to patriotism – to engage in persuading the populace that the enemy is bad, while one's own country, its people, its intentions and its behaviour are fundamentally benign. The potential enemy is a priori guilty, while one's own side must be innocent.[12] In his research for Hitler's Army, Israeli author Omer Bartov realised that due to effective propaganda concerning the alleged perversity and brutality of the opposing side as well as the superiority of one's own claim on morality, the German society managed to turn the question of guilt and responsibility upside down.[13] They found no difficulty in seeing themselves in the rôle of the innocent victims and the enemy they had attacked as the aggressors. This had to do with the fact that from 1933 onwards Nazi images had permeated society to the extent that, as war with the Soviet Union broke out on 22 June 1941, the soldiers resolved the contradiction between abstract enemy images, "made in Germany," and the actual appearance of the foe "by destroying the latter as a manifestation of the former."[14] The Germans perceived, subjectively, a reality which they chose to believe was true, while seeing the objective reality as false. They saw what they expected to see. The national myth and the Nazi creed were omnipresent and had been conceived and propagated so well in advance of the war that very few questioned the accuracy of the official image of the foe.[15] To illustrate, Bartov quotes a particularly revealing picture painted by the Mitteilungen für die Truppe:

> Anyone who has ever looked at the face of a red commissar knows what the Bolsheviks are like. We would insult the animals if we described these mostly Jewish men as beasts. They are the embodiment of the Satanic and insane hatred against the whole noble humanity.[16]

While neither of the belligerents during the First World War had driven their dehumanisation and vilification efforts anywhere near the Nazis'

---

[12] Rampton and Stauber, *Weapons of Mass Deception*, pp. 161-180, and Chris Hedges, *War Is a Force That Gives Us Meaning.* (New York: Anchor Books 2002) p. 142-44.

[13] Bartov, *Hitler's Army*, pp. 124-25 and note 49.

[14] Ibid. p. 127.

[15] The German self-image may actually be traced back to before the beginning of the twentieth century, cf. Brigitte Hamann's description of Hitler's sources of inspiration.

[16] Bartov, *Hitler's Army*, p. 126.

extremes, the French nevertheless published a drawing showing a German soldier eating a little girl's hand. The drawing emerged in the press shortly after rumours had been circulating of Germans bayoneting and chopping up small children, stories that were neither proven nor corroborated. Robert Graves, similarly, described British propaganda as one conveying an image of Germans as being inhumane – a fiction which his front-line experiences of trench warfare did not in any way support. Moreover, Graves tells of an occurrence described in three media with different levels of enmity:

> When the fall of Antwerp became known, the church bells were rung" (*Kölnische Zeitung*). According to the *Kölnische Zeitung* the clergy of Antwerp were compelled to ring the church bells when the fortress was taken" (*Le Matin*). "According to information which has reached *Corriera Della Sera* from Cologne, via London, it is confirmed that the barbaric conquerors of Antwerp punished the unfortunate priests for their heroic refusal to ring the church bells by hanging them... (*Le Matin*).[17]

Interestingly, Hitler, in *Mein Kampf*, praises the British for hate propaganda like that mentioned by Graves: "on the other hand, the English and American war propaganda was psychologically correct. As they presented the Germans to their own people as Barbarians and Huns, they prepared them for the horrors of war..."[18]

During the same war, the Americans sought recruits for the army by using, on one of their posters, a gorilla with obvious German attributes as the synecdoche depicting the enemy.[19]

Probably, the individual horror-story did not have much effect, but the sum of them may well have influenced "the man in the street" at the conscious and subconscious levels. Such stories are not only a matter of the past.

---

[17] Graves, *Goodbye to All That*, pp. 68-69 and 167 (depicting a British propaganda poster)

[18] [My translation from] "Demgegenüber war die Krigspropaganda der Engländer und Amerikaner psychologish richtig. Indem sie dem eigenem Volke den Deutschen als Barbaren und Hunnen vorstellte, bereiteten sie den einzelnen Soldaten schon auf die Schrecken des Krieges vor..." Hitler, *Mein Kampf*, p. 199

[19] Symbols of German brutality: the spiked helmet and the club with the inscription Kultur [culture]. The latter is an allusion to the notion that while other western nation might be civilised, Germany had Kultur [culture]. Used by Spengler, among others (in his magnum opus *Der Untergang des Abenlandes* [*Decline of the West*]).

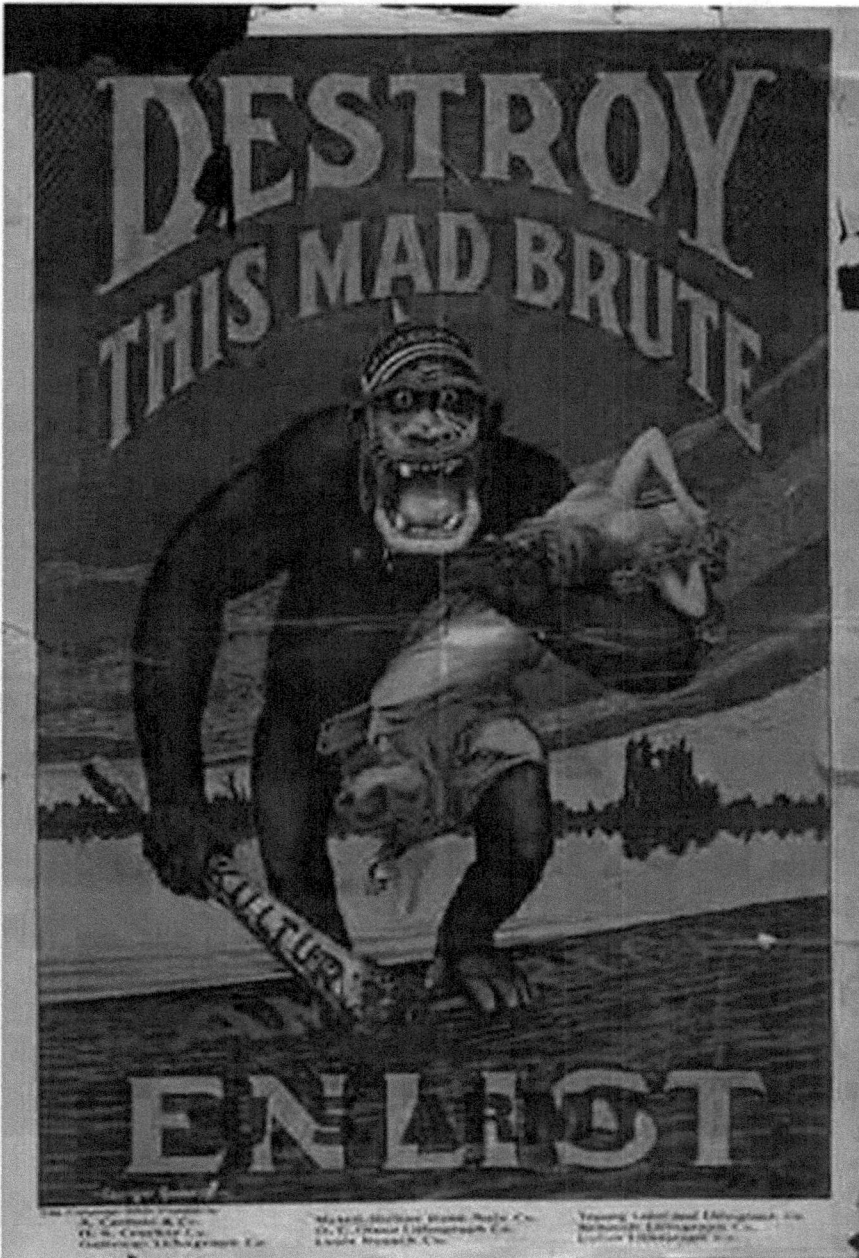

"Destroy this mad brute"

Chris Hedges relates a parallel example of serious demonisation spread by the Americans, the Kuwaiti, or both shortly before the Gulf War in 1991:

> Following the Iraqi invasion of Kuwait, it was widely disseminated that Iraqi soldiers removed hundreds of Kuwaiti babies from incubators and left them to die on hospital floors. The story, when we arrived in Kuwait and were able to check with doctors at the hospitals, turned out to be false. But then it had served its purpose. The source was the 15-year-old daughter of the Kuwaiti ambassador to the United States. It could not be established if she had actually been in the country during the invasion.[20]

Strangely enough, apparently "positive" propaganda serves the same end though directed against other audiences. The American public relations agent John W. Rendon, describing himself as an information warrior having worked for the US Department of Defence and the Central Intelligence Agency, revealed to an audience of air force cadets that when United States' troops entered Kuwait City in 1991 hundreds of Kuwaitis waving small American flags greeted them. For good reasons, he claims, the occurrence was broadcast all over the world to make sure that everybody would get the impression that the Americans were being welcomed as liberators. This, of course, is a subtle kind of propaganda probably intended for home consumption ad modem: "He who is not with me is against me." Rendon asked rhetorically if nobody wondered, "How after seven months of occupation the people of Kuwait were able to get these flags?" Moreover, he informed that this was exactly what he was there to ascertain.[21] Thus, hammering out who was with them, by implication the audience was let in no doubt about the evil forces, which were against them and consequently about the necessity to deal with those.

The information warriors of the public media, whether pro or contra, do not stand idle when war approaches and begins. Governments' needs for support increase as soldiers return home in body bags and the hardships of wartime economy make themselves felt. President George W. Bush's prohibition of televising funeral processions at Arlington Military Cemetary right from the beginning of the War on Iraq was a rather obvious peace of propaganda aimed at preserving public acceptance of the war.

Support is often provided from the most diverse quarters. For example,

---

[20] Hedges, *War is a Force*, pp. 144-45. Also discussed in Rampton and Stauber, *Weapons of Mass Deception*, pp. 77-78.

[21] Rampton and Stauber, *Weapons of Mass Deception*, p. 5.

Graves tells that a British First World War "little Mother" sent a letter to the editor of the *Morning Post*[22] stating:

> To the men who pathetically calls himself 'a common soldier', may I say that we women, who demand to be heard, will tolerate no such cry as 'Peace, Peace!' where there is no peace. The corn that will wave over land watered by the blood of our brave lads shall testify to the future that their blood was not spilt in vain.[23]

More recently, Hedges claims that examples can still be found that, what he terms "the so-called 'free press'" is also a patriotic press and that numerous, though not all, newspapers and broadcasting companies restrain and harness themselves in the service of the country with which their allegiance rest. He further adds that:

> The notion that the press was used in the war [the first Gulf War] is incorrect. The press wanted to be used. It saw itself as part of the war effort. Even those who do go out [those not staying in their hotel rooms] are guilty of distortion. For we not only *believe in the myth* of war and feed recklessly off the drug but also *embrace the cause...* I shed a little light on the lies spread to make the war look like a coalition, but I did not challenge in any real way the patriotism and jingoism that enthused the crowds back home [emphasis added].[24]

With that comment, Hedges states that even in a country with no official censorship the government might get widespread support for military enterprises from segments of the media large enough to make those opposing the official views look ridiculously naïve. His views concur with Stauber and Rampton, who dealt with the issue of American use of propaganda in the 2003 war on Iraq. They quoted the *New York Times* for the revelation that, prior to war, the Pentagon Office of Strategic Influence had begun fabricating news for foreign media consumption and circulated proposals for aggressive campaigns in the press abroad, on the internet and – so they assume – in the form of covert operations as well.[25] Stauber and

---

[22] Very much in the same vein as Alice Miller's German mothers accepting to give their sons for the great cause of the *Vaterland*.

[23] Robert Graves, *Goodbye to All That*, pp. 199-202.

[24] Hedges, *War is a Force*, pp. 143-44.

[25] Rampton and Stauber, *Weapons of Mass Deception*, pp. 66-67.

Rampton further asserted that, in spite of indications from defectors as well as from the United Nations' weapons inspectors, the American administration repeatedly claimed that "the Iraqi were on the brink of developing nuclear weapons." Moreover, they quoted US official sources stating that the Iraqi "had a continued appetite for nuclear bombs, and had a growing fleet of unmanned aircraft, that could be fitted with chemical or biological weapons and used for 'missions targeting the United States'." In the belief of giving credence to the claims, the administration referred to reports, which on some points actually gave evidence to the contrary as, for instance, that the unmanned aircraft actually lacked the range to reach the United States.[26]

Although military and political affairs are not identical, it is irrational to detach one from the other. While employing different means, these spheres serve the same purpose, endeavouring to achieve fulfilment of the state's ambitions, and they are, therefore, interdependent. Clausewitz concludes that, "the conduct of war...is therefore policy itself, which takes up the sword in place of the pen, but does not on that account cease to think according to its own laws."[27] Thus, within the political system extant in a given state the politicians are the standard-bearers of the bellicose party's war aims as well as of the effort to get everyone else on board the man-of-war.

The political endeavours to create, sustain and amplify an enemy image commence before the start of hostilities. This is supposed to support the psychological side of the fight and has, frequently, long lasting effects. Therefore for instance, in 1919 the British electorate preferred that the Kaiser be hanged and, according to historian Margaret MacMillan, the Prime Minister, David Lloyd George, apparently shared these sentiments. However, she also cites a letter from a Foreign Office official, who ridiculed wartime propaganda opining that the newspapers carried on their wartime rôle writing "the greatest rubbish about hanging the Kaiser. They are about as mad as they once were over Jumbo the Elephant."[28]

When the phantom of war has undergone the metamorphosis from fantasy to reality, the battle of words takes on a life and a momentum of its own. During the Second World War, Britain made the facilities of the

---

[26] Ibid., pp. 86-87.

[27] Clausewitz, *On War*, p. 608.

[28] MacMillan, *Paris 1919: Six Months that Changed the World*, p. 163.

British Broadcasting Corporation, the BBC, available to a number of politicians, journalists and others opinion leaders from German-occupied countries to broadcast to their respective home countries. Thus, the Danish conservative politician, John Christmas Møller, who had fled Denmark and settled down in London, supplied the Danes with what was generally perceived as fairly objective news on what was going on at the various fronts. Nevertheless, the Nazi German minister plenipotentiary in Denmark, Dr Werner Best, saw this activity as allied propaganda. Possibly, it was both.

Speeches by war-leaders – which are mostly directly aimed at boosting already existing animosity, gossip and bias – might rightly be perceived as sheer propaganda; as they attempt to enhance the will to fight through forming consistent and comprehensible, but not necessarily true, images of the enemy. To convince their followers, politicians pretend to espouse the conviction that the rest of the world agrees with the righteousness of their cause, and that other enlightened peoples will soon join in the tussle on their side.

During the First World War, Germany was intent on cultivating the impression amongst its citizens that civilised countries were sympathetic to her course and respectful of the decent way in which the Central Powers conducted the war. It came as a nasty surprise that neighbouring countries like Denmark were extremely hard to convince that German military presence in their territories was a kind of peaceful cohabitation, and that no atrocities took place in German occupied countries. Germany, and in particular her Imperial Navy, was worried about possible Entente amphibious landings on the west coast of Denmark and advance through the Jutland Peninsula into the German hinterland. They foresaw and planned an invasion and occupation of Denmark in order to prohibit any such action. This they believed required Danish sympathy for the Central Powers cause, but the Danes were not easily persuaded. Because of the war of 1864, when the German states conquered 1/5 of the Danish territory, anti-German feelings were widespread. Therefore, although Berlin was adamant that intensive propaganda should be conducted in Denmark, the German envoy to Copenhagen, Ulrich Count Brockdorff-Rantzau, was convinced that propaganda would possibly have only negative effects and he did his best to counter his capital's enterprise. The German government was concerned that negative sentiments amongst the Danes might poison the bi-lateral relationship, and they particularly disliked a book published by Johannes Jørgensen entitled *Klokke Roland* (*Bell Roland*), which gave photographic and textual evidence of extensive German atrocities in Belgium. Actually, Jørgensen's book sold extremely well, not least because its message coincided with Entente propaganda, which the Danes more readily believed than that of the Central Powers.[29] Brockdorff-Rantzau had a hard time attempting to sway the opinion of his Foreign Office superiors that fighting anti-German propaganda in Denmark would indeed be very foolish.

If harsh, German First World War propaganda was neither too well planned nor co-ordinated. Conversely, in the 1930s and during the Second World War, the Nazi German propaganda machine was well oiled and carried out a focused and considerably more massive manipulation of facts. The actual effect of this endeavour on their Germany's own population may not be easily appreciated, but Omer Bartov's conversations with ordinary Germans after the Second World War seem to demonstrate a considerable success in brainwashing the populace. Interviews conducted by Bartov many years after the end of the war, to some extent, confirmed that the face of the foe as created in the 1930s and early 40s had been internalised and kept in the minds of those exposed to the Nazi propaganda. He found that a number of Nazi-parlance stereotypes were well preserved among German workers, the group within the Third Reich which he had assumed the least likely to agree with the Nazi dogma. Nevertheless, his interviews revealed that: "They also fought against 'plutocracy,' 'Asiatic barbarism,' 'Judaeo-Bolshevism,' and in 'defence of German culture and Western Civilisation'." Bartov also tells that even memoirs published by German veterans in the 1950s make use of that very phraseology. It is doubtful if the use of that language covers any deeply felt sympathy for Nazi ideology amongst those interviewed, but it shows how pervasive and perennial is the influence on the subconscious.[30]

In the context of appreciation of the foe, the relevance of propaganda is merely the question of whether such half-truths effect the decision-makers' appraisal of information on the opponent. Liddell Hart's interviews with German generals after the war indicate that, to some degree, they do.

Although in many cases war should be avoided, and philosophers like Sun Tzu and Thucydides do indeed warn against all unnecessary armed conflict, one cannot deny its social dimension. In cases of menaces to humanity, like that of Nazi Germany, war seems to be fully justifiable. It appears warranted to assert that because political leaders decide on war by

---

[29] Jesper Düring-Jørgensen, "På listesko i Dänemark (Walking Softly in Denmark)" in *Wekendavisen*, 17-24 April 2008, Ideer, pp. 10-11.

[30] Bartov, *Hitler's Army*, p. 182.

mandates given more or less knowingly by their electorate, the citizens, the perpetrators are in fact societies in their entirety. Whether a warring society is a parliamentary democracy or a more or less authoritarian state, the decision to go to war is always taken on behalf of the citizenry, the country or the nation, although taken in an indirect manner by political elites. These elites, as Hedges points out, rely partly on the press for conveyance of their messages, but they also have more direct ways of transmitting information and propaganda: through politicians themselves.

Churchill and Goebbels

More than once, it has been claimed that bellicose rhetoric and military planning combine to form unhealthy confusion of the martial and the political professions. However, in his *Précis de l'art de la guerre* (*The Art of War*) the Swiss war theoretician Antoine Henri Baron de Jomini claims that you should not *séparer la toge de l'épée* (separate the toga from the rapier) or separate politics and war. While military and political affairs are not identical, it is not rational to endeavour detaching one entirely from the other,[31] and Clausewitz concludes that, "the conduct of war...is therefore policy itself, which takes up the sword in place of the pen, but does not on that account cease to think according to its own laws."[32] Thus, a sensible deduction would be that if policy is reason - which in this context means that it is based on goal-oriented intellectual contemplation, not that it is of necessity reasonable – and war is policy itself; therefore, in fact, war is rational.

But as far as enemy images go, the rationality may – at best – be attributed to the fact that their creation serves the national purpose, if this purpose is to go to war to reach the underlying political aim. Once war becomes reality – the political effort to sustain and amplify an enemy image, which can support the psychological side of the fight – the battle of words takes on a life and a momentum of its own.

When issues of the utmost importance to national survival are at stake, the employment of words becomes a powerful weapon, and history shows an abundance of examples of how this can be wielded with virtuosity by the

---

[31] Mao Tse-tung, *On Guerrilla Warfare*, (Urbana, U.S.A.: University of Illinois Press, 2000), p. 89.

[32] Clausewitz, *On War*, p. 608.

true masters of the trade. However, we shall constrain ourselves to mention but two illustrative ones.

A limited number of speeches by the Prime Minister of Great Britain Winston Churchill and the German Minister for Propaganda Joseph Goebbels from 1941-42 have been selected and juxtaposed. The speeches might rightly be perceived as propaganda, but they are just as much attempts by two leading personalities to form consistent images of their respective enemies for the benefit of, and believed to be taken at face value by, the fora addressed. Here, we shall leave it to psychologists and biographers to judge whether or not these two skilled politicians believed in the truth of their own words, but it seems fair to suggest that they believed in their effect.

Both demonstrated extraordinary eloquence and seemed to be well informed on what was actually going on in the opposing camp – an option which was not open to their audiences. Through their speeches, both performed clever and efficient vilification of the foe and, thus, distortion of the enemy image. In the quotations selected, the propaganda is directly aimed at establishing and sustaining an image of a despicable, ridiculous and evil opponent so as to merit continued fighting. However, their implicit views on which kind of an enemy portrait would most effectively boost the public's enthusiasm are surprisingly different in some respects, less so in others. Both take their points of departure in what their respective audiences may be assumed to swallow as well established truths, building on pre-war reciprocal ethno-phobia. They also employ cleverly selected truthful information on actual current events.

While, in his speeches, Goebbels finds a useful weapon in ridiculing the British leadership on accounts of money greed, drinking and eating habits, poor strategic and operative skills and lack of intelligence; Churchill's ordnance is laid on the atrocities committed by the Germans and the mismanagement by their henchmen, the concentration-camps, the strafing of refugees in France and Flanders, etc. In that respect they develop views already latently accepted amongst their audiences. Whereas Churchill might count on most adult British citizens to be familiar with the brutal realities of the First World War battle-fields, Goebbels chooses to build on the Nazi German literary tradition of, Spengler, Hitler, the Nazi newspapers, and others. He opposes the will to power and triumph with the greed for money and the essential struggle for power. "In History it is about life and only about life, race, the triumph of the will for power, and not about the victory of Truth."[33] They pretended to be convinced that the rest of the world agreed with the righteousness of their causes, and that other enlightened people would soon join their crusade. "The duel between intellect and strength will always be decided to the advantage of strength... On the day the English set free their nine thousand Fascists, these men will tear out the guts of the plutocrats, and the problem will be solved."[34]

On 14 August, 1941, Churchill declared that "another important step will soon be taken in the marshalling of all the peoples of the world against the criminals who have darkened its life and menaced its future (my emphasis)."[35] He goes on to call on:

> ...the good forces of the world against the evil forces which are now so formidable and triumphant and which have cast their cruel spell over the whole of Europe and a large part of Asia. "The most deadly instruments of war-science have been joined to the extreme refinements of treachery and the most brutal exhibitions of ruthlessness (my emphasis).[36]

For a very similar purpose, but in a style adapted to another audience, Goebbels put this into perspective informing the Germans and their allies that the:

> ...*plutocrat powers* try to blame Germany for the war, while the fact of the matter is that *it was they who declared the war in 1939*. And fortunately they have told the Germans which humiliations and suffering they may expect should they lose again. The plutocrat powers envy Germany *her authoritarian socialist state and its social security system* (my emphasis).[37]

Interestingly, Churchill opposing good and evil is more emotional than

---

[33] Spengler, *Der Untergang*, pp. 1194: „Es handlet sich in der Geschichte um das Leben und immer nur um das Leben, die Rasse, den Triumph des Willens zur Macht, und nicht um den Sieg von Wahrheiten..."

[34] Trevor-Roper, *Hitler's Table*, p. 256, table talk on 27 January 1942, midday.

[35] Winston Spencer Churchill, *The War Speeches 1939-45, Vols. I-III*. Compiled by Charles Eade. (London: Cassel & Company Ltd, 1952) 2: 28 (House of Commons, 15 July 1941).

[36] Churchill, *War Speeches. 2*: pp. 59-60 (The meeting with Roosevelt 24 August 1941).

[37] Joseph Goebbels, *Das Eherne Herz: Reden und Aufsätze aus den Jahren 1941/42*. (München: Zentralverlag der NSDAP/Frantz Eher Nachf., 1943) pp. 20 ff. (Speech of 3 October 1941 (3. Winterhilfswerk)).

factual, though what he mentions can be corroborated by newspaper reports. Goebbels, perhaps, is more factual but at the same time more openly propagandist. What he says is mostly correct, but very selective and taken out of its proper context. His first two sentences are not untrue, and it will be difficult for the ordinary German either to prove or falsify the last one. The word plutocrat will have struck a familiar chord with most of his audience, as the Nazi smear campaigns against the well off nuclei of British society – the House of Lords, the City and Jewish bankers like the Rothschild family – had been going on for years.

Churchill, again, knowing the British self-perception of strong anti-authoritarianism, draws attention to the dictatorial character of the adversary's:

> ...rule of the *Herrenvolk* – the master-race – who are to put an end to democracy, to parliaments, to the fundamental freedoms and decencies of ordinary men and women...the iron rule of Prussia, the *universal goose-step*, and a strict, *efficient discipline enforced upon the working-class by the political police, with German concentration camps* and firing parties, now so busy in a dozen lands, always handy in the background (my emphasis).[38]

Again, this is something which must have sounded familiar to British ears. Expressions like *"goose-step"* will probably have called forth a feeling of having to deal with someone who might be evil, but who is first and foremost ludicrous.

In November 1941, Goebbels gave a speech, characteristic of the style, which – we may assume – he estimated would stand a reasonable chance of having impact on audiences at home as well as among Sir Oswald Mosley's[39] selected listeners in the British Isles. "The British Prime Minister Winston Churchill, who – as it is will be remembered – has a *close relationship with alcohol, is no keen lover of the truth*, with which he has been in a constant state of war since his entry into politics (my emphasis)."[40]

---

[38] Churchill, *War Speeches*. 2: pp. 62-63 (The meeting with Roosevelt 24 August 1941).

[39] 1896-1980, leader of the British Union of Fascists.

[40] Goebbels, *Das eherne Herz*, p. 92 (Speech of 23 November 1941 „Der Tönerne Koloß"). It is worth noticing that Hitler, much in the same vein on 18 February 1942, notes: "Churchill is the very type of a corrupt journalist. There's not a worse prostitute in politics. He himself has written that it's unimaginable what can be done in war with the help of lies." Trevor-Roper, *Hitler's Table*, p. 318.

After the Japanese attack on Pearl Harbor, Churchill, much to the annoyance of his opponent, predicted a revolution in Germany. Goebbels, then, politely allowed the English "to say what they please. *They do not understand more of the German people than a cow does concerning x-ray research* (my emphasis)."[41]

Propaganda by ridiculing increases with the progress of the war, and to a certain extent this procedure was exploited by both sides.

This exchange of impolitenesses did not materialise out of the blue. It was a part of the propaganda, which exploited material already subconsciously present in the listeners' minds, and it merits some curiosity if, and for how long, the messages stuck. The interviews, conducted by Bartov many years after the end of the war, show that, in some cases, the effects may indeed be long lasting.

---

[41] Goebbels, *Das eherne Herz*, p. 167 (Speech of 4 January 1942 „Das neue Jahr"). [Translated from] „Wie lassen die Engländer ihr Vergnügen. Sie verstehen vom deutschen Volk soviel wie eine Kuh von der Strahlenforschung."

Chapter VI: Methodology

Know thine enemy and know yourself;
in a hundred battles you will never be in peril.[1]

WHETHER THE WAR aims are conquest, self defence, pre-emption or resources, there will be no war without an enemy. To a state, party to a war or one which is planning the contingency of war, a well defined and precise face of the foe is essential. Therefore, creating a clear and true image of the opposition is necessary. It is the way the warring state may alleviate uncertainty's harmful impact on its decision-making, and intelligence is a key means to obtain this.

The overall enemy image created by intelligence is a product resulting from information on foreign nations, hostile or potentially hostile forces, weather, and milieu of actual or potential military operations. Intelligence materialises as the sum of knowledge and understanding of the environment in which operations are foreseen to be conducted, and it includes knowledge of activities, capabilities and intentions of an actual or potential opponent and of belligerent parties amongst whom peace support operations are being conducted.[2]

However, on the battlefield many disparate elements, not always

---

[1] Griffith, *Sun Tzu*, p. 84.

[2] Land Force Information Operations, *Field Manual, Intelligence (English), B-GL-357-001/FP001*, 2001. pp. 3-4.

strictly relevant to this purpose, influence the process and contribute to blur reality. It is the mission of intelligence to minimise this influence and provide clarity by curbing uncertainty and optimising battle-space awareness. The procedure used for this purpose revolves around what has been termed 'the intelligence cycle' comprising four elements: direction, collection, analysis, and dissemination. These activities are the primary steps, which must be taken in order to obtain a sound basis for creating an image of the face of our foe.

Intelligence historian Michael Herman, a former British intelligence officer, asserts that intelligence in the sense of dedicated institutions may be traced back to the mid nineteenth century, though the term has been used as far back as the fifteenth to cover collection of information, knowledge of events and of military capabilities.[3] However, the human occupation associated with gathering intelligence is much older than that. For centuries if not for millennia the business of collecting information, although keenly pursued, was hampered by slow and cumbersome communications, and for that reason the face of the foe was not always sufficiently sharp and precise. The emergence of telegraphy – optical, electrical and wireless – has done a lot to remedy that problem because it has eased the intelligence-

---

[3] Herman, *Intelligence Power*, p. 9.

communication interaction and brought vital intelligence to the users much quicker than before, making results timelier and more relevant. Today's communications facilities have made it possible that, if it is available, intelligence can be exploited almost anywhere and with minimum delay.

Although once the means of gathering and exploiting intelligence may have been scarce, time-consuming and burdensome, its history shows that the collection of information on the opposition has attracted the attention and perseverance of military commanders, political leaders and war theorists for as long as humankind has thought about war, and written sources confirm that this has happened at least for a few millennia.

Of course, whenever there has been conflict going on amongst societies these have always sought to find out about their enemies' dispositions, strengths, and capabilities. Therefore intelligence is of no recent origin, but it seems justified, nonetheless, to claim that the discipline as a well-defined activity in its own right has not come of age until the beginning of the twentieth century. Although in its core it is probably as old as warfare itself, specialised bureaucracies serving this purpose alone have appeared with the emergence of the general staff, and they have grown and prospered primarily in the 20th century.

From the highest political level down to the individual fighting man or woman, the perception of the foe has had and will, presumably, continue to have decisive influence on how wars are fought. The more truthful, comprehensive, timely and precise this image is, the less wasteful is the war effort – at least in theory. The clearer the portrait develops, the more closely it will coincide with the underlying political cause; the more accurate it can depict the challenge, and the more likely is ultimate success for the belligerent's war aims.

However coveted total comprehensiveness, accuracy, timeliness and precision remain elusive, and military theorists have not been as prolific in their ponderings on this matter as they have in fields which are closer related to front line combat. More often than not, the enemy's characteristics are merely implicitly present in the theory of war. While in his seminal work *Vom Kriege [On War]* Clausewitz spends little more than one page on battlefield intelligence, Jomini in his magnum opus Précis de *l'Art de la Guerre [The Art of War]* devotes a chapter to the matter. Over the last 2500 years, occasionally specific theoretical examination has occurred concerning the adversary as well as the means and methods to be employed for gathering information about him. Thus, in the following we will scrutinise some of the prominent theories on how to handle enemy portrayal.

The steps, which should be taken through the intelligence cycle, aim at providing situational awareness – i.e. knowledge of the opponent, the ground, waters or air space, meteorological details, and the status of own forces. This happens by finding out about the enemy forces' location, strengths, types, directions and rates of movement, and activity, and keeping a watchful eye on one's own resources. Moreover, this process allows us to develop targets, i.e. to pinpoint high value targets, such as the enemy commander, his or her headquarters, and the means of delivery for weapons of mass destruction; and high pay-off targets like artillery concentrations, massed armour formations, vital communication facilities and significant supply resources.[4]

The arrangement of intelligence collection includes the commander's direction to his intelligence staff to provide answers to his priority intelligence requirements, the staff's direction of subordinate formations' intelligence responsibilities, and the staff's direction to collectors through the Intelligence Collection Plan, which will normally appear as an annex to the Operations Order. The intelligence battle procedure includes the Intelligence Preparation of the Battlefield, which is part of the overall decision-action-cycle. As it is of essence to act quicker than the opponent is able to respond – i.e. staying inner-most in the OODA-loop – the intelligence battle procedure must provide the decision-maker with pertinent and accurate intelligence in a timely fashion, allow flexibility in order to meet evolving situations with pertinent response, and to permit integration with the battle procedures of those planning the operations. Anticipation, early warning, focussed activity and rapid development of relevant databases are some of the criteria for success.[5]

The 'Intelligence Preparation of the Battlefield', which is a systematic approach to intelligence, has been developed over the last two or three decades of the 20th century in order to facilitate collection, analysis and presentation of battlefield intelligence. This is a lengthy and iterative process aiming at fusing all known features of terrain, weather, enemy forces' and own forces' situation together in a holistic situational picture. It requires co-operation amongst various functions within the formation or unit headquarters and must be updated concurrently as operations are being prepared and executed.

As to collection of intelligence data today there is a plethora of means

---

[4] *Land Force Information Operations, Field Manual, Intelligence (English), B-GL-357-001/FP001*, 2001. pp. 26-27.

[5] *Land Force Information Operations, Field Manual, Intelligence (English), B-GL-357-001/FP001*, 2001. pp. 31-32

available – or mostly available. Generally, Intelligence Branch (G2) might ask for support from any of the intelligence collectors in and near the area of responsibility, whose assistance would be granted if the asset or capability asked for is currently available. These might include:

- All kinds of unmanned aerial vehicles (UAV) with Full Motion Video, signals intelligence, stills capabilities
- Satellite photos
- Find, feel & understand teams (Human Terrain Mapping)
- Human intelligence
- Counter improvised explosive device teams
- Weapons Intelligence Teams
- Cameras and sensors mounted on blimps
- Various camp surveillance systems
- Subordinate units
- Electronic Warfare (EW)
- CIMIC Support Teams
- Signals Liaison Officer
- Options versus intentions

An enemy image must be a holistic one, comprising information on foreign nations, hostile or potentially hostile forces or elements and areas of actual or potential operations. Such images are primarily derived from a sequence of mutually confirming Intelligence Estimates. The expression "intelligence estimate" is the technical term for everything concerning the foe, the operational milieu and foreseeable challenges. Properly established this will reveal not only composition and disposition of enemy forces and resources but also the courses open to the opponent, i.e. his options. While at the tactical plane of military intelligence enemy options are what intelligence should endeavour to discover, at strategic level the opponent's intentions are of immense importance. However, clever appreciation of such central elements as political aims and their derived military objectives and the intense scrutiny of own vulnerabilities still do not bring about a complete understanding of the enemy's intentions and prospective courses of action. This is so because the process suffers from the insurmountable uncertainty caused by the sheer lack of capacity to calculate human genius, stupidity, will power and general unpredictability.

Although perfect intelligence may be hard to come by, a wide variety of functional specialties combine to bring modern warfare close to that ideal. Apart from open sources such as newspapers, topographical, economical and demographical descriptions, in Clausewitz's active days (ca. 1793-1830) intelligence was primarily human collection actions such as those performed by spies, diplomats, scouts, and light cavalry. This is no longer so. The development of improved means of communications from the telegraph, over landlines, to wireless, and satellite links has facilitated an evolution that has brought military commanders' situational awareness close to real-time perfection. Consequently, in the wake of the recent general development of communications and information technologies, over the years the scope of intelligence has widened and an ample amount of categories other than human and open source intelligence has burgeoned. These include signals intelligence (SIGINT), acoustic intelligence (ACINT), communications intelligence (COMINT), counter intelligence (CI), electronic intelligence (ELINT), image intelligence (IMINT), measurement intelligence (MASINT), technical intelligence (TECHINT), etc.[6] This glut of approaches to collecting intelligence has contributed to making it a highly complex matter, and a useful definition will therefore have to comprise more than simply discovering enemy activity and plans. A contemporary update of the theory of enemy perception can be found amongst the definitions in the NATO Glossary (AAP-6), which states that intelligence is:

> The product resulting from the processing of information concerning foreign nations, hostile or potentially hostile forces or elements, or areas of actual or potential operations. The term also applies to the activity, which results in the product and to the organisations engaged in such activity... Intelligence is a key element of operations and an important component of decision-making.[7]

Today's, or even more so tomorrow's, increasingly detailed images of potential or actual adversaries will be fused with inputs from information technology allowing quick collection, analysis and processing, all of which will be close to real-time. To military commanders this means a higher degree of accuracy of their bases for decisions, as the increasing timeliness decreases the risk that the situation changes drastically before an intended action is actually carried out. In this context, "identification and location of adversary centre(s) of gravity, critical nodes, main axes, second echelons, and weapons of mass destruction will be foci of prime importance."[8] Individual commanders and their staffs may draw upon such

---

[6] Cf.: *Field Manual, Intelligence*, pp. 6-8.

[7] Ibid. pp. 2-3.

[8] Ibid., p. 3.

intelligence as opposed to waiting for higher headquarters to push it forward. Compared with Cold War proceedings, when one had to wait for the intelligence estimates issued routinely by higher headquarters once or twice every 24 hours, this is a novelty which has been facilitated by the recent technological evolution.

Nonetheless, although great progress has been achieved over the last two decades, even the latest high-tech systems are purely "mechanical" with no philosophical amelioration, let alone capacity to gaze into the enemy commander's mind. This dichotomy stems from the fact that modern high-tech information collection and processing, brought about as a part of the so-called Revolution in Military Affairs, almost exclusively falls within the realm of "observational intelligence," meaning all that which can be observed, registered, counted or photographed. Conversely, in military revolutionary context the need for "message intelligence" – which furnishes evidence of thoughts and intentions of enemy personnel – is hardly addressed at all.

Today, the key need appears to be timely appraisal of all relevant factors providing decision-makers with as sound, accurate and comprehensive enemy images as possible so that one's actions will have the designed effect at the right time. It appears that there is a parallel of Sun Tzu's shih and the Clausewitzian notion of *Kulminationspunkt* (urning or culmination point) seen by both of these authors as an important aspect of the overall picture, and modern technology has provided useful tools to pin-point this. However, the Clausewitzian educated intuition or *coup d'œil* has not become irrelevant – quite the contrary. With the technological advances of recent years it has found a much more secure foundation. Decision-makers' quest for multi-faceted images based on near real-time, multiple-source intelligence points to improved probability of inferring important elements of the opponent's intent. The modern ways and means of automatic fusion and processing of intelligence seem to be significant aids to that aspiration, but the final interpretation of the image of the enemy still remains a matter of the commander's *coup d'œil*.

Uncertainty Inherent in the Image of the Enemy

In their quest for rationales war theorists have devoted considerable effort to studying the nexus of intelligence, uncertainty, and decision-making. They have done so because the overwhelming majority, if not all, of their maxims on war depend on their successful application of knowledge of the influence on the battle-space milieu and insight into what the adversary intends to do – or is capable of doing – and, hence, on reduction of uncertainty.

Sun Tzu observed "that which depends on me, I can do; that which depends on the enemy cannot be certain."[9] Although his primary advice was that one should rather not engage in war unless victory was certain, he realised that uncertainty to a greater or lesser extent would always influence battle because "as water has no constant form, there are in war no constant conditions."[10]

Like Sun Tzu, Thucydides thought that war should be avoided, at least until it had been carefully prepared. He warned:

> Consider the vast influence of accident in war, before you engage in it. As it continues, it generally becomes an affair of chances, chances from which neither of us is exempt, and whose events we must risk in the dark. If the war is prolonged, it will usually be prone to the whims of luck; but these might reach both of us, and how they will develop is a dangerous and daring game, whose result nobody can foresee.[11]

Machiavelli observed that uncertainty for lack of adequate information was an influential factor in any battle, but that it could and should be reduced by means of skirmishes, allowing the troops to find out what the enemy was really worth. Jomini found that obtaining perfect information of the enemy's proceedings should be the basis for "forming good combinations in war."[12] Nowhere, however, did he claim that uncertainty was likely to be overcome in its totality. Clausewitz insisted that, at the moment of battle, knowledge of enemy strength and intentions are normally scarce and fraught with uncertainty. He warned that one should not "aim at fixed values; [for] in war everything is uncertain, and calculations have to be made with variable quantities." Further, he drew attention to sources of uncertainty in war, which are embedded in the fact that "military action is

---

[9] Sun Tzu, *The Art of War*, p. 85 quoted in Handel, *Masters of War*, p. 30.

[10] Ibid., p. 101 quoted in Handel, *Masters of War*, p. 29.

[11] Thucydides, *Thukydides's. Historie* [*Thucydides' History (of the Peloponnesian War)*]. M. Cl. Gertz (trans). Vols. I-III. (København [Copenhagen]: Selskabet til Historiske Kildeskrifters Oversættelse, 1897-98), Book 1, Section 78, p. 103.

[12] Jomini, "Grand Military Operations" in Michael I. Handel, *Masters of War*, p. 250.

intertwined with psychological forces and effects." For Claus[13]witz, uncertainty seemed to take up a far more prominent place in the theory on war than it did to Sun Tzu, Machiavelli or Jomini: "War is the realm of uncertainty; three-quarters of the factors on which action in war is based are wrapped in a fog of greater or lesser uncertainty...war is the realm of chance. Chance makes everything more uncertain and interferes with the whole course of events."[14]

Unlike Clausewitz, Moltke was not daunted by the prospects of attempting to lift the fog of war. He may not have imagined achieving intelligence superiority, as we would want nowadays, but he certainly expected to be able to get a considerable lead over his adversary. As chief of the Prussian Great General Staff, Moltke accepted uncertainty – he merely wished to be sufficiently well informed to provide his army commanders with a basis for their operational judgement, thus relegating uncertainty to a remote corner of the operational field. For example, Moltke cleverly exploited the intelligence and communication means at his disposal at Königgrätz, during the Prussian war against Austria in 1866. Here his superiority was not only due to a modern communications system and to having a high level Hungarian spy, the Baron von Schluga, on the Prussian payroll, but also to the Byzantine Habsburg decision-making body, which together with the poor Austrian railroad system gave a clear advantage to the Prussians in the form of shorter response time.

Chinese revolutionary leader and Communist Party Chairman Mao tse-Tung (Mao Zedong), 1893-1976, thought that one might be "comparatively certain about [one's] own situation, [but] very uncertain about the enemy's." However, he found that:

> There are signs for us to read, clues to follow, and sequences of phenomena to ponder... These form what we call a degree of relative certainty, which provide an objective basis for planning in war... Even though future changes are difficult to foresee and the farther ahead one looks, the more blurred things seem, a general calculation is possible and an appraisal of distant prospects is necessary.[15]

---

[13] Clausewitz, *On War*, p. 136, quoted in Handel, *Masters of War*, p. 27.

[14] Ibid., p. 101, quoted in Handel, *Masters of War*, p. 244.

[15] Mao tse-Tung, *Selected Writings*, pp. 242-243 and p. 131, quoted in Handel, *Masters of War*, p. 246.

The precision of that "general calculation" depends on the extent and incisiveness of intelligence.

Despite today's ingenuity or access to information there appears to be a common acceptance amongst the theorists about the rôle of the ever-present uncertainty. These days, some of the earlier impediments have been overcome while some remain. It has not always been possible to get and transmit information in time, and even now when technology offers a near frictionless delivery, there is no guarantee that every aspect is taken into account, or that nothing changes in the time that elapses from presentation of the picture to its utilisation. However, of course, shorter response time increases the chances that the picture is unchanged when action can be taken. As demonstrated above, uncertainty has always been a key corollary of warfare omnipresent in the milieu of decision-making. Therefore it must be a task for theory and practical research to find ways to deal with that challenge and, to the extent possible, to find remedies.

Despite technological achievements in limiting the influence of uncertainty, one can never be absolutely sure. War is an affair of chances from which neither party is exempt. If the war is prolonged, it will usually be prone to accidental developments whose results nobody can foresee with any kind of certainty. The sources of uncertainty in war are embedded in the fact that military action is intertwined with psychological forces and effects and, according to Clausewitz, a great many factors are wrapped in a fog of greater or lesser ambiguity. Future changes will always be difficult to foresee; but a general appraisal of distant prospects is necessary, and modern technology does facilitate forecasts with less uncertainty than what was possible merely a few decades ago.

The methods employed in the collection of information with a view to creating images of the enemy rest increasingly on technology, which leads to an expectation of a drastic reduction of that particular kind of uncertainty that is caused by subjective assessment. The technical development facilitating this trend is not very old, but the wish to create a true picture has been the same for ages.

Lifting the Veil from the Face of the Foe

Although the drive towards creating a clear picture has recently been intensified, very few seriously believe that all fog and friction of war will ever dissipate completely. Amongst the few who do seem to believe in having found an approximation to that goal are Arthur K. Cebrowski, John J. Gartska, and David S. Alberts. Their basic assumption is that, like the commercial sector, the military moves away from centralised control towards a networked modus operandi. The synergy, thus generated, will allow an overview of the theatre of action, which is continuously updated and so near to being complete that it makes battle-space awareness all encompassing, accurate and real-time.[16] They foresee that full dominance of all niches of the electro-magnetic spectrum will allow entry into an opponent's decision-action cycle with the possibility of predicting future dispositions. With full insight no question needs to be left unanswered, and through this achievement the process of creating accurate and timely enemy portrayal is ridded of ambiguity and uncertainty.

In their opus on network centric warfare, Alberts et al. work on the assumption that "operational concepts of dominant manœuvre, precision engagement, full-dimensional protection, and focused logistics will be enabled by information superiority" with the ultimate aim of "full-spectrum dominance."[17] They claim that this superiority can be achieved through information operations that protect one's ability to collect, process, and disseminate an uninterrupted flow of information and, at the same time, deny the opponent the possibility of doing the same. The way towards elimination of uncertainty, and with it the fog of battle, they argue, is by fusing sensors. What cannot be detected with sufficient precision and timeliness by one sensor might be so by simultaneous employment of a number of sensors of different types and locations linked together in a network. Such sensor fusion will contribute to reducing uncertainty of positions of high value targets – and targets in general.[18]

Proponents of network centric warfare assert that, in the future, decision-making being eased by the high quality and timeliness of the available information may be "proactive and agile" rather than reactive: "Increased levels of battle-space knowledge mean that we can bound accurately our adversary's capabilities," which implies less focus on reaction to sudden or unexpected changes and more attention to shaping the battle-space.[19] This ability to respond rapidly to changing circumstances allows command and control to become less time-consuming and better able to look ahead in time. One's level of uncertainty drops as a

---

[16] Cebrowski and Gartska, "Network Centric Warfare."

[17] David S. Alberts, et al., *Network Centric Warfare*, p. 54.

[18] Ibid., p. 150.

[19] Ibid., p. 159.

consequence of more time and resources for "monitoring the situation and looking ahead to ensure that problems are identified and resolved as quickly as possible, perhaps even before the actor entities realise they exist (emphasis added)."[20]

However, that kind of perfect overview is closely linked to contemporary state-of-the-art technology, which only comes to full fruition in its own milieu. It is primarily a matter of observational intelligence, requiring something to observe. If there are no troops to be seen and no electronic emission to register, there will be little observation. An adversary choosing to act completely out of the box in a truly asymmetrical fashion rid of electronic forewarnings severely hampers the surveillance and big-brother-scrutiny of a high-tech electronic superpower.

To Clausewitz, daring was essential in circumstances of uncertainty making up for insufficient intelligence. If the modern high-tech commander grows accustomed to a near perfect, technologically gathered, analysed, and fused intelligence as his sole basis for action and consequently becomes less than keen on using his informed intuition – his *coup d'œil* – then the initiative will shift to his asymmetric opponent, who – in this way – proves to be the one in possession of this precious Clausewitzian quality. However, if one fights an opponent on close to equal terms the risk exists that sources and means of intelligence are destroyed or manipulated. Both sides may try to and succeed in, partially at least, blinding each other and the classic notion of uncertainty will reappear as the Phoenix from the ashes.

Change and Permanence

As we have seen, the methods used for the creation of an enemy image have followed in the footsteps of the invention of new means – rarely the opposite way round. Methods have been adapted to new technological inventories. Exploitation of sources has been improved by the advent of dedicated staffs, computers and the Internet, and indeed by meta-system concepts like ISTAR (Intelligence, Surveillance, Target Acquisition and Reconnaissance), which will be explored further in the next chapter. In that context, one also observes that, as a consequence of the immense development in the field of communications, Clausewitz's doubts as to the usefulness of intelligence at the operational and tactical levels have largely

---

[20] Ibid., p. 160.

been superseded. The technological progress of the two world wars and post-1945 computer development has provided sophisticated new tools. The near real-time day and night situational awareness seen on the coalition side in the 2003 war in Iraq was brought about by the combination of imagery, electronics, signals and human intelligence, and improved communications and command facilities. As for theories, there seems to have been a reasonable degree of consistency over the years. Central to them all is the need for timely appraisal of all relevant factors contributing to accurate and comprehensive enemy images. Multi-faceted pictures based on sound multiple-source intelligence are key to the demand for automatic fusion and processing of intelligence.

Today, with the need for near complete battle-space awareness, the enemy image must be a comprehensive one, comprising information on foreign nations, hostile or potentially hostile forces or elements and areas of actual or potential operations. It remains unchallenged that what depends on the enemy cannot be absolutely certain. The sources of uncertainty in war are embedded in the nature of the phenomenon being an affair of chances, and they include the psychological forces and effects that are intertwined with military action. Therefore, in war a great many factors remain wrapped in a fog of greater or lesser uncertainty. Future changes will always be difficult to foresee, but a general appraisal of distant prospects is necessary, and modern technology does indeed facilitate forecasts with a higher degree of certainty than ever before. The recent development in the technology employed in the creation of enemy images has led some to expect a drastic reduction of uncertainty in war. However, presently the vast array of preconditions needing fulfilment to allow perfection of this progress does not seem to have been met. This was amply demonstrated by coalition losses in the latest wars in Iraq and the difficulties currently encountered in Afghanistan. Even the best modern technology has shortcomings.

Moreover, there is bound to be an element of subjectivity in all human appraisals. The British historian, Richard Holmes, observes:

> The soldier goes to war with an abstract image of the enemy in his mind's eye, an image sometimes sullied by officially inspired propaganda and almost always spattered by the mud thrown by the popular press. His training will have featured aggressor forces or 'terrorists', and the very language he is encouraged to use will suggest that he is dealing, not with another human being thrust by the turn of the dice into another uniform, but with a mere object of hostility

belonging to some different tribe – almost to another species.[21]

While methods and organisations tailored to collecting, processing and disseminating intelligence have developed over the last two hundred years, the gear which has allowed today's increasingly penetrating familiarity with the face of the foe is mainly a consequence of the technological breakthrough in intelligence gathering and processing, as well as of the revolutionary progress in precision technology and communications. The trend, which we have seen developing since the atrocities in the beginning of the twenty-first century and the recent war in Iraq, indicate that a degree of precision and timeliness hitherto unknown in warfare and allowing a nearly complete awareness of the enemy, the environment, and the battle conditions might materialise sometime in a not too distant future. During the latest war in Iraq, quite a few Americans even expected to see a promising demonstration of the achievements in this field. This expectation, however, was only partially fulfilled.

---

[21] Holmes, *Firing Line*, p. 360.

Chapter VII: Approaching Clarity

ALTHOUGH THEORISTS HAVE found out what is important to know about one's enemy, the broader picture, which we have seen so far, is mostly composed of some highly precise as well as numerous more or less opaque details – a naturalistic painting with streaks of impressionism in it, so to speak, and in many instances there are good reasons for regarding it as a product of art rather than science.

We shall now turn to the practical aspects of creating a picture of the enemy and examine the means and methods employed to bring about precision and reliability or, to stick to metaphors, to create an image that comes closer to photography than to art.

In the Middle Ages, by and large European warfare concerned the Emperor, kings, princes, their lieges and the relatively small military forces within the capacity of the sovereigns' coffers. However, wars from the Enlightenment up to and including the Cold War have increasingly permeated most corners of any belligerent country's economic, social, and mental life. After the end of the Cold War, armed conflicts seem to have again become more limited in their aims as well as in scope – at least as far as the comparatively affluent societies are concerned. Nonetheless, today's fighting affects both the civilian and the military spheres, and the reach of modern weaponry makes the whole world a potential battlefield, although almost every single conflict is restricted in space and participation.

Moreover, with respect to perception of the enemy, no clear-cut division can be established between the civilian and military sectors. Images based on assessments of political intentions or war aims, economic interests, resources, and industrial output appear to fall primarily within the realm of the former, while topographical and climatic details, military strength ratios, and dispositions of forces, boundaries between units, combat efficiency, and operational and tactical intentions lie in the latter. Both have as their primary objectives limiting or, preferably, dissipating uncertainty. However, between these spheres there are several points of interface: the hostile society's economic and industrial potential, enemy recourse to reserves of personnel and resources, and possible alliance options, to mention but a few.

The creation of an image of the adversary includes incorporation of both the civil and the military dimensions. While the former may be described as the process of net assessment, the latter remains the province of military intelligence. Intelligence per se has a bearing on both, and sound intelligence estimates are of crucial importance to the decision-maker at any level.

Strategic and Tactical Intelligence

Nowadays, strategy comprises elements as diverse as politics, economy, security, and sociological and ecological considerations. The strategic aims, the means and the ways to achieve them and the objectives to be reached en route form a complex setting, and the decision-maker needs sound and precise evaluation of the challenge as a basis for his or her strategy conception. This is where intelligence matters.

Intelligence can be either strategic, which in this context simply means that it concerns the national leadership of the user state, or tactical, which similarly refers to all other levels whether military or otherwise. Both levels may be based on single- or multiple-source approaches. Terminology differs slightly depending on civilian or military usage. In the armed forces' parlance unprocessed single-source data are "information," while "intelligence" is the product resulting from collection, evaluation, analysis, fusion, and interpretation of the material. In the larger, partially civilian, intelligence community the information gathered, be it single- or multiple-source, is often referred to as "intelligence" right from the moment it is gathered.[1]

Although intelligence can be divided between strategic national level intelligence on one hand and everything else described as tactical intelligence on the other, for the general purpose of establishing an image of the adversary, such division is hardly relevant. Moreover, the United States have begun studies into the feasibility of linking together the wider aspects of intelligence with surveillance and reconnaissance – the latter two often being categorised as combat information rather than intelligence – in a meta phenomenon which they call ISR (intelligence, surveillance and reconnaissance).[2] In parallel, the North Atlantic Treaty Organisation (NATO) works on the further inclusion of target acquisition into the concept, thus calling their meta-system ISTAR. These elements all contribute to the creation of the enemy depiction, and we shall therefore address them jointly.

Intelligence Estimates

Intelligence serves the decision-maker by providing sound estimates of the hostile environment, the enemy's likely situation and his intentions. Ray Cline, a former CIA Deputy Director for Intelligence (DDI) and head of the State Department's Bureau of Intelligence and Research, explained that: "Estimates are careful descriptions of the likelihood that certain things will exist or occur in the future... An estimate tries to reduce the inevitable degree of uncertainty to a minimum in making calculations about future situations."[3] Consequently, Sun Tzu's appreciation of the need for intelligence estimates is still relevant. Today, this need is defined by the decision-maker's "primary intelligence requirements" and it forms the basis for the planning process.[4] Provision of consolidated intelligence estimates is the task of the intelligence community, which fulfils it by relying not only on "state-of-the-art" technologies providing "observational

---

[1] Michael Herman, *Intelligence Power*, p. 96.

[2] Michael Herman, *Intelligence Services in the Information Age* (London: Frank Cass, 2002), p. 12.

[3] R.S. Cline, "Secrets, Spies and Scholars: Blueprint of the Essential CIA" p. 65 quoted in Herman, *Intelligence Power*, p. 258.

[4] Handel, *Masters of War*, p. 231.

intelligence," but also on a wide variety of "message intelligence" sources. Human and Open Source Intelligence are disciplines for collection of the latter and have survived centuries of technological progress. Although of later occurrence, signals intelligence, too, may serve that purpose. These disciplines remain of vital importance when it comes to acquiring knowledge of enemy intentions.

Net Assessments

To gauge the likeliness of victory any responsible government will seek to make a sound net assessment of the balance between the prospective enemy's and one's own potentials and capabilities before preparing for, let alone going to, war. Although good intelligence is a precondition for realistic net assessments, it is not the only one. The quality of a net assessment depends on the nature and dependability of the data which the intelligence agencies have provided, and on the appropriateness of the methods they have employed. Poor quality results from inappropriate methods and lack of scepticism, as was the case in the run up to the War on Iraq in 2003, when CIA copied information provided by one of the British intelligence services, who had simply gleaned it from an undergraduate student's term paper with no attempt on verification. Conversely, prior to the outbreak of the Second World War, the British Industrial Intelligence Centre provided precise and pertinent net assessments on the German aircraft production that actually induced, however reluctantly, the British government to start rearming.

The value of a net assessment, however, depends not only on the producers. It varies considerably depending on the intellectual capacity and education of the users, the decision-makers. Making them understand the importance of the logical enterprise of defining options and unmasking the unknown and known factors is crucial, and clarifying difficult choices is part of this process.[5]

Williamson Murray and Allan R. Millet ascribe the term "net assessment" to the post-Second World War period acknowledging, however, that processes of a similar kind have been attempted earlier than that. While in Britain in the 1930s, "no explicit organisations existed...government leaders had little choice but to move beyond the

---

[5] Williamson Murray and Allan R. Millet, "Net Assessment on the Eve of the Second World War" in Murray and Millet, *Calculations*, pp. 1-3.

Approaching Clarity

elementary data provided by their intelligence agencies and...make the best net assessments they could."[6] In this period, the entire process suffered from the lack of a formal organisation, which might fuse the findings of individual information collecting agencies. Further, the military, naval, and air intelligence were single-service agencies with no joint appreciation of enemy strengths and weaknesses. It was unusual to see an independent balancing process of enemy vis-à-vis own forces, though the Germans, through their frequent Kriegsspiele (war games), might have approached such a force-on-force comparison.[7]

However, at the strategic level many of the great powers established successful interdepartmental organisations to fuse diplomatic, military and political information and considerations. As an example of such a bureaucracy, the British system is illustrative. Necessitated by the need to defend a global empire against regional threats – be they American, French or German – and influenced by the experiences of the Second Boer War (1899-1902) and the First World War (1914-18), the British established institutions such as the Committee for Imperial Defence, the Chief of Staff Sub-Committee, and the Minister for Coordination of Defence. Although the government was not centralised to the extent of those of the American, Soviet or German systems, the British political leadership had a relatively free hand between general elections and had the benefit of a cabinet system of governance, which worked on a collective basis.

British Intelligence Co-ordination

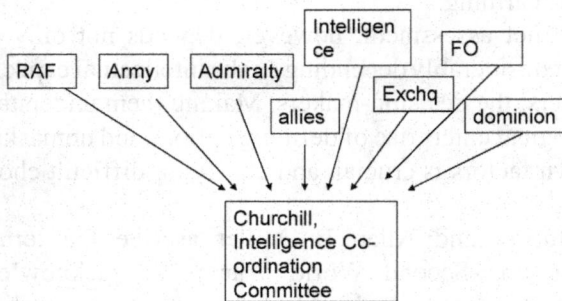

---

[6] Ibid., pp. 4-5.

[7] Ibid., p. 9.

Assessments were arrived at by co-operation in the cabinet or in its various committees and sub-committees and, subsequently, decisions were taken and executed by senior civil servants and military officers who themselves had, usually, taken part in the assessment process.[8] Although in comparison with other systems of that era, by a superficial glance the British committee concept seems to provide evidence of an extremely well oiled machinery, the need for consensus was time consuming and was bound to delay action when swift measures were required. By comparison with Fascist decision-making, the British committee system was cumbersome, though perhaps more likely to find the right answers.

The British assessment process would be initiated by a political request to the Chiefs of Staff to prepare a strategic survey, lists of comparative force strengths, estimates of the services' prospects in case of war and – possibly – submissions for funds.[9] Then the War Office, the Admiralty and the Air Ministry would assemble data from, among other sources, the service attachés' and civilian diplomatic assessments and supplement these by inputs from radio decrypts, accounts from visiting businessmen, and reports from secret agents. Although, theoretically, this approach seems logical and straightforward, there were difficulties arising from the problems of penetrating the Fascist dictatorships' obsessive secrecy. Problems arose in finding out about specific quantities and qualities of production as well as intangibles such as military, naval and air doctrines. In this context intentions as to possible theatres of operations reflecting the potential enemy's geo-strategic ambitions mattered a lot and were difficult to fathom. For example, it took considerable time for the Royal Navy to find out that the *Kriegsmarine* (the German navy) did not intend to stay in the Baltic, but rather looked for westward opportunities.[10]

Apart from the services, intelligence inputs into the assessment process were contributed by the Foreign Office, the Secret Intelligence Service, the Treasury, the dominions, the Industrial Intelligence Centre, and the Prime Minister's Office; all the inputs were fused and their interpretation agreed upon at the Committee for Imperial Defence or Cabinet levels. For many reasons, as an instrument for political action the assessments were not

---

[8] Paul Kennedy, "British' Net Assessments' and the Coming of the Second World War," in ibid., pp. 19-22.

[9] The following is based on Kennedy's examination of the matter in ibid., pp. 23-25.

[10] Ibid., pp. 23-27.

always sufficiently precise. This shortcoming emanated, inter alia, from colonial fixation with the Far East, reluctance to doctrinal innovation amongst the services, and inability to read the true intentions of the Fascist powers.

In the pre-Second World War period, the agency that appears to have most efficiently and innovatively contributed to the net assessment process was the Industrial Intelligence Centre, which had been set up in 1931. This institution assessed foreign powers' economic strength and weaknesses, their armaments capacity and their vulnerabilities.[11]

German net assessment lagged behind the British endeavours in the same period, and this was not only because of their failure to appreciate enemy strength. The Nazi German state was organised in such a Byzantine manner that it was impossible for German authorities to keep tabs on own resources and capabilities. Williamson Murray opines that the Germans, though coming close to winning, lost the Second World War largely because of an inability to appraise their own military capabilities and capacity in relation to those of their actual and potential opponents.[12] The Nazi German society was a truly convoluted organism plagued by competing bureaucracies.[13] As for net assessment of foreign powers, the trouble started right at the top with parallel state and party foreign services, a handicap which was only marginally alleviated by the amalgamation in 1938 of these institutions and the appointment of the Nazi-party foreign expert Joachim von Ribbentrop as Minister for Foreign Affairs.[14] Unlike the British system, a German Cabinet hardly existed – ministers were personal advisors to the Führer, who normally consulted them individually – and neither did they constitute a decision-making body, nor did any institution exist similar to that of the British Chiefs of Staff Committee.[15] The *Oberkommando der Wehrmacht*, or OKW was in reality Hitler's personal military staff rather than a truly joint supreme command, as the services' commanders-in-chief more often than not dealt directly with the head of state. The OKW was created by Hitler when, at the time of his

---

[11] Ibid., pp. 30-33.

[12] Williamson Murray, "Net Assessment in Nazi Germany in the 1930s" in ibid., p. 60.

[13] Ibid., p. 68.

[14] The "official" foreign minister until 1938 was Konstantin von Neurath.

[15] Murray and Millet, *Calculations*, p. 69.

dismissal of von Blomberg as Minister for War, the ministry was converted into a tri-service military staff serving the supreme commander, viz. himself. Hitler reserved strategic insight and decisions for himself and used this staff, the OKW, for support in that field. The operational military leadership remained in the hands of the services high commands *Oberkommando des Heeres*, OKH (the army high command), *Oberkommando der Kriegsmarine* (the admiralty), OKM, and *Oberkommando der Luftwaffe*, OKL (the air force high command). No overall strategic evaluation took place within the OKW, and the intelligence collection and analysis of information was equally atomised. General Walter Warlimont (1894-1976), chief of operation at OKW headquarters, noted in his memoirs that: "the advice of the British Chiefs of Staff and the American Joint Chiefs was a decisive factor in Allied strategy. At the comparable level in Germany there was nothing but a disastrous vacuum."

German Intelligence Co-ordination

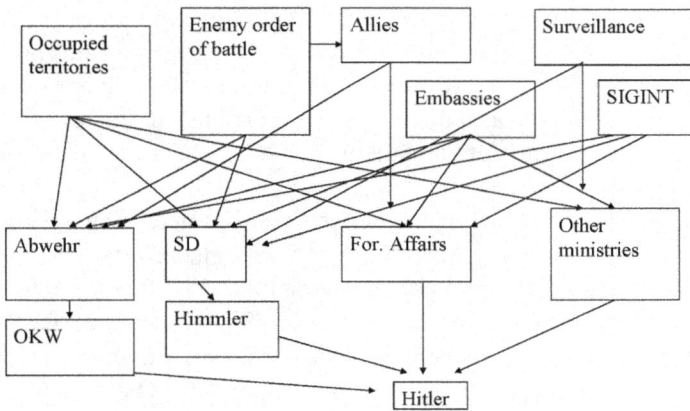

Occupied territories	Enemy order of battle	Allies		Surveillance
			Embassies	SIGINT
Abwehr	SD	For. Affairs		Other ministries
OKW	Himmler			
		Hitler		

The official strategic intelligence service, the *Abwehr*, lost the battle for supremacy as the primary net assessor of the state through a slow but inexorable takeover by the *Sicherheitsdienst*, or SD, the security service of the SS. But also, most other departments within party as well as state had their own individual intelligence gathering and evaluation. Thus, the final net assessment was made not only formally, but often also practically, by the Führer personally.[16]

While under the British system at the time questions were passed from Cabinet through the bureaucratic system where thorough analyses were performed by a number of agencies, the German system's support of Hitler's assessments rested almost entirely on individuals.[17] However, Hitler's assumptions did not always go unchallenged – at least not in the early war years. Among others, the Chief of the German General Staff, General Ludwig Beck, in connexion with the Czechoslovakia crisis in 1938 vehemently claimed that Germany risked a war with France and Britain for which the Reich was unprepared. Despite the reasonableness of Beck's warning, Hitler overruled his objection as he found that the Western powers had already written off Czechoslovakia.[18] Thus it seems appropriate to suggest that while the British leadership attempted to assess the Empire's abilities against those of its potential opponents, Germany relied to a large extent on the Führer's personal intuition. British net assessment developed and improved throughout the war not least because of Churchill's insistence on a centrally co-ordinated intelligence community.[19] During the war, the German military and civilian bureaucracies experienced increasing difficulties in challenging Hitler's personal, intuitive, and impulsive assessments because of the formidable trust and prestige he enjoyed in the general public as well as amongst large portions of the officer corps brought about by his early achievements and his success with blaming most of the setbacks on his generals.[20]

The Second World War demonstrated the need for reliable net assessments and the experiences led to refinements and also proliferation of the systems used and found useful during that war. Therefore, today the British Joint Intelligence Committee and the US National Security Council make assessments, which are similar to those described above.

As a niche, perhaps, in the net assessment business, the American

---

[16] Williamson Murray, "Net Assessment in Nazi Germany in the 1930s" in Murray and Millet, *Calculations*, pp. 69-70.

[17] Ibid.p. 71.

[18] Ibid., pp. 75-76. Beck was subsequently sacked.

[19] Christopher Andrew, *Secret Service: The Making of the British Intelligence Community*, Sceptre Edition Second Impression (Sevenoaks: Sceptre: 1987) pp. 675-78.

[20] Liddell Hart, *The German Generals Talk*, pp. 294-98.

authors Richard Neustadt and Ernest May deserve mentioning for having published a compilation of thoughts on how, in a number of cases, history might have served and may serve in future as a useful guidance to proper appreciation of possible courses of action. They suggest that their own country is somewhat remiss in that respect. To appreciate ongoing developments they recommend that one analyses the situation on hand by dissolving it into "known," "unclear", and "presumed" factors and, subsequently, compares with historical parallels.[21] To some extent this scheme runs counter to the maxim that History never repeats itself, an idea which seems to be generally accepted, although we can find instances where a certain similarity of event springs to the eye (such as the difficulties encountered in the Crimean and Vietnam wars, Hannibal's envelopment of the Romans at Cannae (216 BC) and von Schlieffen's attempt on this in his contingency plan for war against France (1905) etc). On the other hand, historical comparison may be relevant as it appears that the undergrowth of institutions busying themselves with elements of the net assessment process is as tortuous in today's United States as it was in Germany of the 1930s – an interesting historical parallel, albeit not an encouraging one. The authors indicate that in a remarkable number of cases either American decision-makers have not managed to pose the right questions or the bureaucracy has not provided pertinent answers. Among many examples of insufficient and faulty net assessment, May and Neustadt mention China's rôle in the Korean War, the Vietnam War in general, the Bay of Pigs Affair, and the abortive attempt in 1980 to rescue the hostages at the American embassy in Tehran. It appears that precisely the bureaucratic complexity – and the number – of the assessing organisations have combined with inefficient top-level co-ordination to make the assessments inadequate.[22]

Military Intelligence

Information technology, developing rapidly over the last few decades, has been an enabler of the impressive improvements in precision and communications allowing accurate and near real-time battle-space

---

[21] Richard E. Neustadt and Ernest R. May, *Thinking in Time: The Uses of History for Decision-makers* (New York: The Free Press, 1988), p.38.

[22] Ibid., passim.

awareness. In much of the theoretical and conceptual literature of recent years on the Revolution in Military Affairs, precision has been hailed as a key to future warfare (For an explanation of the meaning and origin of the term "Revolution in Military Affairs" see footnote 10 on page 15). The Canadian Forces' Field Manual, Intelligence, tells us that:

> Intelligence, as an activity, is a core competency within the realm of Information Operations...and the centre co-ordinating function in the Intelligence, Surveillance, Target Acquisition, and Reconnaissance (ISTAR) system of systems.[23]

In other words, intelligence fuses and processes the information gathered and, thus, decisively supports a commander's decision-making and the execution of his or her mission.

Quoting the NATO Glossary (AAP-6), the Field Manual, Intelligence, further defines intelligence as "concerning foreign nations, hostile or potentially hostile forces or elements, or areas of actual or potential operations."[24]

As indicated above, today's, and most certainly tomorrow's, computerised intelligence technologies permit quick collection and processing through fusing meta-systems like ISTAR.[25] Thanks to modern communications, subsequent dissemination is mostly a matter of minutes if not seconds. Although the collection and fusing meta-systems are not fully developed, let alone implemented, they are probably within realistic reach. No doubt this development will enable future decision-makers to gain even more quickly than today the situational awareness needed for successful and speedy execution of their plans. Future networked systems may allow "identification and location of the opposition's centres of gravity, critical nodes, main axes, second echelons, and weapons of mass destruction" – some of the decision-maker's primary concerns.[26]

To be able to apportion and employ resources effectively, a military

---

[23] *Field Manual, Intelligence*, p. 1.

[24] Ibid., p. 1-3.

[25] ISTAR is a NATO project aiming at establishing a "meta-system" fusing systems of Intelligence, Surveillance, Target Acquisition, and Reconnaissance to present to the end-user a comprehensive picture of the hostile environment. Ibid., *Field Manual, Intelligence*, p. 3

[26] Ibid., *Field Manual, Intelligence*, p. 3.

commander must analyse thoroughly the opponent's capability, courses open, and other factors potentially influencing events. Having made his or her intelligence preparation of the battlefield concerning the struggle ahead, he or she has established a sound basis for forming a realistic appraisal of what the enemy can do, and where and when he will be able to act. But this will rarely be enough for a decision-maker responsible for drawing crucial conclusions. He or she will also like to know the adversary's intention. Human intelligence efforts like interrogation of prisoners, conversations with locals or refugees, liaison work in liberated or occupied areas as well as signals intelligence may be helpful in that respect but hardly sufficient and as close to real-time as the decision-maker needs.

Even if one has precise knowledge of the enemy's intention, that intention may have changed before the information can be put to proper use. Moreover, although the timeliness of intelligence and communications has improved considerably, the speed of battle and the need for quick decisions have also increased. One thing that has not become more plentiful is the time available for making judgements and decisions. Today, the decision-maker needs far more information much quicker and on a wider range of matters than in the past. The closer the intelligence user is to the military units' front, the more pronounced this need becomes. Most information can be acquired, but though intelligence, now, is abundantly available, the difficulty lies in sifting through it, sorting crucial from casual and avoiding the risk of information overload. In an article in 1995, John Ferris and Michael Handel drew attention to the dilemma of "modern uncertainty" and the self-confident tendency to interpret an otherwise unmanageable mass of material solely through preconception.[27] In that context, they divided uncertainty into two groups: "Type A" uncertainty characterised by ignorance and the inability to receive accurate, useful and timely intelligence good enough to allow acting upon it, and "Type B" uncertainty stemming from the power of modern command, control, communications, and intelligence (C3I) systems, which collect and communicate anything and everything that can be collected and communicated simply because it can be done.[28]

---

[27] John Ferrris and Michael I. Handel, "Clausewitz, Intelligence, and the Art of Command in Military Operations." *Intelligence and National Security*, vol. 10, No 1 (January 1995): pp. 1-58.

[28] Ibid., p. 49. This is further elaborated by Dixon as a consequence of 'cognitive dissonance'. Norman F. Dixon, *On the Psychology of Military Incompetence* (London: Futura, 1988), p. 166.

Regarding the contemporary intelligence landscape, Michael Herman has made a number of useful observations. According to Herman – and as briefly addressed earlier – intelligence may be divided into two major groups, observations and messages.[29] Observations provide evidence, which cannot "speak" by itself, i.e. evidence similar to that found by an archaeologist, requiring careful interpretation to make sense. Likewise, observations of imagery, measurements and other descriptions must be interpreted and conclusions inferred. Messages, on the other hand, are the results of disciplines like human intelligence and communications intelligence that do indeed "speak," such as the British and Allied use of Operation Ultra information during the Second World War.[30] Messages are evidence like that used by many historians. They derive them from interviews, archival studies, letters and official documents. While the former category is concerned with presence, quantities, quality, and location of things, the latter is intelligence concerning minds, thought and meaning, which in the best of cases might enable the user to determine the opponent's intentions, although limited to the time of the delivery of the message. While observational intelligence might be provided without the knowledge of the target, messages require contact or inside access because they are provided by the target itself, orally or written, in one way or another. It has been claimed that the Japanese decision to expand the country's engagement in South-East Asia in 1940 was taken, at least partially, on the background of intercepted British Cabinet documents. The material had been captured by the Germans and handed over to Japan, and it disclosed British intentions not to reinforce forces in the region because of the paucity of naval, army, and air force units in Europe.[31]

Collection of intelligence – other than "open source" – may be divided into some main constituent disciplines. Human intelligence covers information gathered by the activity of human beings through espionage, interrogation of prisoners of war, casual conversations, etc. Signals intelligence comprises communications intelligence directed against diplomatic post, telephone lines, wireless and satellites; and electronic intelligence concerned with electronic emission from, among other things, radars and radio beacons. Imagery can be everything from satellite

---

[29] Herman, *Intelligence Power*, pp. 82 ff.

[30] Decoded messages from the German Enigma machine cipher; see Andrew, *Secret Service*, pp. 628 ff.

[31] Herman, *Intelligence Power*, p. 83.

depictions, beamed to the earth in near real-time over aerial photography, to sketches.[32] A striking example of the usefulness of the latter is the ingenuity demonstrated by General Sir (later Lord) Robert Baden-Powell, who, under the guise of an entomologist, drew sketches hidden in the wings of butterflies of Austro-Hungarian forts along the Dalmatian coast.[33] Apart from these major methodological categories, there are niches like acoustic, radar, and nuclear intelligence, seismological measuring, remote sensing of sound, heat, smell and vibration. There is also surveillance and finally battlefield military intelligence collected mainly by forces in more or less close contact with their opponents.[34]

While the material placed at the intelligence users' disposal may be broken down into the observation and message categories, the process of providing it has similarly evolved around two interlocking components. These are collection and evaluation. The first comprises the methods described above as well as the means by which information is obtained. This may be secret intelligence from spies, radio interception, code-breaking, covert photography and the like, as well as the exploitation of open sources. Intelligence collectors at the national level include institutions such as the British Secret Intelligence Service (SIS or MI6) and Government Communications Headquarters (GCHQ), and in North America the Canadian Security Intelligence Service (CSIS), U.S. Central Intelligence Agency's Directorate of Operations for human sources, and its Directorate for Science and Technology for advanced technical collection, U.S. National Security Agency for signals intelligence, and the U.S. National Reconnaissance office and U.S. National Mapping Agency for satellite imagery. However, every level has collection agencies specific to its tasks, though not always to the full satisfaction of individual decision-makers. These agencies are assumed to possess expertise on their particular techniques and fields such as combat information, unmanned aerial vehicle operation, satellite utilisation, photo reconnaissance, radars, etc. The second, much smaller, component is responsible for the evaluation of reports from different secret sources weighed against each other, and against non-covert ones: press reports, radio broadcasts, diplomatic reporting, and all the other information at a government's, as well as its

---

[32] Ibid., pp. 61-81.

[33] Richard Deacon, *A History of the British Secret Service* (London: Panther Books, 1984), pp. 175-76.

[34] Ibid., pp. 61-81.

lower level authorities', disposal. It is the object of evaluation to provide the best possible and most versatile picture of the adversary and make credible forecasts.[35]

While intelligence collection has been described above by the various intelligence subject categories, processing comprises the five following steps of action: collation (recording, grouping), evaluation (reliability of source and credibility of information), analysis (identifying significant facts, comparing with existing knowledge, drawing conclusions), integration (of all analysed material to form patterns), and interpretation (meaning what is likely to happen).[36]

Output may be divided into three categories according to its probable use: current-reportorial, basic-descriptive, and speculative-evaluative. Most fall into the first category. Of the longer-term output, a lot can be categorised in the basic-descriptive category (e.g. order of battle). The third is the least voluminous and is geared to specific users.[37] The use of intelligence may be seen as comprising the exploitation of all information pertinent to drawing the picture of the adversary. Intelligence may also be regarded in a processing context. Whether single-source or all-source, most intelligence outputs have a significant element of 'processing', as reflected in the military distinction between unprocessed data of every description, information, and the product resulting from the processing of information, intelligence.[38] While some decision-makers want unprocessed or hardly processed single-source products to judge for themselves, as for instance Churchill did, others may need well-analysed and interpreted all-source information.[39] Thus the degree of processing varies. Some covertly acquired documents and intercepted messages need analysis, while others are more transparent – in the case of more or less exotic languages, translation may be needed. A fitting example of exploitation of the latter kind is the Soviet acquisition of intelligence on Western nuclear programmes, which consisted primarily of original documents and scientists' explanations. To

---

[35] Herman, *Intelligence Services*, p. 32.

[36] Herman, *Intelligence Power*, p. 100.

[37] S. Kent, "Strategic Intelligence for American World Policy, p. 8 quoted in Herman, *Intelligence Power in Peace and War*, pp. 105-06.

[38] Herman, *Intelligence Services*, p. 10.

[39] Andrew, *Secret Service*, pp. 627-78.

the informed reader, the Soviet nuclear specialists, these rarely needed interpretation. However, many intelligence products incorporate intensive processing, often of a fairly complex kind. In particular, the relatively 'soft' evidence available amidst concealment and deception provide little information unless carefully evaluated requiring specific intelligence skills such as measurement, signature, traffic analysis and imagery interpretation.[40]

A distinction may be made between secrets that are potentially 'knowable' facts and mysteries that have no clear-cut answers. Processing is necessitated by the need for intelligence to fulfil its forecasting rôle as a guide to the future. To fill that rôle, the analysts must discover the secrets and try to solve the mysteries, and the future is bound to be a mystery as even if opponents have plans these may change or not materialise at all. Therefore[41] short of total transparency, governments and military headquarters have to make assumptions about future possibilities and uncertainties, and intelligence must provide them with a sound basis for doing so. As Herman states:

> ...the English-speaking countries have developed the concept, with some influence on Western intelligence as a whole, of intelligence as a two-stage process of single-source collection followed by all-source analysis, with the implicit principle that intelligence collectors should not have the responsibility of final assessment. This is quite contrary to what was the KGB's view of intelligence, as covert single-source information fed directly to policy-makers – perhaps still the policy of its successor, the SVR.[42]

Intelligence and the Revolution in Military Affairs

Not only the collection of data but also most of the processing is benefiting enormously from the information revolution, a key enabler of the Revolution in Military Affairs.[43] The slow advent of "artificial intelligence" may slightly hamper the stride but cannot stop the march towards more and

---

[40] Herman, *Intelligence Services*, p. 10.

[41] Ibid., p. 11.

[42] Ibid., p. 33.

[43] See Introduction, note 7.

more complete and timely information. The Revolution in Military Affairs is a beneficiary from the general technological development, and it has introduced computerised management and processing into the intelligence world. Computer technology reduces the human involvement in intelligence collection and processing as far as the observational elements are concerned. Message intelligence will always depend on language and human contacts and will therefore be less affected by the technological advances. Intelligence from satellites, unmanned sensors, unmanned aerial vehicles and other high-tech gadgets can now provide intelligence material for immediate operational use, theoretically even in automated sensor-to-shooter loops. The Revolution in Military Affairs allows users to draw on satellites for information built on communications as well as on non-communications interception. That development facilitates multi-sensor integration giving to the user the benefit of highly automated integration of the flow from various sensors and of processing of the information collected.[44]

As to the wealth of intelligence now available, Herman observes that those tasked with evaluation and interpretation have to strike a delicate balance between timely warning and alarmism. Extreme caution, Herman finds, as well as a sense of daunting responsibilities seem to pervade the intelligence community:

> The power of the 'enemy image' links with some facets of intelligence psychology. For collectors as well as analysts there is an attractive self-image of the intelligence practitioner as a warner, jolting policy-makers out of complacency and make them listen... Something of the emotional shock of war...spills over into the assessment of potentially hostile forces; underestimation is less readily forgiven than overestimation, and the analyst in any case has his own inherited compulsion not to let the fighting men down. English-speaking agencies were deeply influenced in the Cold War by national folk memories of the payment in blood for underestimation in the 1930s...[45]

Herman points to the existence of two different mental models of intelligence provision. According to some writers on the Revolution in Military Affairs, observation of things and quantities seems to provide the sole foundation for appraising the opposition. Another model focuses on thoughts, minds, intentions and textual messages. This model, which is less

---

[44] Herman, *Intelligence Services*, p. 52.

[45] Herman, *Intelligence Power*, p. 247.

easily satisfied by technological innovation alone, appears to be absent from their debate. The first provides all-source collection and fusion of geo-positional displays of current situations from radar sources and television based on surveillance devices:

> It is not clear how far this model counts on near real-time imagery interpretation; images distributed electronically to commanders still have to be interpreted by someone. A single-source surveillance satellite on a 15 minute pass produces enough material to occupy 100 analysts with conventional tools for a week. Presumably it is thought that automatic target recognition will speed up processing dramatically.[46]

The emphasis seems to be on seeing and pictures. Commanders and subordinates will have a shared timely image of the ongoing battle – an accurate, near real-time situational awareness.[47] Herman observes that in this way, the common operating picture will "put the commander back in command making him see the battle-field himself, with a modern equivalent of Napoleon's and Wellington's *coup d'œil*."[48]

However, while awareness means, roughly, being able to locate, identify, and track major items of military equipment and units, knowledge requires an ability to relate such activities to each other and to operational schemes. This requires more than mere observational intelligence.

It has been claimed by some – among others Alberts and Cebrowski – that a world where many decisions can be taken with something approaching perfect knowledge is not very far away. This is linked to a belief in the possibility of achieving dominant battle-space knowledge.[49] However, establishing knowledge requires not only observations but message intelligence as well, and only in the rarest of circumstances will that be anything close to "real-time." On the contrary, the advent of public-key encryption and digital signatures in electronic communication may severely hamper the ability to exploit radio frequency and other messages. Strongly encrypted messages will soon be the norm and will be unbreakable within the timeframe of useful exploitation on the battlefield. Thus,

---

[46] Ibid., pp. 53-54.

[47] Ibid., pp. 53-54.

[48] Ibid., p. 54.

[49] Ibid. p. 54. Among those is D.S. Alberts.

information will have to be extracted, for example, directly from enemy headquarters at either the sending or the receiving end, as signals intercepted in-between will be meaningless.[50]

Cebrowski, Alberts and others claim that the fog of war may eventually dissipate. As discussed above, their basic assumption is that a network centric modus operandi will allow an overview of the theatre of operations, which is continuously updated and so near to being complete that it makes battle-field awareness all-encompassing, accurate and in real-time – it becomes knowledge.[51] They further anticipate the possibility of full dominance of all niches of the electro-magnetic spectrum, which will allow entry into the opponent's decision-action cycle with the possibility of predicting future dispositions, which will help minimise uncertainty. Alberts et al. work on the assumption that dominant manœuvre, precision engagement, full-dimensional protection, and focused logistics are under way and enabled by information superiority followed by "full-spectrum dominance."[52] Moreover, it has been argued that the move towards elimination of uncertainty travels via fusion of sensors of different types, simultaneously employed, and linked together in a network.[53]

Albert's prophesy seems one-sided. One is bound to ask to what extent, if at all, it addresses the aspects of the aforementioned second model that focuses on minds rather than things. Knowing one's enemy fully requires access to his thoughts, but to make optimal use of it you must also have access to flows of information about your own organisation. The raw evidence of this process is language, not observation.[54] According to Herman, textual sources are not addressed by the Revolution in Military Affairs discussion and seem to play no part in its concepts. Alberts, for one, seems to grant little attention to this aspect. Therefore, one may say that a Revolution in Military Affairs commander might be well sighted, but deaf as well as illiterate in assessing his enemy – hardly a desirable condition for

---

[50] M.C. Libicki, *The Mesh and the Net: Speculations on Armed Conflict in a Time of Free Silicon* (Washington D.C.: National Defense University, 1996), pp. 140-1 and 26. Quoted in Herman, *Intelligence Services*, p. 58.

[51] Cebrowski and Gartska, "Network Centric Warfare."

[52] D.S. Alberts et al., *Network Centric Warfare*, p. 54.

[53] Ibid., p. 150.

[54] Herman, *Intelligence Services*, p. 55.

lifting the fog of war.

Nevertheless, the Information Revolution does spill over to the technological and conceptual aspects of the intelligence world. From having had a prominent rôle in traditional war fighting, intelligence has now become decisive in exploiting the speed and precision which are currently practicable. Utilising intelligence, networking and communications, weapons systems might be employed on a much more precise and concurrently updated basis than ever before, thus limiting ammunition and fuel consumption as well as collateral damage.

The 2003 war in Iraq provided a test ground for Revolution in Military Affairs equipment, and interviews with US intelligence officials conducted by this author in the early summer of 2003 revealed that on that occasion the United States actually tested systems for automatic fusion and processing of intelligence. However, these turned out to be in immature stages of development.[55]

Anthony Cordesman's *The Instant Lessons Learned* communicates some pertinent observations: the "combination of imagery, electronic intelligence, signals intelligence, and human intelligence...and improved communications and command and intelligence fusion at every level gave it near real-time day and night situational awareness."[56] Further, the effectiveness of air support benefited from "a combination of new I[ntelligence,] S[urveillance, and] R[econnaissance] assets, new precision weapons, and...precision strike operations with excellent targeting, an emphasis on 'effect based' strikes, and careful limitation of collateral damage."[57]

Today, intelligence sources abound, and the Iraq lessons indicate that in a not too distant future they may be accessed even more easily, timely, and by many more users than hitherto, but the very same lessons also indicate that uncertainty and friction do not necessarily vanish. The development suggests a future where intelligence officers will be able to access databases around the world "internet style," attaining all the open source intelligence they might wish, and additionally have access to a wide variety of secret information. Communications technology will allow a free choice between processing on the spot or by one's home country just as

---

[55] Interviews conducted May 2003 with senior officials at military institutions in the United States (their names and affiliations are known to the author).

[56] Anthony H. Cordesman, *The Instant Lessons*, p. 5.

[57] Ibid., p. 8.

quickly, collated with new and combat decisive information achieved in real-time and relevant to the battle that is in progress.[58] It remains unclarified, however, if the users will be able to select only pertinent intelligence and exploit it in an adequate manner. The ordinary internet abounds with casual and often faulty information. Similarly, it is likely that an intelligence internet will provide such a wealth of haphazard information that the risk of misapprehension and unlucky combinations might endanger the entire project. There will be a severe risk of faulty deductions and decisions which, possibly, only diligent application of message intelligence, code breaking and other old fashioned and rather time consuming methods might help avoid.

In order to move to an almost total and immediate transparency of the war environment, the modern intelligence community needs "artificial intelligence" good enough to fuse and process the information gathered and present a "weeded," tidy image of the enemy as he really looks at the moment. The above mentioned American intelligence fusion systems mark an important step forward, but they still appear to be in an experimental stage of development.

The task of translating readings into militarily useful data is even more difficult and calls for analysis of individual outputs, effective fusion of disparate readings and, ultimately, integration of them into seamless, comprehensive systems. Automatic integration will depend, in part, on the progress of artificial intelligence, which will always be difficult to predict.[59]

The information revolution, being the fundamental enabler of economic globalisation, also influences the ratio of power to price of information technologies.[60] Thus, the fruits of the Revolution in Military Affairs are not necessarily to be reaped only by the most affluent powers. Recent actions by non-state actors – not least in post-war Iraq – indicate that the sophistication of the weapons used as well as their remote control systems are rapidly increasing.

Warfare was once almost exclusively a military and economic matter. Modern war, though mostly limited in scope and participation, is

---

[58] Interviews with United States officials (their names are known to this author).

[59] Thierry Gongora & Harald von Riekhoff. *Toward a Revolution in Military Affairs? Defense and Security at the Dawn of the Twenty-First Century* (Westport, Greenwood Press, 2000) p. 42.

[60] Ibid., p. 41.

potentially all encompassing and makes its impact felt in many corners of a belligerent society's civilian as well as military sectors. Intelligence serves the decision-makers in both fields by providing sound estimates of the enemy's likely situation and intentions, reducing the inevitable degree of uncertainty to a minimum. Strategic intelligence and net assessment serve to compare the state's potential with that of its prospective opposition and describe the courses open. Tactical intelligence is a core competency within the realm of information operations. It serves collection, fusion and processing of information and, thus, decisively supports the decision-maker in the execution of his or her mission.

The Information Revolution enables users to draw on satellites for images, communications and non-communications interception, and it allows them to integrate the flow from various, widely distributed, sensors and to process the collected information. This opportunity is today's equivalent of the *Feldherrenhügel* – the tactical vantage point – whence the commander may again behold the battlefield and appraise it with this modern equivalent of Napoleon's and Wellington's *coup d'œil*.

According to some experts, a network centric modus operandi will allow an overview of the theatre of operations, which will be continuously updated and so near to being complete that it makes battlefield awareness all encompassing, accurate and real-time. Textual sources, however, appear neither in the Revolution in Military Affairs discussion nor in connexion with the Network Centric Warfare concept, and this may prove to be a major stumbling block in the endeavours to reach full battlefield knowledge. Therefore, as suggested above, one may say that assessing his enemy today's decision-maker may have a clear vision, but he or she will frequently be ignorant of the opponent's thoughts and intentions, and this is a significant shortcoming when the ambition is lifting the fog of war.

Observational intelligence and technical development

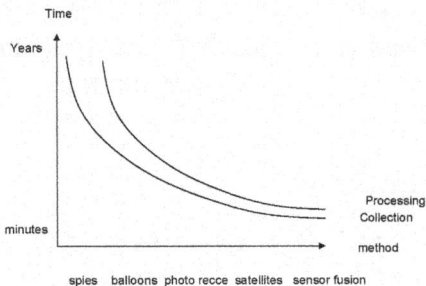

To illustrate this challenge the figure on the bottom of page 181 shows how observational intelligence along with the technical development has approached real-time.

Notionally, the next figure depicts the similar progress of message intelligence, showing an interesting relapse towards lower performance under the present technological regime, which allows for an encryption so strong that many messages will hardly be available within a timeframe that is realistic with a view to supporting ongoing operations.

The progress of message intelligence

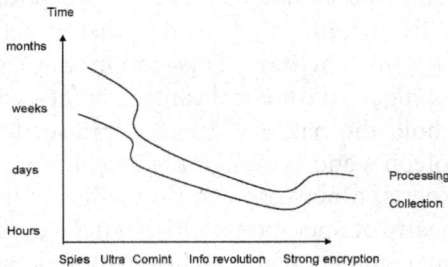

Time

months

weeks

days

Processing

Collection

Hours

Spies   Ultra Comint   Info revolution   Strong encryption

A future land combat scenario might be that of a near perfect battle-space awareness giving ground troops the opportunity of commanding ordnance from ships, missiles or manned and unmanned aircraft held ready at a safe distance.[61]

It is possible that large parts of future battle-space awareness will be derived from sources which are not secret, but open. Intelligence will be information defined as high quality understanding of the world using all available sources. Secrets will matter less than hitherto, and selection and speed will be the critical challenges, as response time may shrink considerably.[62] Keeping in step with the proliferation in technological opportunities may require adjustments to the intelligence organisation. The centralising efforts once important for making agencies communicate and co-operate, may not be particularly helpful in the creation of enemy images of post-2010 conflicts. Intelligence's future may be that of a loose

---

[61] Gregory F. Treverton, *Reshaping National Intelligence for an Age of Information* (Cambridge: Cambridge University Press, 2001), p. 63.

[62] Ibid., p. 98.

confederation of overlapping networks connecting sources, producers and consumers, of which military planners will be prominent ones.

Considering that, as intelligence consumers are the institutions of the entire belligerent society and not only its fighting forces, it is no given thing that intelligence, awareness or knowledge should not in future – at least partially – be provided by commercial enterprise. The private open intelligence system mentioned earlier, Wikileaks, may be an indicator of a trend of which we have, so far, seen only the beginning. In future, much intelligence will probably be available to all and sundry, although the task as far as warfare and security are concerned will be to ensure that as many intelligence networks as possible serve military, national and alliance purposes.[63]

Moreover, we should not forget private enterprises of yesteryear. The forces of the condottieri were commercial businesses, and for many years artillery and train were driven by civilians. It is not unlikely that intelligence might be the commercialised venture of tomorrow. As Gregory F. Treverton wrote: "If intelligence has a niche, it will be to add to the understanding by being open...and by being in touch with the best of experts outside government."[64]

The object of intelligence is to prevent too many surprises and to permit commanders to shape battle plans.[65] However, cancelling uncertainty is not only a question of near-perfect intelligence. As we have discussed in earlier chapters there are mental barriers in addition to the technological difficulties, which can hardly be overcome completely. It will always remain difficult to look into the opponent's mind and forecast his dispositions, and there is some way to go before full exploitation of artificial intelligence for purposes of fusion, collation and appraisal of data becomes possible. Napoléon and a few other great captains possessed a unique Fingerspitzgefühl, or common sense, allowing them to read the minds of their enemies and foresee their actions.[66] But few decision-makers possess that capacity, and as Elinor C. Sloane notes, though "advanced technology can go a long way towards decreasing the fog and friction of

---

[63] Ibid., pp. 64-5.

[64] Ibid., pp. 27-8.

[65] Ibid.

[66] Ibid., p. 64

war...it cannot eliminate them altogether."[67]

Unlike Alberts et al., Ferris and Handel seem to be clear that intelligence can never achieve complete and absolute perfection, for by definition, even with excellent intelligence, friction and the reciprocal nature of war ensure that uncertainty will still exist, even if in a different form and, perhaps, to a lesser degree.[68]

To reach a near flawless enemy image a method must be found for filtering the component details of one's enemy impression to get rid of non-factual elements and irrelevant detail, and one needs to "get inside the enemy leadership's 'brain'" to be able to forecast his decisions and actions and, thus, cancel uncertainty entirely. That, however, may not happen in near future – or, indeed, it may never happen at all.

Human Intelligence and the End of Osama bin Laden

Regardless of the near-perfection of computer networks, satellites, sensor-to-shooter loops etc, there will always be knowledge which cannot be obtained by technological means alone. As briefly touched upon in previous chapters, human intelligence (or HUMINT) requires human contact in the form of spies, interrogation teams, commercial activities, interception of couriers etc. It may include interviews with local civilians, interrogation of prisoners of war, and various random contacts. More often than not, it is carried out in an environment where the interviewed individual is, or believes him/herself to be, under severe duress because of imminent danger, fighting, confinement, threats of violence, or actual physical pressure. Just as no intelligence will be close to perfect without also employing HUMINT techniques, HUMINT alone will rarely deliver the whole picture. Near real-time day and night situational awareness must be brought about by diligent efforts of a combination of imagery, electronics, signals and human intelligence. However, one must bear in mind that, even if a fairly precise picture has been obtained, precise knowledge of the enemy's intentions is short-lived, because such intentions may change before the information can be put to purposeful use.

Modern intelligence is highly dependent on electronic emission, but in

---

[67] Elinor C. Sloane, *The Revolution in Military Affairs*. (Montreal, McGill-Queen's University Press, 2002), p. 30

[68] Ferris and Handel, "Clausewitz, Intelligence, and the Art," pp. 41-42.

the rare cases when an opponent manages to operate entirely without use of wireless equipment, satellites, internet or telephones, HUMINT is the only possible approach to get close to the target's location, intention or activity. And that, in a way, was how the long drawn out quest for the world's leading terrorist, Osama bin Laden, was brought to a successful conclusion.

As early as in September 2001, when the al-Qaeda perpetrated their atrocities in New York and Washington, Osama bin Laden was already a high-profile terrorist. Thus, in the beginning of 2002, it was obvious that bin Laden would not be found easily, and it was decided to cast the net wide and start mapping the whereabouts of those close to him: family and associates. Moreover, intelligence officers scrutinised the video-tapes that he released occasionally to find out about his state of mind and health and to look for possible changes in attitude.[69]

In 2005, a Central Intelligence (CIA) employee suggested working to a four pillars approach: Tracking bin Laden's family members who might want to get in touch, tracking couriers, surveying his communication with senior al-Qaeda leaders, and finally monitoring his press activity. Since for years the family, al-Qaeda and press pillars yielded nothing, the CIA chose to focus on the courier line of approach. As over time the area where bin Laden's hideout might be found was narrowed down to the border areas between Afghanistan and Pakistan, it was also becoming clear that the courier must be a person speaking, or at least understanding, Arabic as well as one of the local languages.

In 2010, in co-operation with Pakistani military intelligence, the CIA managed to locate mobile phone numbers known to be linked to members of an al-Qaeda "facilitation network."[70] Conversations on one of these phones, which was switched on only in and around the northern Pakistani city of Peshawar, were held exclusively in Arabic and Pashto. Locating the mobile, a Pakistani CIA-collaborator was able to find the owner and his motor vehicle and follow it to Abbottabad. This led the CIA to a large fortress-like compound, which turned out to be entirely without electronic links with the world around it, indicating that the inhabitants wished to stay undetected. Subsequently, in order to be able to establish a more close and continuous observation, the American pursuers discretely set up a safe

---

[69] Peter Bergen, *Manhunt: from 9/11 to Abbottabad – the ten-year search for Osama bin Laden* (London: The Bodley Head, 2012), pp. 74-83.

[70] Bergen, *Manhunt*, p. 122.

house in Abbottabad and started piecing together a pattern of daily routines of the compound and its occupants.

The intelligence thus gathered by HUMINT as well as by various high-tech means of surveillance made it increasingly likely that, apart from various family members and collaborators, bin Laden himself was actually living in the compound. Although the picture did never become absolutely watertight, in early 2011 as it became clear that the golden opportunity to strike would not remain forever, the time seemed ripe for action. Thus, in mid March 2011, American President Barrack Obama sanctioned a raid by Navy SEALs in order, once and for all, to eliminate the threat posed by Osama bin Laden. On the basis of the intelligence thus gathered the raid went ahead around midnight on 1/2 May 2011. A twelve year long intelligence effort was at an end as, in the early hours of 2 May, this operation achieved its primary objective, viz. to capture and kill bin Laden. This is a fascinating story, but the minutiae of it lie beyond the scope of this book.[71]

The hunt for Bin Laden and his eventual elimination shows an example of the obvious value of thorough and patient intelligence work over many years. I implied strategic as well as tactical intelligence efforts; it employed HUMINT, COMINT old-fashioned spy activity as well as prisoner interrogation and meticulous analysis of the various data. The intelligence cycle spun round over and over again as the field of search narrowed ever closer and finally zoomed in on the compound in Abottabad. Seen in this context and considering the availability of all conceivable sorts of modern revolution-in-military-affairs-resources, it is remarkable how decisive a rôle was played by low-tech and century old methods like surveillance, interrogation, HUMINT and spying.

---

[71] A detailed and, to some extent, critical description may be found in Peter Bergen's *Manhunt*.

Afterword

> *Take ye heed; watch and pray: for ye know not*
> *when the time is.*[1]

IN CASE OF war we should probably all like to have a clear impression of the face of the foe, not to mention precise, timely and comprehensive knowledge of his actions. Like the lines in a perspective painting meeting in the vanishing point, which is beyond the canvas, the achievements in information and precision technologies make us approach a situation when all our lines of enquiry meet; where all our needs for timely intelligence are fulfilled. We approach it, but the vanishing point – the all-encompassing knowledge – still remains beyond reach.

The development of enemy portrayal historically, methodologically and theoretically, and the considerations which are pertinent to the depiction of the foe allow us to see trends towards near-perfect, continuously updated and real-time battle-space awareness: an exact face of the foe. However, juxtaposing the contrasting aspects of the increasingly clear enemy image provided by more and more sophisticated technological means and the intangible but equally real process going on in the minds of each belligerent and every bellicose society, it may dawn upon the contemplative character that there are reasons to assume that uncertainty and friction in war will hardly be totally overcome. Even an operation as sophisticated as the hunt

---

[1] Mark: 13, 33.

for bin Laden did eventually go ahead without complete assurance of time, place and possible opposition. The influence of uncertainty and friction still contribute to the creation of composite images providing the background for actions of individual combatants as well as for decisions taken in war rooms, at headquarters, or at command posts.

There is a range of issues to consider when deciding whether an enemy image is realistic, objective, and precise or not. Timeliness and credibility are central conditions for the creative process, which has military as well as civilian dimensions. While the civil effort is an intellectual one emphasising net assessments, fusion of sources, and inference of intentions, the military process concentrates on collecting and evaluating topographic, materiel, numerical and capability data, and the overall aim is to create a naturalistic portrait of the opponent – an image which is sufficiently timely, incisive and precise to be used as a basis for decision-making in war.

Therefore, the image of the enemy ought to serve decision-makers by providing sound estimates of the adversary's situation and likely intentions, thus reducing the degree of uncertainty to a minimum. The aim is to limit the occurrence of surprise, ease decision-making and, as a result, permit war leaders to shape and execute their plans successfully. The Revolution in Military Affairs has provided easy access to information from a wide variety of sensors spread ubiquitously over the area of responsibility and beyond, which allows commanders to look, so to speak, through the eyes of each fighting man and woman. Given such a potential wealth of information, uncertainty caused by overload has materialised as an obvious risk. The Clausewitzian "ignorant uncertainty" seems to have found a modern replacement. There is a delicate balance between on the one hand having all relevant and necessary information, and on the other being overwhelmed by superfluous details. Clausewitz's observation that most intelligence is contradictory has not yet vanished completely. But further systems development in the sphere of command, control, communication and intelligence systems will probably increasingly facilitate automated fusion and analysis. At a certain point, this development will help dissolve the appearance of contradiction as one approaches a true picture. True information cannot be contradictory, as it simply represents reality, but of course, the proper evaluation of it depends on its comprehensiveness and one's own ability to process and understand it all.

Central to theories on the construction of images has been the need for timely appraisal of all relevant factors contributing to a truthful and comprehensive enemy depiction, putting together what might be called a mosaic of one's foe. Over the years there seems to have been a reasonable degree of consistency in the desire to achieve this objective. Methods employed in the process of putting together the mosaic have concurrently been adapted to new technological opportunities, but at the same time the influence of human attitudes and interference have contributed bias to the outcome.

For thousands of years, rulers and captains have shown a keen interest in acquiring the best possible situational awareness. However, an effective instrument for exploitation of the information has not been available until the creation of organisations dedicated to the task. That development, initiated probably by Napoléon, did not really get underway until the Boer War, but has since thrived, coming to a temporary apogee in the war on Iraq in 2003.

Clausewitz's doubts about the usefulness of intelligence at the operational and tactical levels have largely been superseded. The technological innovations of the world wars and the post-Cold War revolution in information technology have provided sophisticated new tools guaranteeing timeliness unthinkable in the early nineteenth century.

During the 2003 war in Iraq, on the coalition side the combination of technology and human efforts brought about near real-time day and night situational awareness. Despite this, intelligence assessments continued to be coloured because of the preconceived picture of, and subconscious attitudes towards, the enemy, his capabilities and his weaponry. That which depends on the enemy we can never be absolutely certain about. The Iraq War once again confirmed that the sources of uncertainty are embedded in the facts that war is an affair of chances, and that military action is intertwined with psychological forces and effects on both sides.

In addition, there is bound to be an element of subjectivity in all human appraisals. Inevitably, a country's politicians and officers alike go to war with abstract and highly subjective images of the enemy in their minds' eyes. Prior to outbreak of conflict they have been influenced by preconceptions and propaganda actively promoted by the public opinion shapers like press, politicians and others and frequently underpinned by national heroic myth and artistic imaging. Thus, the cultural, psychological and societal aspects of enmity modify the clear, sharp, "scientific" picture. What everybody at the sharp end wants, presumably, is a clear, user-friendly, and timely picture suitable as a point of departure for decision-making and action. But what is always lurking in the background, blurred and biased, is a wide variety of more or less subjective features with roots in diverging – primarily attitudinal and political – preconceptions. These are mostly to be found in the realm of the subconscious, which makes them hard to combat. To some extent, they are present and actively influencing the perception of the foe all the time, the way all subconscious material constantly influences any person's behaviour without necessarily being registered at the conscious level.

With our knowledge of the psychological, religious and societal factors and of the influence of propaganda we may now understand the possibilities and limitations involved in putting an enemy image together today and, probably, for the foreseeable future.

As most paintings, the depiction of an adversary will have a background and a foreground – and perhaps a centre ground – it will have some parts with a high degree of clarity and some with lesser. As has been amply demonstrated by centuries of warfare and most recently in Iraq in 2003, home-grown political and cultural preconceptions influence one's battle-situational awareness. One may have a highly precise notion of enemy dispositions, but here and there in one's mental landscape the image is blurred as if one were approaching the foe through a smoke screen. General Wallace's candid statement to the press in late March 2003 indicated that, even with modern and highly developed technological means of intelligence collection, and regardless of the professionalism of the fighting forces, the individual's mental baggage as well as his or her shortcomings still played a rôle.

The subconscious elements are likely to continue to influence the process of assessing a potential adversary. In the centre and foregrounds of the picture, metaphorically speaking, modern technology provides a lot of very timely and highly accurate material. Thanks to artificial intelligence this will become fused increasingly quickly, evaluated, and interpreted automatically, and brought to the consumers or weapons systems in synchronisation with battle plans. However, these pieces of the mosaic will all be based on observational intelligence giving precise accounts of things and locations, but hardly any certain knowledge of enemy intentions. Primarily, that knowledge will remain in the realm of message intelligence. As timely code breaking gets less and less promising in modern cryptology, to a large extent message intelligence will have to rely on bugging enemy headquarters, on employing spies and on prisoner of war interrogation, which give results close to certainty at the time the intelligence is collected. However, these are slow methods in comparison with the whole panoply of means brought about by the revolutionary developments in computer, precision and information technologies. Moreover, history shows that the use of physical pressure, or torture, as a shortcut to achieving quick results is a tempting but a dangerous path to thread.

Human intelligence, or HUMINT, includes interviews with prisoners of war and various other human contacts, and it is carried out, frequently, in an environment where the interviewed individual is under severe duress because of fighting, confinement, threats of violence, or actual physical pressure. Although the Geneva Conventions prohibit the use of torture, the distinction between persuasion and violence lends itself to interpretation by the power conducting the interview. According to Henrik Rønsbo of the Danish Centre for Torture Research and Rehabilitation of Victims (RCT), torture may occur when states suffer from inner weaknesses. He claims that while, previously, Western colonial powers applied electrical torture by means of field telephones (a French method) or beating with canes (British), these methods are still being used by a range of the former colonies. Western countries have invented more sophisticated techniques such as sleep deprivation, noise, exposure, imprisonment in isolation, etc – the so-called "clean methods." While US schemes like water boarding and various other procedures used during the conflicts of the Bush administration are regarded by most other countries – allies and opponents alike – as traditional torture, at the time the Americans themselves do not categorise them that way.[2]

Torture is an effective means of intimidation and oppression, but it is hardly likely to produce valid intelligence. During the War on Terror, the argument has been heard over and over again that if we can save the lives of thousands by applying physical pressure to one or a few persons we should do so. However, it has been claimed that the War in Iraq in 2003 was initiated on the grounds of information on weapons of mass destruction obtained under torture, and as we now know, these were never found.

There is more to HUMINT than interrogation of prisoners. Human intelligence sources generally and human intelligence agencies are important providers of information. This is particularly true as far as the opponent's intentions are concerned, but also relevant in environments of reduced usefulness of electronic equipment, aircraft and satellites -- such as operations under bad weather, lack of friendly air superiority, scarce means of aerial reconnaissance, or dense vegetation. Moreover, conflicts at the lower end of the spectrum of combat intensity (when targets emitting electronically are few and far between), conflicts underlying political restrictions, and operations in urban areas where the usefulness of sensors and communications are limited, are all prone to increased emphasis on human intelligence. To exploit properly the human intelligence sources, the intelligence operatives must normally question them directly.

It will, therefore, be understandable if the future may witness a trend

---

[2] Heidi Laura, "Den selvfølgelige vold [the natural violence]" in *Wekendavisen*, Nr. 24, 2009, pp 1-2.

towards taking the photographically sharp and timely technological picture as the most important and decisive information in creating an enemy portrait and the predominant basis for action. Conversely, the clearer and more incisive analysis based on additional intelligence of the message category risks being neglected because it will be regarded as unnecessarily time-consuming. Subconscious matters might be dismissed because they are intangible. This, however, will provide images of the enemy, which are not true depictions of reality; after all it is within the realm of reality that wars are fought. If you toss a coin into a bowl of water and then try to pick it up by stretching out your hand along the perceived line of sight, it is unlikely that you will hit the coin in the first attempt. The deviation may be small, but it is sufficient to make you miss the object. With decision-making in war small deviations may prove disastrous. Decision-makers will have to decide on the right balance between time and accuracy. Wherever they choose to place their emphasis, their picture of the enemy will always be imperfect.

The figure below illustrates the connexion between technological sophistication and focus, and the influence by these two on precision. While lower technological influence combined with other factors and a broad perspective may lead to a blurred image, and high technological performance and a narrow focus will yield good observational precision, it is assumed that most real world enemy depictions will lie somewhere in between.

The technology-focus-precision connexion

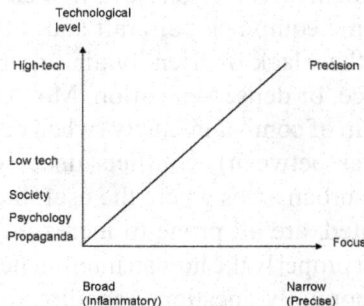

Advances in communications may allow automated targeting and delivery of weapons, or give an opportunity of commanding ordnance from ships, missiles or manned and unmanned aircraft held ready at a safe distance. However, sublime technology, new doctrines and adjusted organisation will not guarantee a flawless enemy image. The sources of bias and uncertainty are ubiquitously present, and will make the dream of complete information dominance and perfect real-time knowledge of the opponent unrealistic.

To create perfect, timely and all encompassing enemy portraits a method must be found to get rid of non-factual, biased and casual elements. Additionally, one needs to get inside the enemy leadership's Ooda-loop to be able to forecast its decisions and actions in time. As long as that does not happen, it will be difficult, if not impossible, to rid warfare of uncertainty. Doing away with uncertainty is not likely in the near future – or, indeed, at all.

"The Fighting Téméraire"

Returning to the art metaphor, it seems justified to claim that modern technology has increased and improved some parts of the picture to almost photographic clarity, as it has been found with the old naturalistic painters, but still these parts do not cover the whole canvas. There are, of course, intermediate steps on the road from naturalism to expressionism. J.M.W. Turner has painted an impressive view of a man of war, "The Fighting Téméraire," being towed away on her last voyage in the haze of the setting sun.[3] The ship herself, as well as the tug and other central parts of the painting, are sharp and precise, but the further one's eyes move from the centre towards the frame, the mistier the background and the fewer the details. The enemy image materialise similarly. While the central combat-decisive parts are mostly clear, accurate, and timely, and take up an increasing part of the canvas, lots of psychological, societal, mythical fringe elements, uncertainty, and simple ignorance blur the impression outside the viewer's focus. Although the latter elements may decrease in number and prominence, it seems evident that they will never disappear entirely. In other words, uncertainty and chance will continue to influence warfare as it has done in the past.

---

[3] Joseph Mallord William Turner, 1775-1851. Turner painted the fighting Téméraire in 1838 depicting the old wooden man of war, the Téméraire, being dragged to her last home by a little steamer. A mighty red sun amidst a host of flaring clouds, sinks to rest on one side of the picture, and illumines a river that seems interminable, and a countless navy that fades away into such a wonderful distance as never was painted before. From http://www.victorianweb.org/authors/wmt/turner2.html accessed 29th September 2003.

Bibliography

Speeches, Memoirs and Official Publications

Alberts, D.S. et al., *Network Centric Warfare: Developing and Leveraging Information Superiority 2nd Edition*. CCRP publications Series, 2000.

Best, Werner and Siegfried Matlok, ed. *Dänemark in Hitlers Hand: Der Bericht des Reichsbevollmächtigten Werner Best über seine Besatzungspolitik in Dänemark mit Studien über Hitler, Himmler. Hezdrich, Ribbentrop, Canaris u.a.* Husum: Husum Verlag, 1988.

Bourgogne, Adrien-Jean-Baptiste-François. *The Retreat from Moscow: the Memoirs of Sergeant Bourgogne*. London: The Folio Society, 1985.

Churchill, Winston Spencer. *The War Speeches 1939-45, Vols. I-III*. Compiled by Charles Eade. London: Cassel & Company Ltd, 1952.

Cordesman, Anthony H. *The Instant Lessons of the Iraq War: Main Report, Third Working Draft*. Report by the Center for Strategic and International Studies. Washington D.C.: Center for Strategic and International Studies, 2003.

Goebbels, Joseph. *Das Eherne Herz: Reden und Aufsätze aus den Jahren 1941/42*. München: Zentralverlag der NSDAP/Frantz Eher Nachf., 1943.

Graves, Robert. *Goodbye to All That*. London: The Folio Society, 1981.

Hitler, Adolf. *Mein Kampf*, 626-630. Auflage. München: Verlag der NSDAP, Franz Ehers Nachfolger, 1941.

Jünger, Ernst. *In Stahlgewittern*. Stuttgart: Klett-Cotta Verlag, 1990.

Saint Exupéry, *Antoine de. Krigsflyver [Pilote de guerre]* (København: Jespersens og Pios Forlag, 1943).

Thukydides. *Thukydides's Historie [Thucydides' History (of the Peloponnesian War)]*. M.Cl. Gertz (trans). Vols. I-III. København (Copenhagen): Selskabet til Historiske Kildeskrifters Oversættelse, 1897-98.

Military Manuals

Land Force Information Operations, Field Manual, Intelligence (English), B-GL-357-001/FP001, 2001.

Additional Sources:

Monographs and Anthologies

Alberts, David S., John J. Gartska, and Frederick P. Stein. *Network Centric Warfare: Developing and Leveraging Information Superiority*. 2nd Edition (Revised). CCRP, 2002.

Andrew, Christopher. *Secret Service: The Making of the British Intelligence Community*, Sceptre Edition Second Impression. Sevenoaks: Sceptre, 1987.

Bartov, Omer. *Hitler's Army*. New York: Oxford University Press, 1992.

Bergen, Peter. *Manhunt: from 9/11 to Abbottabad – the ten-year search for Osama bin Laden*. London: The Bodley Head, 2012.

Childers, Erskine. *The Riddle of the Sands*. Virginia: IndyPublish.com McLean, no year.

Clausewitz, Carl von. *On War*. Princeton, New Jersey, U.S.A.: Princeton University Press, 1976.

Deacon, Richard. *A History of the British Secret Service*. London: Panther Books, 1984.

Dixon, Norman F. *On the Psychology of Military Incompetence*. London: Futura, 1988.

Frankl, Viktor E. *Psykologi og eksistens* [*Psychology and Existence*]. Copenhagen: Gyldendal 2002.

Frankl, Viktor E. Man's *Search for Meaning*. New York: Pocket Books, 1985.

Gat, Azar. *Fascist and Liberal Visions of War*. Oxford: Clarenden Press, 1998.

Gongora, Thierry & Harald von Riekhoff. *Toward a Revolution in Military Affairs? Defense and Security at the Dawn of the Twenty-First Century*. Westport, Greenwood Press, 2000.

Gooch, John and Amos Perlmutter, eds. *Military Deception and Strategic Surprise*. London: Frank Cass, 1982

Greenwald, Glen. *No Place to Hide*. New York: Metropolitan Books Henry Holt, 2014.

Griffith, Samuel B. *Sun Tzu: The Art of War*. London: Oxford University Press, 1971.

Grossmann, Dave. *On Killing: The psychological Cost of Learning to Kill in War and Society*. Boston: Little, Brown and Company, (paperback) 1996.

Hamann, Brigitte. *Hitlers Wien: Lehrjahre eines Diktators*. München: R. Piper, 1996.

Handel, Michael I. *Intelligence and Military Operations*. London: Frank Cass, 1990.

Handel, Michael I. *Leaders and Intelligence*, London: Frank Cass, 1989.

Handel, Michael I. *Masters of War: Classic Strategic Thought*, Third revised and expanded edition. London: Frank Cass Publishers, 2001

Handel, Michael I. *Strategy and Intelligence*. London: Frank Cass, 1989.

Handel, Michael I. *Intelligence Services in the Information Age*. London: Frank Cass, 2002.

Hedges, Chris. *War Is a Force That Gives Us Meaning*. New York: Anchor Books, (paperback) 2002.

Herman, Michael. *Intelligence Power in Peace and War*. Cambridge: Cambridge University Press, 1999.

Herman, Michael. *Intelligence Services in the Information Age*. London: Frank Cass, 2002.

Herzog, Chaim and Mordechai Gichon. *Battles of the Bible*. London: Greenhill Books, (paperback) 1997.

Holmes, Richard. *Firing Line*. London: Jonathan Cape, 1985.

Holmes, Richard. *Nuclear Warriors*. London: Jonathan Cape, 1988.

Holmes, Richard et al. *The Oxford Companion to Military History*. Oxford: Oxford University Press 2001.

Howard, Sir Michael. *Krigene I Europas Historie* [Danish translation of *War in European History*]. Aalborg, Denmark: Fremad, 1977.

Hughes, Daniel J., ed. *Moltke and the Art of War*. Novato; Presidio, 1993.

Huntington, Samuel. *The Clash of Civilizations*. New York: A Touchstone Book. Simon and Schuster, 1997.

Jervis, Robert. *Perception and Misperception in International Politics*.

Princeton University Press, 1976

Jomini, Antoine Henri baron de. *The Art of War*. London: Greenhill Books 1996.

Kahn, David. Hitler's Spies: *German Military Intelligence in First World War*. USA: Da Capo Press, 2000.

Kaplan, Robert D. *Warrior Politics: Why Leadership Demands a Pagan Ethos*. New York: Vintage Books, 2003.

Keegan, John. *A History of Warfare*. New York: First Vintage Book Edition, 1994.

Keegan, John. *The Face of Battle*. London: Penguin, 1978.

Kershaw, Ian. *Hitler: 1889-1936*, two vols. New York: Norton and Company, 2000.

Lewis, Bernard. *What Went Wrong? The Clash Between Islam and Modernity in the Middle East*. New York: Oxford University Press, 2003.

Liddell Hart, B. H. *Strategy*. New York: Meridian, 1967.

Liddell Hart, B. H. *The German Generals Talk*. New York: Perennial, 2002.

Lidegaard, Bo. *Jens Otto Krag 1914-61*. Copenhagen: Gyldendal, 2001

Luckszat, Jan. *Der Weg zur Reichseinigung* [*The Road to Reich Unification*]. Potsdam: Militärgeschichtliche Forschungsamt, 2008

Machiavelli, Nicolo. *The Art of War*. Cambridge, MA: Da Capo Press, 1965.

Machiavelli, Nicolo. *The Discourses*. London: Penguin Group, 1998.

Machiavelli, Nicolo. *The Prince*. London: Penguin Books, 1999.

Miller, Alice. *Am Anfang war Erziehung*. Frankfurt am Main: Suhrkamp Taschenbuch, 1983.

MacMillan, Margaret. *Paris 1919: Six Months that Changed the World*. New York: Random House Trade Paperback Edition, 2002.

Mailer, Norman. *Why are we at War*. New York: Random House, 2003.

Mao tse-Tung. *On Guerrilla Warfare*. Urbana and Chicago: University of Illinois Press, 2000.

Markus, Georg. *Der Fall Redl*. Frankfurt am Main: Ullstein, 1986.

Matthews, Ron & John Treddenick, eds. *Managing the Revolution in Military Affairs*. Chippenham: Palgrave Publishers, 2001.

Maurois, André : *Les silences du colonel Bramble*. France: Grasset, 1921.

Munro, Hector Hugh. *The Complete Stories of Saki*. Ware: Wordsworth Classics, 1993

Murray, Williamson and Allan R. Millet. *Calculations: Net Assessment and the Coming of the Second World War*. Toronto: The Free Press, 1992.

Neustadt, Richard E. and Ernest R. May. *Thinking in Time: The Uses of History for Decision Makers*. New York: The Free Press, 1988.

Paret, Peter; with the co-operation of Gordon A. Craig and Felix Gilbert, eds. *Makers of Modern Strategy*. Princeton, New Jersey: Princeton University Press, 1986.

Parker, Geoffrey. *The Military Revolution*. Cambridge: Cambridge University Press, 1988.

Paulsen, Adam. *Overvindelsen af Første Verdenskrig: Historiepolitik hos Ernst Troeltsch, Oswald Spengler og Thomas Mann* [*Overcoming the First World War: History Politics with Ernst Troeltsch, Oswald Spengler og Thomas Mann*]. Copenhagen: Museum Tusculanum Publishers, 2014.

Porch, Douglas. *The French Secret Services*. New York Farrar, Straus and Giroux, 1995.

Rampton, Sheldon and John Stauber. *Weapons of Mass Deception: The Uses of Propaganda in Bush's War on Iraq*. New York: Jeremy P,

Tarcher/Penguin, 2003.

Ranke, Leopold von. *Preussische Geschichte*. Essen: Phaidon Verlag GmbH, n.d.

Rieber, Robert W., Ed. *The Psychology of War and Peace: The Image of the Enemy*. New York and London: Plenum Press, 1991.

Rip, Michael Russell and James M. Hasik. *The Precision Revolution: GPS and the Future of Aerial Warfare*. Annapolis: Naval Institute Press, 2002.

Safranski, Rüdiger. *Goethe: Kunstwerk des Lebens [Life as a Work of Art]*. Cologne: Carl Hanser Verlag, 2013

Sawyer, Ralph D. *The Tao of Spycraft*. Canada: Harper Collins, 1998.

Sloane, Elinor C. *The Revolution in Military Affairs*. Montreal, McGill-Queen's University Press, 2002.

Spengler, Oswald. *Der Untergang des Abendlandes*. München: Verlag C.H. Beck, 1990.

Sun Tzu. *The Art of War. The Denma Translation*. Boston: Shambhala Publications Inc, 2000.

Toland, John. *Adolf Hitler*. Ware: Wordsworth Edition, 1997.

Treverton, Gregory F. *Reshaping National Intelligence for an Age of Information*. Cambridge: Cambridge University Press, 2001.

Trevor-Roper, Hugh R. *Hitler's Table Talks 1941-1944: His Private Conversions*. New York City: Enigma Books, 1988.

Vissing, Lars. *Machiavel et la politique de l'apparence*. Paris: Presses Universitaires de France, 1986.

West, Nigel. *Venona: The Greatest Secrets of the Cold War*. Glasgow: Harper Collins Publishers, 2000.

Wirtz, James. *The Tet Offensive: Intelligence Failure in War*. Ithaca: Cornell University Press, 1991

Zeev, Maoz and Azar Gat, eds. *War in a Changing World*. Ann Arbor: The University of Michigan Press, 2001.

Articles

Aagaard, Charlotte. "Kold Krig i Blikkenslagerbanden [Cold War amongst the Plumbers' Gang] *Information*, 21 November 2005.

Andersen, Lars Erslev. "Asymmetrisk krig, ny terrorisme" [Asymmetric War, New Terrorism]. *Militært Tidsskrift* (March 2002): pp. 48-66.

Belbutowsky, Paul. "Strategy and Culture." *Parameters* (Spring 1996): pp. 32-42.

Ben-Zvi, Abraham. "Between Warning and Response: The Case of the Yom Kippur War," *International Journal of Intelligence and Counterintelligence* 4, 2 (Summer 1990), 227–42

Betts, Richard K. "Analysis, War, and Decision: Why Intelligence Failures Are Inevitable," *World Politics* 31, 2 (October 1978), 61–89

Beyerchen, Alan. "Clausewitz, Nonlinearity and the Unpredictability of War," *International Security*, 17:3 (winter, 1992), pp. 59-90.

Bramming, Pernille. "Hvorfor frygter vi Islam?" *Militært Tidsskrift* (March 2002): 23-34.

Cebrowski, Arthur K. and John J. Gartska, "Network-Centric Warfare: Its Origin and Future" in *U.S. Naval Institute Proceedings*, articles 1998.

Clausewitz, Carl von. "Krigsføringens vigtigste Grundsætninger" [Core Maxims of War]. *Militært Tidsskrift*, Det Krigsvidenskabelige Selskab, 1992.

Coker, Christopher. "Asymmetrical War" in *IFS Info* No 1, 2001. p.7.

Düring-Jørgensen, Jesper. "På listesko i Dänemark [Walkiong Softly in Denmark]" in *Wekendavisen*,Nr. 17-24 April 2008, Ideer, pp. 10-11.

Ferrris, John and Michael I. Handel "Clausewitz, Intelligence, and the Art of Command in Military Operations." *Intelligence and National Security*, vol. 10, No 1 (January 1995): pp. 1-58.

Fulghum, David A. "Intel, Anti-Stealth Part of Tanker Spinoff" in *Aviation Week and Technology*, 4 March 2002, No 43.

The Guardian, Saturday, 29 March 2003: General Sir Mike Jackson acknowledges that the invading troops have not seen "displays of a welcoming population."

Handel, Michael I. "Intelligence and the Problem of Strategic Surprise," *Journal of Strategic Studies* 7, 3 (September 1984), 229–81

Handel, Michael I. "Technological Surprise in War," *Intelligence and National Security* 2, 1 (January 1987), 1–53

Mignot, B. "Le renseignement stratégique" in *Penser les ailes françaises*, No. 10, June 2006, pp. 82-85.

Mozaffari, Mehdi. "Bin Laden and Islamist Terrorism," *Militært Tidsskrift* (March 2002): 35-47.

Norton-Taylor, Richard. "Commanders admit unexpected resistance has put paid to 'quick war' plan." *The Guardian*. Saturday, 29 March 2003.

Observer reporting team. "The reality of war." *The Observer*. Sunday, 30 March 2003.

Rasmussen, Per Husman et. al. "Feasibility-Studie: Inelligente Systemer." *Forum for Forsvarsstudier* (March 2003).

Watt, D.C. "An Intelligence Surprise: The Failure of the Foreign Office to Anticipate the Nazi-Soviet Pact," *Intelligence and National Security* 4, 3 (July 1989), 512–34

Williams, Thomas J. "Strategic Leader Readiness and Competencies of Asymmetric Warfare." *Parameters* (Summer 2003): 19-34.

Internet

Al Qaeda. *The Al Qaeda Manual*. Computer file impounded by British Police in Manchester. From internet, accessed 1st November 2002. www.disastercenter.com/terror.

Gudmundsson, Bruce I. *The Revolution in Military Affairs*. From internet, accessed 1 April 2003.
http://mca.marines.org/Gazette/2002/02Gudmundsson.html

Livy. *The History of Rome*, Book 22: 4-6. From internet, accessed on 1 April 2003. http://www.barca.fsnet.co.uk/trasimene-text.htm

Martyn, Robert. *Canadian Military Intelligence and the Revolution of Military Affairs of 1914-1918*. Queen's University. From internet, accessed 1 March 2003.
http://members.shaw.ca/keepinga/smss/pdf/martyn_smss2001.pdf.

Cebrowski, Arthur K. and John J. Gartska. "Network-Centric Warfare: Its Origin and Future" in *U.S. Naval Institute Proceedings* articles 1998. http://www.usni.org/proceedings/articles98/procebrowski.htm accessed 22nd August 2003

http://ns-gedenkstaetten.de/nrw/de/wewelsburg/thema_3/ss_esoterik.html, accessed on 30 November 2003.

http://www.wewelsburg.de/startscreen/startframes.html, accessed on 30 November 2003.

http://www.salon.com/news/feature/2002/02/07/tehran/index_np.html, accessed on 6 November 2003.

http://www.scrappleface.com/MT/archives/000608.html, accessed 6 November 2003.

http://www.rferl.org/nca/features/2003/01/24012003172118.asp, accessed on 6 November 2003.

http://www.pbs.org/wgbh/amex/vietnam/trenches/mylai.html. Accessed on 28 January 2004.

http://www.herodote.net/histoire06101.htm. Accessed on 28 January 2004.

http://www.thestate.com/mld/thestate/news/nation/5510716.htm. Accessed on 27 January 2004.

http://www.apsanet.org/PS/sept00/snyder.cfm

206

Index

212

About the Author

KJELD HALD GALSTER, born 1952, is a military historian and a retired military officer. He has held positions as senior researcher, Royal Danish Defence College and (external) associate professor of the Saxo Institute, University of Copenhagen. He has lectured at Trinity College, Dublin and The Royal Military College of Canada; and he has published widely in Canada, Ireland and Denmark.

Also available from Legacy Books Press

Crucial Coalition
Anglo-Danish Military Collaboration and the Message of History

By Kjeld Hald Galster

ISBN: 978-0-9880192-8-7

In the summer of 2010, a unit of Danish soldiers known as ISAF-10 deployed to Afghanistan under British command. In Helmand Province, they tried to secure a fragile peace while dealing with the challenges of training an often apparently indifferent Afghan police and army, ensuring a functioning collaboration with the British despite insufficient military intelligence and divergent military cultures, and fell under frequent attack by an increasingly sophisticated and deadly Taliban.

In this remarkable book, Kjeld Hald Galster tells their story. He also looks at the wider picture, examining coalitions ranging from Ancient Greece to the Cold War. Exploring the millennia-long history of coalition warfare, he looks at what makes them work, the lessons they teach us, and how they reflect - and predict - the rise and downfall of the coalitions of the willing in Afghanistan and Iraq, and those yet to come.